Gustav Mahler and the New York Philharmonic Orchestra Tour America

Mary H. Wagner

THE SCARECROW PRESS, INC.
Lanham, Maryland • Toronto • Oxford
2006

SCARECROW PRESS, INC.

Published in the United States of America
by Scarecrow Press, Inc.
A wholly owned subsidiary of
The Rowman & Littlefield Publishing Group, Inc.
4501 Forbes Boulevard, Suite 200, Lanham, Maryland 20706
www.scarecrowpress.com

PO Box 317
Oxford
OX2 9RU, UK

British Library Cataloguing in Publication Information Available

Library of Congress Cataloging-in-Publication Data

Wagner, Mary H., 1965–
  Gustav Mahler and the New York Philharmonic Orchestra tour America / Mary H.
Wagner.
    p. cm.
  Includes bibliographical references and index.
  ISBN-13: 978-0-8108-5720-9 (pbk. : alk. paper)
  ISBN-10: 0-8108-5720-0 (pbk. : alk. paper)
  1. Mahler, Gustav, 1860-1911—Performances—United States. 2. New York
Philharmonic. 3. Conductors (Music)—United States. 4. Concert tours. I. Title.

ML410.M23W2 2006
784.206'07471—dc22

                                                          2006009389

~

Contents

~

Tables

~

Foreword

For almost a century, Mahler's American career gave rise to legends, unverified statements, and distorted facts that badly needed to be set right, yet until now few biographers have attempted to take a closer look at this late period of his life. The events that occurred during his last weeks in New York, including the outbreak of his final illness, were open to a good deal of misunderstanding. At the time, the seriousness of Mahler's condition had to be kept secret, so long as there was still some hope of a recovery. However, New York's musical community was already aware that a meeting of the Philharmonic Committee had taken place, at which certain of its members had taken Mahler to task. Consequently, when he took to his bed and had to cancel several concerts, it was initially believed that the meeting had upset him to such a degree that he feigned illness and decided to abandon his post as musical director.

Several weeks later, while Mahler was being treated in Paris—with little hope of recovery—Alma was interviewed there by an American music critic. She was understandably distraught at the time, and made a dramatic statement claiming that the New York Philharmonic's committee of women had humiliated Mahler and destroyed his morale: "To his amazement," she explained, "he had ten ladies ordering him about like a puppet. He hoped, however, by hard work and success, to rid himself of his tormentors. Meanwhile he lost health and strength." Almost everything that was later written on Mahler in America was influenced by this sad episode, and by the shameful obituary that Henry Krehbiel wrote two weeks later for the *New York Tribune*.

It was a very long piece, which Max Smith, in the *New York Press*, described as "one of the most savage attacks on a dead man's memory ever printed in this city" and one that "has outraged the feelings of every reader possessed of a grain of common decency."

Krehbiel had overlooked so many facts, and distorted so many others, that one would hardly have expected anyone to take such a vicious assault seriously, especially since it was launched in an obituary. But, surprising as it may seem, Krehbiel enjoyed quite a high reputation in New York, and his piece did much to tarnish the image of Mahler's years at the Philharmonic. Traces of this critic's most prejudiced and unreliable statements concerning Mahler's career can still be detected in several of the books and articles published in America after Mahler's death.

Fortunately, Mary Wagner's superbly researched book now sheds light on one of the least known, yet most successful and most interesting episodes in Mahler's American years: his tours with the New York Philharmonic. Whereas a few New York critics, especially the influential Krehbiel, had never ceased to berate Mahler for weeks and months on end, and seized every possible pretext to do so, the critics of such cities as Cleveland; Pittsburgh; Buffalo; Springfield, Massachusetts; and Boston went out of their way to praise him. Yet the contents and style of their reviews show that they were every bit as cultured, discerning, and sophisticated as the New York critics were. Furthermore, the details of the organization of the tour, and the assessment of the role these concerts played in the musical life of each city, are fascinating contributions to the historical record. We also learn that Mahler had insisted on traveling with ninety-two musicians, and that some of these cities were thus hearing a full symphony orchestra perhaps for the first time in their history. In contrast, the Boston Symphony, which toured widely every year, never did so with more than fifty to seventy musicians. Traveling every day and conducting every night in a different hall must have been a trying experience for Mahler, yet the result was worth his while: his tours to the Great Lakes area, to New England, and to large cities on the East Coast were so successful that they made a significant contribution to the orchestra's financial recovery. From our present perspective, it is clear that the ambitious policies of the rejuvenated orchestra could not have been economically viable during the first two seasons that Mahler conducted it. But at the end of the third year, 1911, the whole situation changed, thanks to the large sum bequeathed to the orchestra by Joseph Pulitzer. However, by that time Mahler had died, not because the "committee women" had misused him, but because bacterial endocarditis was still then an incurable disease.

Henry-Louis de La Grange

Acknowledgments

Although this book bears my name, it would not exist without the wonderful individuals who encouraged me along the way. In particular I give thanks to my family, relatives, friends, and colleagues who provided supported for my research and read through multiple drafts. I am grateful as well to the University of Michigan–Flint Office of Research and the Annual Fund for their support on this project. Throughout the process of putting this book together numerous people and libraries cooperated and provided material including: Henry-Louis de La Grange at Bibliothèque Gustav Mahler, Paris; Boston Public Library; Barbara Perkel and Bridget Carr at the Boston Symphony Orchestra Archives; Buffalo and Erie County Public Library; Buffalo Symphony Orchestra; Gino Francesconi at the Carnegie Hall Archives; Carnegie Library of Pittsburgh; Carol Jacobs at the Cleveland Orchestra Archives; Cleveland Public Library; Connecticut Historical Society; Connecticut State Library; Margaret Humberston at the Connecticut Valley Historical Museum; Hartford Public Library of Connecticut; Internationale Gustav Mahler Gesellschaft; Kent State University Library; Library of Congress; James A. Matthews; New Haven Free Public Library; Astor, Lenox, and Tilden Foundations, Music Division of the New York Public Library; Richard Wandel and Barbara Haws at the New York Philharmonic Archives; Oneida Historical Society, New York; Onondaga County Public Library, Local History Division; Onondaga Historical Association; JoAnne Berry at Philadelphia Orchestra Association Archives; Philadelphia Public Library; Rhode Island Historical Society Library; Rochester Public Library; Ann Schafer at the

Rochester Historical Society; Joe Deneen and Herb McCullagh at Saginaw Railway Museum; David Peter Coppen at Sibley Music Library, Eastman School of Music; Springfield Historical Society; Springfield City Library; State University of New York at Syracuse Library; Henry Z. Steinway at Steinway Music Hall; Lesa A. Quade at University of Michigan–Flint Library; Utica Public Library of New York; and Richard Boursy at Yale University Library. Furthermore, I would like to thank Andrew Wagner, Clara Wagner, Andy Joseph Wagner, Wilma Cleveland, Joseph Cleveland, Theodore Albrecht, Henry-Louis de La Grange, and James Zychowicz for their steadfast support.

~

Introduction

Gustav Mahler's name is most often associated with monumental composi-
tions such as the Eighth Symphony or *Das Lied von der Erde*. Although
Mahler was remembered as a composer, he helped reshape and transform the
New York Philharmonic into a leading orchestra with greater artistic recog-
nition and stability. Unfortunately, the achievements of his final years in
New York have often been neglected and need closer examination.

From 1909 until his death in May 1911, Gustav Mahler became known in
America as the director of the New York Philharmonic. In 1909 when the
orchestra reorganized from a cooperative plan, based on ownership by the
musicians, to a guarantor plan, based on ownership by a group of guarantors,
they needed a new leader to rejuvenate and reshape the crumbling orchestra.
Mahler eagerly accepted the challenge and focused on making the New York
Philharmonic the best orchestra "in this country and the equal of any in the
world."[1] To accomplish this objective the orchestra instituted regular rehearsals, developed a season of forty-six concerts, and began touring the
United States. This book documents Mahler's tours with the New York Philharmonic during the 1909 and 1910 seasons—the preparations for the tours,
the outcome of each concert, and the perceptions of audiences beyond New
York City.

With almost a decade spent at the Vienna Hofoper and several years of directing the Vienna Philharmonic, Mahler brought valuable experience to
the Philharmonic. Mahler used that experience to work with the New York
musicians to raise the quality of the orchestra to a level that competed with

the Boston Symphony Orchestra and the New York Symphony. He developed several concert series to appeal to a broader demographic of the population, including "All Beethoven," "Historical," and "Popular Concerts" series. The Philharmonic's managerial reorganization allowed Mahler to expand the number of concerts from sixteen to forty-six in the 1909–1910 season and to increase the number to fifty concerts in the 1910–1911 season.

Touring

At the turn of the twentieth century, many opera companies, soloists, and orchestras, including the Boston Symphony Orchestra and the New York Symphony, toured the country on a regular basis. With Mahler as conductor, the Philharmonic hoped to develop a national reputation and gain more recognition. Each tour capitalized on Mahler's talent not only as a conductor but also as a composer and performer. These tours were effectively marketed, offered affordable tickets, and encouraged individuals to attend the concerts to watch the famous Gustav Mahler conduct America's oldest orchestra.

During Mahler's first season with the Philharmonic (1909–1910), the orchestra traveled with approximately one hundred musicians to Philadelphia, New Haven, Boston, Providence, and Springfield, Massachusetts.[2] Never before had so many musicians in one orchestra traveled to these cities to perform. Before the next season, a number of changes increased the success and profitability of touring. Through reducing traveling expenses, touring with a smaller orchestra of eighty-five musicians, and duplicating the programs, the Philharmonic offered more concerts and improved their economic picture. In Mahler's final season (1910–1911) the orchestra traveled to Pittsburgh, Cleveland, Buffalo, Rochester, Syracuse, Utica (New York), Philadelphia, and Washington, D.C.[3] Before Mahler became deathly ill and left the Philharmonic at the end of February 1911, he had nearly quadrupled the number of programs in the season and developed an expanded audience base that reached far beyond Manhattan to include Brooklyn and more than thirteen cities.

Current Literature on Mahler in America

While many scholars have addressed Mahler's compositional accomplishments and conducting legacy in Europe, little research has previously covered his contributions to the development of the symphony orchestra. The majority of books related to Mahler's final years focus on his period in Toblach, the premiere of the Eighth Symphony in Munich, and Alma Mahler's infidelity.

For the most part, Mahler and his tours with the New York Philharmonic find little place in literature focusing on American history, culture, and music. Verification of tour dates reveals inaccuracies in some of this literature, such as *Music is My Life* by Adella Prentiss Hughes.[4] This is not surprising, since the history of these tours is not easily accessible. Unfortunately, when the Philharmonic reorganized it retained very few records related to the tours. Furthermore, New York periodicals only occasionally printed news pertaining to the tours and, even then, only briefly indicated when the orchestra departed from or returned to New York.

In 1973 Marvin von Deck, in his dissertation "Gustav Mahler in New York: His Conducting Activities in New York City, 1908–1911,"[5] began exploring articles surrounding this period. In 1989, Zoltan Roman completed *Gustav Mahler's American Years 1907–1911*,[6] which thoroughly documented and reproduced portions of articles from several newspapers and periodicals focusing on Mahler's period in New York City. Twelve of the records mentioned Mahler's tours with the Philharmonic, but more material remained to be researched. Henry-Louis de La Grange's *Gustav Mahler: chronique d'une vie*,[7] soon to be available in a more extensive English edition, further documents this final era in Mahler's life. Even so, the background, role, and the success of Mahler's tours with the orchestra deserve to be further explored.

Methodology

This book focuses on the tours themselves, the conditions surrounding the tours, the planning and process of touring, and the results of these concerts. It intends to demonstrate for the first time the importance of the tours in both Mahler's career and the Philharmonic's history. Since many of the documents and references have never been compiled before, this book presents the history of each concert outside of greater New York.

To retell the history of Mahler's Philharmonic tours, I reviewed more than one thousand documents from roughly thirteen cities. I gathered information from numerous newspaper articles, promotional materials, and even contracts associated with various concerts. Since indices were not available for newspapers from the turn of the twentieth century, I pored over microfilm from approximately eighty newspapers for relevant articles. When placed together, these documents restore a thorough record of the conditions surrounding classical music in each city and the impact of the performances by Mahler and the Philharmonic. Within each chapter, I examine the preparations, reviews, and success of each concert.

Overview

Chapter 1 provides the historical background of Mahler's acceptance of the Philharmonic position. It addresses the struggles and obstacles forcing the New York Philharmonic to reorganize in 1909 and Mahler's move from the Metropolitan Opera House to the New York Philharmonic. Although Mahler began working at the Metropolitan Opera House in 1908, changes in the management, the death of Met manager Heinrich Conried, and Toscanini's arrival in 1909 convinced Mahler to consider other options. With the help of Mary Sheldon and several influential New Yorkers, the Philharmonic gained a stronger financial position and hired Mahler as the new music director.

Chapter 2 describes the touring conditions in America in the early twentieth century and the economic impact of touring on an organization's revenue. Readers will gain a more thorough understanding of how musicians incorporated touring as part of their livelihood. The chapter details how tours were organized on a local level, grouped into series, and promoted through the media. The positive and negative impacts of touring locally are also addressed. Finally, the chapter presents the conditions and logistics of traveling by railroad throughout the country. Based on the expansion of the rail system and its affordability, touring became a popular and economically feasible method for musicians to earn a living.

Chapter 3 presents Mahler's style of programming music for the Philharmonic and, more specifically, for the tours. This chapter devotes a considerable section to Mahler's arrangement of the Bach Orchestral Suites and reveals how the newly arranged composition became a trademark of the Philharmonic's season. Additionally, it provides background on how Steinway and Sons reconfigured a piano to sound like a harpsichord. The chapter discusses the works Mahler selected for the tours. It also addresses the use of soloists and the order and length of programs.

The next four chapters present the preparations, conditions, and reviews from the performances on tour. Chapter 4 provides the details surrounding the New England Tour of 1910, followed by the Great Lakes Tour of 1910 in chapter 5. Chapter 6 offers insights on tours to Philadelphia and Washington, D.C. Mahler's final tour to New England in 1911 is the focus of chapter 7. These chapters offer selected quotations from various reviews that have not been previously available to readers. They also examine the level of cultural development in each city, explain how the media promoted each concert, and record the impact of each concert. Each city along the tours supported roughly six to eight daily newspapers, so these reviews and promotions offer a comprehensive evaluation of each concert.

Several appendixes provide detailed information about the tours. The programs have been reconstructed and include detailed information on the date, place, and time of each performance. Since many of these concert halls are no longer in existence, another appendix provides information pertaining to the size, location, and description of each facility.

Conclusion

Mahler's tours with the New York Philharmonic had a lasting effect on the programming of the Philharmonic. After his departure and death in 1911, the tours continued to thrive and expand until the decline of the railroad industry in the mid-1920s. The tours also impacted the cities where they were presented by sparking interest in orchestral music, encouraging the development of local orchestras, and exposing listeners to a greater repertoire of classical music. Moreover, Americans witnessed Mahler as a conductor, performer, and composer for the last times in his life.

Notes

1. "Nation's Best Orchestra, Mahler's" *Musical America*, 30 October 1909, 31.

2. The orchestra presented concerts in Philadelphia on January 17, 1910, New Haven on February 23, 1910, Springfield, Massachusetts, on February 24, 1910, Providence on February 25, 1910, and Boston on February 26, 1910.

3. The orchestra performed in Pittsburgh on December 5, 1910, Cleveland on December 6, 1910, Buffalo on December 7, 1910, Rochester on December 8, 1910, Syracuse on December 9, 1910, Utica on December 10, 1910, Philadelphia on January 23, 1911, and Washington, D.C., on January 24, 1911.

4. Adella Prentiss Hughes, *Music Is My Life* (Cleveland: World Publishing Company, 1947), 130. Hughes incorrectly stated the year of the concert as December 6, 1908, rather than the actual year of December 6, 1910.

5. Marvin L. von Deck, "Gustav Mahler in New York: His Conducting Activities in New York City, 1908–1911" (Ph.D. diss., New York University, 1973).

6. Zoltan Roman, *Gustav Mahler's American Years 1907–1911* (Stuyvesant, NY: Pendragon Press, 1989).

7. Henry-Louis de La Grange, *Gustav Mahler: chronique d'une vie.* 3 vols. (Paris: Fayard, 1973–84).

CHAPTER ONE

Mahler in New York

A number of circumstances brought about Mahler's arrival at the New York Philharmonic in 1909 and eventually his tours with the orchestra. Mahler's education and career in Europe provided the skills and background to develop audiences, procure guarantors, and create more artistic renditions of opera and symphonic music. Disenchanted with conditions at the Metropolitan Opera House, Mahler decided to accept the position of conductor at the New York Philharmonic Society in 1909. As part of the reorganization of the Philharmonic, Mahler expanded the number of concerts and led the orchestra on its first concert tour.

Mahler's Career in Europe

Throughout the world Mahler is known primarily as a composer and secondarily as a conductor. Hundreds of books, recordings, symposia, and articles focus on the structure, complexity, and advancements of his music. During Mahler's lifetime, however, he was first recognized as a conductor, and he progressed through several positions that eventually led him to accept the role as director of the New York Philharmonic in 1909.

Born to Bernhard and Marie Mahler on July 7, 1860, in the Bohemian village of Kaliště, Gustav was the second of fourteen children and the first of six to survive infancy. Gustav spent much of his childhood in Iglau, where he studied piano and music theory. After an unsuccessful year at Prague's Neustädter Gymnasium in 1871, he returned to Iglau. Nevertheless, Mahler continued to develop his skills, and in 1875, the Vienna Conservatory accepted him as a student. After studying piano, harmony, and composition, Mahler decided to concentrate on composition. Although he graduated from the conservatory in 1878, Mahler supplemented his training with history and philosophy courses at the University of Vienna.[1]

Determined to be a composer, Mahler worked as a teacher and conductor to earn an adequate income so that he could devote his spare time to composition. Although historians focus less on Mahler's conducting career, his achievements and recognition as a conductor complemented his composing career and fostered opportunities for performances of his own works. Prior to arriving in America, Mahler progressed through several posts to chief conductor at the Hamburg Stadttheater and finally reached the summit of European posts as a conductor at Vienna's Hofoper. With discipline and a strong work ethic Mahler quickly advanced his career. To begin with Mahler was noted for improving the financial condition of several despairing opera houses and organizations. Secondly, Mahler became involved with many aspects of performance, from rigorous rehearsal schedules to production details such as lighting. Finally, rather than merely conduct a work, Mahler treated each piece as his own composition and never hesitated to make changes and enhancements to notes, dynamics, phrasing, or tempo. These characteristics served Mahler well when the New York Philharmonic considered him as a candidate for their director.

After Mahler received his first conducting post at Bad Hall in upper Austria during the summer of 1880, he became engrossed with conducting. A year later he accepted the Kapellmeister position at the Landestheater in Laibach and conducted his first opera, Verdi's *Il trovatore*.[2] Mahler's stern discipline proved effective when he accepted the next Kapellmeister post in January 1883 at Olmütz and revitalized its financially depressed condition. Despite some initial press criticism, he quickly demanded high standards and improved performances.

These accomplishments soon led the way to the position of Royal Music Director and Choral Director at Kassel in August 1883. Unfortunately, Mahler soon became dissatisfied with the restrictions of this position, but he continued to refine his conducting skills. Although the press offered mixed reviews and believed that his conducting gestures appeared excessive and the tempos seemed irregular, concertgoers applauded his enthusiasm and the ensemble's precision.[3] Triumph finally arrived when Mahler conducted five hundred musicians in a festival performance of Mendelssohn's *St. Paul*.[4]

In July 1885 Mahler joined Ludwig Slansky and manager Angelo Neumann[5] as they hoped to rescue Prague's Deutsches Landestheater from bankruptcy. With the departure of Anton Seidl,[6] Neumann decided that Mahler and Slansky would share conducting duties equally. Supporters and critics soon sided with Slansky and offered biased criticism of Mahler. Although conductors a generation before him took great liberties with the music, critics at the end of the nineteenth century began condemning individuals for tampering with the music, especially historical works. Although his definition of authenticity varied drastically from the critics, Mahler focused on remaining musically and dramatically loyal to the score. With experience as a conductor and composer, Mahler believed adaptations and alterations to the score were sometimes necessary. Based on the soloists, conditions of the house, and modern instrumentation, he implemented changes for a successful production. Nevertheless, he also continued to modify scores in order to emulate the composer's true intentions.

With mounting disputes between Slansky and Neumann, Mahler left Prague in 1886, after only one year, and joined the Neues Stadttheater in Leipzig. Headed by the great conductor Arthur Nikisch,[7] this house offered larger audiences and better equipment. Mahler soon intended to resign, but when Nikisch suddenly fell deathly ill, he stepped in as conductor in a performance of a *Ring* cycle. The critics instantly applauded Mahler's interpretation and praised him as a genius.[8] During this period he became acquainted with Richard Strauss and Carl von Weber, the grandson of Carl Maria von Weber. Mahler completed and published Weber's sketches for his opera *Die drei Pintos*. He also conducted initial performances of the opera throughout Europe, which enhanced his reputation and fame.[9]

In May 1888 Mahler resigned the position in Leipzig. During the summer he prepared for the Prague premiere of *Die drei Pintos*. Several weeks after the performance, the Royal Hungarian Opera in Budapest offered him a conducting position. Despite being entrenched in a financial crisis, the opera house still offered one of the "most modern and best equipped theaters in central Europe."[10] Mahler quickly transformed the company as he staged opera in Hungarian, engaged native singers, and reduced the costly price tag linked to international guest singers. Beginning in October 1888, the opera house consumed Mahler's energy, and by the end of the second season, the theater achieved higher performance standards and a profit. After a major shift in politics and a new prime minister, Count Géza Zichy emerged as intendant of the theater. Zichy soon demanded absolute control over artistic decisions, and in March 1891 Mahler decided to leave for a better opportunity in Hamburg.[11]

Mahler held the position as first conductor at the Stadttheater in Hamburg from 1891 until 1897. The modern impresario Bernhard Pollini[12] engaged the best performers in Europe, managed most of the artistic responsibilities, and attracted large audiences. Thus, Mahler focused his energies on creating a theatrical idealism and maintained a concentrated rehearsal schedule involving singers and players.[13] The grueling schedule kept Mahler conducting up to nineteen operas per month, which left little time for thorough rehearsals. Nevertheless, he impressed critics with his ability as a superior conductor, and over the next few years he rose to international acclaim.

With his sights set on eventually obtaining a position in the Catholic city of Vienna, Mahler finally converted to Roman Catholicism in February 1897. With strong recommendations from colleagues, nobility, and society connections, he obtained the coveted post of Kapellmeister in Vienna in April 1897 at the age of thirty-six. Mahler's era in Vienna marked the longest and most prosperous period of his tenure, which stretched until 1907. By September 1897 he was promoted to the pinnacle position in Europe of the director of the Hofoper, also known as the Vienna Court Opera, and began to transform the operas from their declining public appeal. Mahler attempted to invigorate the productions to attract audiences, which had been declining in more recent years. Similar to the challenges Mahler would eventually encounter in New York, he managed to please the critics, administrators, managers, patrons, and musicians. As one of the three resident conductors at the Vienna Hofoper, he quickly established a niche as an interpreter of Wagner and Mozart operas. He also gained the attention of the critics and the public and even became a controversial subject in the press.

When Hans Richter[14] resigned from the Vienna Philharmonic Concerts in 1898, Mahler accepted these additional duties. Unlike conditions at the opera house, however, the musicians themselves managed the Philharmonic through a cooperative plan. Their disapproval of Mahler's authoritarian manner and insensitivity with musicians fostered disagreements and triggered negative reviews. After Mahler underwent emergency surgery for internal bleeding in April 1901, he resigned from these philharmonic responsibilities but continued in his role at the Hofoper.[15]

During these years Mahler set high operatic standards in Vienna as he introduced "animated stage direction, imaginative scenery, and a nightly norm of performance that was never allowed to fall below his personal expectations."[16] He extended control over all aspects of the opera, including the costumes, casting, repertoire, audience behavior, stage design, abolishing press tickets, and denying entrance to latecomers. Furthermore, he removed incompetent musicians from the orchestra and forced singers to act out their roles rather than just enter and exit the stage.[17]

While in Vienna, Mahler established important relationships with musicians, artists, and Alma Schindler, a woman soon to become his wife. Although Mahler continued to compose symphonies during this period, the press paid more attention to his accomplishments as a conductor. Not everyone, in particular the critics, approved of Mahler's ultimate power, treatment of musicians, and musical alterations. Several articles even exhibited anti-Semitic cynicism, which continued to appear and flourish in local newspapers during Mahler's final years in Vienna. By 1906, Mahler realized his era in Vienna would eventually end, but before officially resigning, he secured a new and well-paid position in America at the Metropolitan Opera House.

Opportunities in America

With the Hofoper as part of the imperial court, the emperor appointed Mahler as a lifelong civil servant, but the press continually scrutinized his actions. Early on, Mahler realized that although he achieved the pinnacle position in Vienna and gained popularity, some admirers might become potential enemies. This led him to remark, "I know very well that those who praise me to the skies today will be stoning me to death tomorrow."[18] He also believed a theater director should not remain at the same post much longer than five years. His insight into the situation proved accurate. Compared with the responsibilities of music directors today, Mahler's administrative duties required an unprecedented amount of time. This directed his focus away from musical endeavors such as score preparation, rehearsals, and composition. Moreover, he even had to negotiate contracts with artists, cope with absences, and resolve conflicts among personnel.

These duties even surfaced during a performance of *Tristan* that Mahler directed in May 1907. In attendance at the performance, the famous German soprano Lilli Lehman recalled that by the end of the second act Anna von Mildenburg,[19] who played Isolde, reported that she could no longer perform because she lost her voice. As it turned out, what Mildenburg really lost was her temper with Erik Schmedes,[20] who played Tristan, and she refused to continue with the performance. Lehman noted that Mahler "exploded as if someone had thrown a lighted match into a powder barrel."[21] Lehman spontaneously volunteered to play Isolde, and with some changes the production continued. This vignette reflects only one of the many incidents that Mahler needed to handle as an administrator.

At the same time Viennese critics spoke ill of Mahler's ability to manage the Hofoper's finances. Although allegations of a deficit proved unsubstantiated, they caused irreparable harm to Mahler's reputation. The house's expenditure significantly rose for the 1906–1907 season but increases in ticket prices offset these expenses. Furthermore, a complete analysis of the opera's financial position could not be determined until the end of the season.

Unfortunately, critics often made predictions based on the financial information from the preceding season.

A number of articles discussed the deteriorating relationship between Mahler and the staff. The press continued to attack Mahler throughout the 1906–1907 season. As the *Allgemeine Zeitung* noted, "Conspirators are prowling around the Opera. No paper dagger is too dirty to be launched against the hated director. Industrious as ants, they assemble and pile up one snippet after another."[22]

Although the critics continuously criticized Mahler's performance as an administrator and artist, he believed that conditions were declining for repertory opera. Throughout the season fewer patrons from central Vienna and more from the suburbs attended performances, as electric trains could easily and quickly transport the public to the opera hall. In a note to Julius Korngold, critic for the *Neue Freie Presse*, Mahler wrote that if he wanted to leave his post, it would not be based on the critics or the desire to solely compose but because of the conflicts of the present operating condition of the theatre.[23] The demands of creating numerous productions became strenuous and never-ending. During the 1905–1906 season Mahler had a repertoire of fifty-three works and during the 1906–1907 season he had fifty-eight works. By the end of his Viennese period he had conducted 649 operatic performances, averaging sixty-four performances per season.[24] Clearly the responsibilities for producing so many operas in a nine-month period and the director's duties left little room for composition. Even Mahler's successor, Felix Weingartner, held the Hofoper position for only two and a half years and left extremely discouraged. In addition to the Hofoper commitments, Mahler agreed to guest conduct throughout Europe for various festivals and to promote his own music.

By the time Mahler contemplated leaving Vienna, several critics realized the insurmountable demands put upon one individual. The *Illustrites Wiener Extrablatt* went so far to remark that the Hofoper's needs could "be looked after by two or three conductors, and first class, gifted stage managers."[25] A model similar to this, with multiple conductors and administrative assistance already existed in America at the Metropolitan Opera House.

The Metropolitan Opera

The timing of Mahler's decline coincidentally occurred as the director of the Metropolitan Opera, Heinrich Conried,[26] began looking for an internationally renowned conductor to head German opera for the 1907–1908 season. Opened in 1883, the New York Metropolitan Opera House soon became the primary venue for opera in America with emphasis on Italian and German opera. As the city prospered Oscar Hammerstein opened the Manhattan Opera in 1906 and broke the Met's monopoly on opera in New York. Hammerstein diversified his productions by offering current opera and premieres. In the first month of operating, Hammerstein trumped the Metropolitan by offering the New York premiere of *Aida*. The Met soon realized it needed to compete with the Manhattan Opera not only for patrons but also for performers.

Believing New York City could not support two first-class opera houses, Conried and the Met implemented several tactics to crush and abolish the Manhattan Opera House. First, the Met notified managers and singers that any dealings with Hammerstein could endanger their future relationships with the Met.[27] Secondly, the Met decided to hire more full-time employees, including stage hands and musicians for the orchestra. The Metropolitan lured musicians who had previously put their careers together piecemeal, New York Philharmonic members, and those willing to leave Hammerstein.

As part of Conried's strategy he redefined the responsibilities of the Met's board of directors from a passive to a more active role. Previously, board members simply allowed the Met to use their names, but in October 1907 changes in the opera company became "more important than any since the formation of that body."[28] Several members resigned and the board expanded from fifteen to seventeen members. New members became actively involved and financially supportive. In addition to William K. Vanderbilt joining the board, several new foreign directors associated with the Covent Garden Royal Opera in London and the Opera Comique in Paris also became members. These foreign board members planned to assist in exchanging singers and help to "reduce the present high salaries paid to singers."[29]

Since Hammerstein owned his plush new Manhattan Opera House, he accrued the revenue from ticket sales directly. Prior to 1908, the Metropolitan Real Estate Company, representing the stockholders, leased the building to the Metropolitan Opera Company. Shareholders, who owned their boxes, rented them out and accrued personal dividends. If losses accumulated from a production, the Metropolitan Opera Company became liable, not the owners of the Metropolitan Real Estate Company. In an effort to hold the shareholders more fiscally responsible, Conried initiated a new arrangement in October 1907. The new contract enabled the Metropolitan Opera Company to secure more resources to compete against Hammerstein, heightened the stockholders' position, and limited Conried's personal liability.[30]

To compete artistically with Hammerstein, the Met clearly needed an international celebrity to cultivate and expand German opera. Conried feverishly scouted Europe, and soon a rumor that Arturo Toscanini might come to the Met circulated in the *New York Sun*. The news proved premature. Conried identified Gustav Mahler as the best candidate to fill the position several months later. Determined to defeat the Manhattan Opera, Conried offered Mahler a four-month contract for 100,000 kronen, along with traveling and living expenses. Compared with the Viennese payment of 36,000 kronen for approximately nine months of work, Mahler realized he remained undervalued in Europe. After several negotiations, Mahler agreed to three months of work at 25,000 kronen per month. Conried agreed to work with Mahler so that Mahler could possibly conduct other concerts. Mahler also placed a stipulation in the contract that if for any reason Conried left as director, the contract could be dissolved. In June 1907, Mahler signed the Met contract for three months of work at a salary of $20,000. Announcements soon flooded New York newspapers confirming Mahler would arrive in time to conduct the opening opera on January 1, 1908.[31]

Mahler's new position at the Met relieved him of administrative tasks and allowed him to focus on the musical aspects of the productions. Besides saving for retirement, the position provided him a more balanced lifestyle during the working months and considerably more time off to focus on composition. Before he departed Vienna he expressed some apprehension to Richard Strauss about the unknown working conditions at the Met. Having recently appeared in New York and in other American cities, Strauss reduced Mahler's anxiety as he replied, "Over there you get up on the podium and do this—(he waved an imaginary baton) and then you go to the cashier and (a gesture of counting money)."[32]

In the months preceding his European departure, Mahler conducted several concerts. After arriving in New York in December 1907, Mahler soon learned of Conried's ailing medical condition, noted as sciatic neuritis,[33] and of a reorganization with the Metropolitan administration. Giulio Gatti-Casazza,[34] artistic director, and Andreas Dippel,[35] administrative manager, would control the direction of the opera house and report to the holding company, presided over by Otto H. Kahn.[36] Mahler signed a contract with this management to ensure his position and future with the Metropolitan.

When Mahler made his first Metropolitan appearance conducting *Tristan and Isolde* on January 1, 1908, the critics gave the performance overwhelming positive remarks. Richard Aldrich of the *New York Times* commended Mahler for revealing the score's "complex beauty, with its strands of interwoven melody always clearly disposed and united with an exquisite sense of proportion and an unerring sense of the larger values."[37] Later in the season Mahler toured with the Metropolitan to Philadelphia and Boston.[38] Both critics and many prominent supporters, representing various musical societies, observed Mahler's capabilities. In New York Mahler could attract large audiences, turn around the financial conditions of an organization, and devote his energies to the music. Furthermore, Mahler brought international acclaim to the city and to the Met.

Luring Mahler to the Philharmonic

During Mahler's first season in New York several organizations invited him to guest conduct, including the New York Symphony. In April 1908 Walter Damrosch secured Mahler for three concerts during the following season on November 29, December 8, and December 13, 1908, which would take place prior to the beginning of the opera season.[39]

Before Mahler left for the summer, a group of wealthy concertgoers also approached him about conducting three festival concerts for March and April 1909. This party consisted of Mrs. George R. Sheldon, Mrs. Samuel Untermeyer, Mrs. William Douglas, Mrs. George M. Tuttle, Mr. Patrick Valentine, and Mr. Felix Warburg, people who eventually formed the backbone of the restructuring group of the New York Philharmonic.[40] This committee raised money for the concerts and authorized Mahler to select and train his own orchestra. Although final details still needed clarification, he planned to conduct his Fourth Symphony and Beethoven's Ninth Symphony for these events. In his new contract with the Met, he demanded a provision for him to conduct several concerts in America the following year.

In November 1908, when Mahler arrived back in New York for his second season with the Metropolitan Opera, he shared the conducting load with a rising Italian star, Arturo Toscanini. Giulio Gatti-Casazza and Toscanini soon controlled the Italian and French repertoire while Andreas Dippel and Mahler led the German repertoire. As musical directors, Mahler and Toscanini would share responsibilities and conduct roughly two performances a week, and each would receive a salary of $25,000. On the average, however, Toscanini usually conducted three performances a week, and Mahler directed one performance per week.[41] In October 1909, Toscanini arrived in New York and chose to conduct *Tristan und Isolde*. Under Mahler's strong objection he yielded and conducted *Die Götterdämmerung* in December.[42]

Although a rumor appeared in the *Musical Courier* that Mahler seemed dissatisfied with his position at the Met and sought a position with the Berlin Royal Opera, he returned to New York and opened the season with a performance of the *Marriage of Figaro* on January 13, 1909.[43] By the middle of February the *New York Sun* reported that Mahler intended to remain at the Metropolitan for the 1909–1910 season and conduct at least twenty performances.[44] However, Mahler would conduct only four times at the Metropolitan during the next season since he found a better opportunity in New York.

As Conried and the Met restructured their board, some cultural institutions in New York had reorganized and others had migrated toward a structure headed by a board of directors. This system differed drastically from Europe, where the development of an orchestra served a court theater and the opera house. To create and sustain a permanent resident orchestra in America, an arrangement evolved where "musicians devote their energies to an organization which is controlled by a layman board of directors and artistically directed by a conductor."[45] The stability of this structure played a critical link to Mahler's accepting the role of music director of America's oldest orchestra, the New York Philharmonic.

The Background of the Philharmonic

The New York Philharmonic Society prided itself on being the oldest orchestra in the United States. Formed in 1842, the Philharmonic initially consisted of primarily German musicians and heralded notable conductors including Theodore Thomas (1877–1891), Anton Seidl (1891–1898), and Walter Damrosch (1902–1903).[46] At the turn of the twentieth century the most prominent orchestras in the United States also included the Boston Symphony Orchestra, the Theodore Thomas Orchestra, the New York Symphony, and the Pittsburgh Orchestra. Compared with its Boston counterpart, the Philharmonic faced several obstacles. In Boston, the wealth of one major tycoon, Henry Lee Higginson, subsidized the orchestra. In 1900, Higginson also helped build Symphony Hall as the permanent home for the orchestra, which eliminated the expenses for hall rental, rehearsal space, and office space.[47] Furthermore, several businessmen led the management of the Boston ensemble and coordinated ticket sales, marketing, promotions, and tours. This financial stability allowed the orchestra to travel throughout the country and gain recognition as the leading American orchestra. New Yorkers had the opportunity to first hear the orchestra by 1887.[48]

In New York City entertainment consisted not only of orchestral music, but even more so of theater and opera. By 1909, New York prided itself on having two major opera companies, the Metropolitan Opera and the Manhattan Opera House. Other orchestras also formed when Leopold Damrosch established the New York Symphony Orchestra in 1878. Formed in 1904, the Russian Symphony Orchestra offered a third active orchestra in New York City during the first two decades of the twentieth century.[49] Although the

New York Philharmonic was the oldest orchestra, the New York Symphony Orchestra and the Russian Symphony Orchestra offered equally challenging seasons and toured extensively throughout the United States. Without a hall of its own, and dependent on the availability of Carnegie Hall, the Philharmonic competed with the events of other organizations.

For example, during the 1909–1910 season the New York Symphony under the direction of Walter Damrosch planned to provide sixteen Sunday afternoon concerts at the New Theater and eight more concerts at Carnegie Hall.[50] Furthermore, Frank Damrosch organized a number of Symphony Concerts for Young People,[51] of which six were to be offered on Saturday afternoons under the direction of his brother, Walter Damrosch. Meanwhile, the Russian Symphony Society led by Modest Altschuler planned eight concerts at Carnegie Hall, and the Boston Symphony Orchestra under the direction of Max Fiedler offered ten concerts at Carnegie Hall.[52]

Until the Philharmonic reorganized in 1909, they managed themselves in accordance with the cooperative plan. Based on this management style, the musicians acted as shareholders or owners of the orchestra and selected the conductor, promoted concerts, and scheduled the season. Musicians divided the profits generated from concerts, but since they depended on box office receipts, they received no guaranteed amount. Therefore, many musicians counted on other employment to maintain an adequate level of income. Prior to the 1909 restructuring, a position with the Philharmonic Society represented only part-time employment. Furthermore, the season consisted of only eighteen or so concerts on Thursday and Friday evenings between the months of January and March. During the 1908–1909 season only fifty-seven musicians were registered as actual members of the society, and of these, only thirty-seven consistently played in the orchestra that boasted one hundred men.[53]

Prior to Mahler's arrival, musicians frequently missed rehearsals and concerts to meet other obligations, which forced the Philharmonic to hire substitute musicians. By the 1907–1908 season, these expenses peaked, as the Philharmonic spent more than $8,400 for substitute players.[54] It was no surprise that the caliber of the Boston Symphony Orchestra remained significantly higher than the Philharmonic. If the public and supporters desired a more refined, financially secure, and permanent orchestra, several major changes needed to be rapidly completed to turn around the organization's quickly accruing deficit. These changes included reliance on the newly formed Guarantors Fund, a restructuring of procedures, the hiring of a renowned conductor, the expansion of concerts and of the length of the season, and broadening the base of concertgoers inside and outside New York City.

A First Attempt to Restructure the Philharmonic

Although the Philharmonic restructured in 1909, Walter Damrosch had attempted a similar reorganization several years earlier. Throughout the country Damrosch became known as the leader of the New York Symphony Orchestra. He enjoyed ties to wealthy and political circles in New York that included his father-in-law, James G. Blaine, a congressman and secretary of state.[55] In addition, Andrew Carnegie supported the Damrosch family as president and chief patron of the Oratorio Society of New York from 1877 until 1918. Leopold Damrosch began the society in 1873, and Walter conducted the organization during various periods from 1885 to 1898 and 1918 to 1920.

During Damrosch's brief tenure as the New York Philharmonic director for the 1902–1903 season, he realized several inadequacies in the ensemble. For example, fewer than half of the one hundred musicians were members of the governing society. Moreover, the musician roster changed with each concert, creating inconsistencies in rehearsals and performances. Damrosch also noticed that many members had aged, diminishing their technical skills and resulting in musicians "no longer fit to play first violin."[56] Other non-members in the wind section were less faithful to the Philharmonic's schedule and their attendance proved undependable. Musicians frequently committed their time to other ensembles that offered better pay and simply found substitutes for the Philharmonic concerts. Based on these difficulties, Damrosch concluded that for the Philharmonic to survive a number of changes were mandatory, including the resignation of less competent musicians.

By December 1902, Damrosch envisioned a plan to do the following: place the orchestra on solid financial ground, sustain concerts over the next four years, create consistency among players, improve the caliber of playing, and convert the organization to a permanent status. Damrosch then recruited eight supporters to form the Committee of the Permanent Orchestra. In January 1903, Damrosch, Samuel Untermyer, John Notman, and E. Francis Hyde drafted new terms of the trust for the orchestra.[57]

This trust defined a board consisting of roughly fifteen members, adding another seven members from the subscribers of the fund. The plan outlined an expansion from eight evening and afternoon concerts to roughly forty concerts per season, with the musicians attending regular rehearsals and meetings for seven months per season. To accommodate younger aspiring players, the new plan called for the resignation of several older musicians, and included moving August Roebbelin and Richard Arnold from the position of concertmaster to a lower ranking in the violin section.[58] In addition, this plan reduced the liability of the Philharmonic members for handling any deficits.

Under the existing cooperative plan, however, the society members voiced little enthusiasm in modifying a structure that adequately functioned for more than half a century. Not only were Roebbelin and Arnold well respected as senior members of the orchestra, but Arnold also served as the vice president of the society. The society primarily objected to the forced resignation of musicians and the older members unanimously agreed. In addition, players had become accustomed to only eight pairs of concerts per season and had supplemented their income through forming other orchestras and ensembles, and by performing with other organizations.[59] Musicians further expressed concern over being eventually replaced, resented more disciplined rehearsals, and felt subsequent changes would be implemented if they relinquished their voting rights.[60]

On February 28, 1903, the society formally declined the offer and stated that the changes would interfere too seriously with the democratic system of the society. Speaking on behalf of the society, Felix F. Leifels, secretary to the Philharmonic, delivered a statement to local newspapers indicating that the reorganization "would so change the nature of the society and interfere with the control of its affairs by its members, which has always been its vital principle, that the future of the society would be thereby imperiled."[61] Leifels further indicated the society did not automatically oppose any future proposals, but that any new proposition should not reference previous negotiations. Damrosch quickly requested that Arnold not forward his name as a candidate for the following season. In his memoirs Damrosch stated, "The changes which I had proposed were necessary, however, if the society expected to continue its existence as an orchestral body."[62]

The years prior to Mahler's arrival at the Philharmonic continued to reflect inconsistencies in conductors. From 1903 to 1906 a number of guest conductors appeared with the orchestra, including Victor Herbert, Richard Strauss, Felix Wiengartner, Vassily Ilyich Safonoff, and Edouard Colonne. To pay for the exorbitant conductor salaries, E. Francis Hyde raised roughly $50,000. When the Philharmonic agreed to hire Safonoff for the 1906–1907 season, he requested a salary of $20,000, the largest amount ever paid to a Philharmonic conductor.[63] Unfortunately, the number of concerts per season remained at eight pairs, and over the course of the next three seasons the box offices receipts steadily declined, beginning with $55,000 for the 1906–1907 season; $50,000 for the 1907–1908 season; and $40,000 for the 1908–1909 season.[64] At the same time advertising costs, hall rental, and the soloists' fees continued to rise, and it became clear another method of supporting the Philharmonic needed to be carefully considered.

After being rejected by the Philharmonic, Damrosch returned to the New York Symphony Society in 1903, and brought his restructuring plan to this organization. Some guarantors from the Philharmonic followed Damrosch and assisted financially in supporting the orchestra. Among the supporters was Harry Harkness Flagler, a millionaire oil magnate heir, who personally managed to help finance the New York Symphony musicians on full-time, permanent salaries starting in 1907. By 1914, he assumed the entire financial responsibility of the orchestra. Over the years the New York Symphony continued to prosper with the aid of wealthy moguls such as Flagler, who contributed more than a million dollars of his fortune to the orchestra.[65]

During this era competition grew as rival orchestras, such as Modest Altschuler's Russian Symphony Orchestra, thrived in New York City. In addition, visiting orchestras, such as the Philadelphia Orchestra and Boston Symphony Orchestra, expanded their Carnegie Hall offerings. As union wages for musicians continued to rise, opera companies and ensembles threatened the Philharmonic's cohesiveness as they lured players away. Although there was a gentleman's agreement that New York orchestras and out-of-town orchestras would "not steal each other's players," ensembles still lured musicians with better pay and working conditions.[66]

The Economic Panic of 1907 further influenced musicians to seek secure employment. As the economy slowed down over the summer, the stock market declined, interest rates significantly increased, several large corporations declared bankruptcy, and a recession loomed on the horizon. By October 1907 a financial panic swept through New York City as depositors withdrew more than $47 million from the Trust Company of America. The impact of the 1907 Panic was soon reflected in the instability of major industries, such as United States railway, whose earnings fell $300 million by 1908.[67]

As the 1908–1909 season approached, a number of wind players left the Philharmonic for full-time positions with union wages at the Metropolitan Opera. These players included: the first and second flutes, the first clarinet, first bassoon, first trombone, first trumpet, tuba, tympani, several violins, and the first and second cellos.[68] Although a number of players became dissatisfied with Safonoff, the primary cause for their resignations proved to be a desire for permanent positions with good salaries. Speaking on behalf of the society, Arnold could not condemn the musicians' leaving and emphasized that "a man's first duty is to his family."[69] Some players had served the Philharmonic for twenty-five to thirty years, but a guaranteed full-time salary became a priority.

Despite the Philharmonic's recognition as America's oldest orchestra, it did not earn the definition of a "permanent" orchestra until 1909, since it lacked a full-season contract, full membership, regular rehearsals, and a financial base. Until this point the orchestra also failed to serve as the principal means of employment for its members, and musicians failed to treat the orchestra as a top priority.[70]

Sheldon Leads the Transition

Mary Sheldon's offer to Mahler to conduct several concerts marked the pivotal beginning of the Philharmonic's reorganization. Notes from an informal meeting at Sheldon's home in April 1908 further outlined how the Mahler concerts could be the beginning of a new permanent orchestra, different from the New York Philharmonic or any other orchestra. To accomplish this objective, Sheldon needed to secure funding by November 1908. Sheldon's ties to the wealthy elite of New York proved advantageous in raising capital. Her husband, George R. Sheldon, served as president of the United States Trust Company and treasurer of the Republican National Committee for more than ten years. Throughout his life he served on the board of directors of eighteen companies including the American Locomotive Company and the Bethlehem Steel Company.[71]

Safonoff completed his second year of a three-year contract with the Philharmonic in March 1908, and even though some people believed his contract might not be renewed, the newspapers ran a different story. Based on some "excellent authority," the *New York Times* reported in July 1908 that despite some opposition, the Philharmonic Society engaged Safonoff for another three years after the expiration of his contract in 1909.[72]

Unfortunately, Sheldon and her committee opposed this direction. While in Europe during the summer of 1908, Sheldon adamantly stated that if Safonoff conducted past the expiration of his initial contract, she would "simply go ahead and form another orchestra" so that New York would have the "greatest orchestra America has ever heard."[73] Sheldon also confirmed that in addition to engaging Mahler for several concerts the committee also had "an option on his services for the following year."[74]

In response to Sheldon's determination to create a new orchestra, Richard Arnold indicated New York could not support another orchestra and suggested the two organizations, namely the New York Philharmonic and Sheldon's new orchestra, should be placed together, and conducted by Mahler. Sheldon further noted that upon returning to America, she would work with the Philharmonic Society to form a new entity and that some personnel changes would be imperative.[75]

The Philharmonic's New Plan for Survival

As the 1908–1909 music season opened, the society outlined plans for re-structuring, with a new board and eventually a new conductor. As early as November 1908, news circulated regarding the formation of the New York Philharmonic into a permanent orchestra modeled on the Boston Symphony Orchestra. Although the society and the guarantors had not yet arrived at a decision, it appeared that their plans would succeed and Gustav Mahler would become the new conductor.[76] In a letter to the editor of the *New York Times*, Sheldon indicated her primary concern was to "establish the old Phil-harmonic Society on a living and substantial basis."[77] Her supporters offi-cially formed the "Guarantors of the Fund for the Permanent Orchestra of the Philharmonic Society of New York" and aimed to "raise enough money to rebuild the Philharmonic into an orchestra of first rank, paying sufficient salaries to the players and the conductor to enable them to give their full time to the orchestra during the concert season."[78]

Sheldon encouraged contributions to the orchestra of ten, fifteen, and even thirty thousand dollars from business tycoons such as J. P. Morgan, John D. Rockefeller, Joseph Pulitzer, and Thomas Ryan. Sheldon's group soon raised $100,000, and by March 29, 1909, the *New York Times* reported, Shel-don and her committee of backers guaranteed more than $90,000 annually for a three-year period, thus accounting for a substantial amount of the or-chestra's operating budget.[79]

When the guarantors met on February 6, 1909, they detailed the steps for the orchestra's reorganization. The restructuring offered musicians twenty-three weeks of concerts and an increase from eighteen to forty-six concerts each season. Furthermore, the committee and a newly appointed conductor would approve of each musician. The Philharmonic would no longer be "governed by its democratically elected Board of Directors, but by the Com-mittee of Guarantors who would designate the directors, three of which could be orchestral members."[80]

Many of the changes outlined in the plan reflected those presented in Damrosch's 1903 plan. This time, however, members of the society adopted the plan because they desired a steady income rather than an uncertain fu-ture. Concertmaster Richard Arnold, who opposed the earlier plan, further explained that in previous years musicians risked uncertain profits for the honor of playing with the Philharmonic, but as other organizations began to demand their services, the musicians were less willing to take this risk.[81]

With this newfound financial security the Philharmonic could attract more qualified, full-time musicians and recruit a renowned conductor. By early 1909 Mahler and the committee privately reached an agreement regarding his position as director of the orchestra. By the end of January 1909 the search progressed for a new concertmaster, and Arnold soon planned to retire.[82] The newspapers finally announced Gustav Mahler would lead the newly reorganized Philharmonic in the middle of February 1909. A month later the committee approved a formal contract for Mahler's appointment.[83]

Mahler Joins the Philharmonic

Mahler's new position at the New York Philharmonic offered several advantages compared with his position at the Vienna Philharmonic. First of all, since the cooperative plan no longer governed New York musicians, Mahler could select the best musicians. Unfortunately, in Vienna the musicians still owned the orchestra under the cooperative and determined the music director.

In New York the Philharmonic became the musicians' main focus and under the new plan rehearsals became a priority. In Vienna, however, the musicians provided the music for the opera productions, and the Philharmonic performances became a second priority. Previous Vienna Philharmonic conductors, such as Hans Richter, had not insisted on numerous rehearsals, and this conflicted with Mahler's expectations.[84] In New York, critics and orchestra supporters viewed Mahler's desire for perfection as a positive point and a way to move ahead culturally of other orchestras.

Mahler gladly accepted the Philharmonic position with an attached salary of $25,000, worth roughly $494,000 in 2005 dollars.[85] Although some critics declared his fee too high, Mahler conducted more than twice the number of concerts in Manhattan as his predecessor Safonoff, to whom the Philharmonic paid a salary of $20,000.

Although Mahler chose Theodore Spiering[86] as the new concertmaster and selected new musicians, the so-called new players represented many members from the Manhattan Opera Orchestra, the Victor Herbert Orchestra, and the Boston Symphony Orchestra. Even a horn player left the Metropolitan Opera Orchestra to join the Philharmonic.[87] As Henry Finck of the *New York Evening Post* noted, "It used to be the other way; the best Philharmonic players being enticed away by offers of a bigger salary."[88] Furthermore, changes in the new system stipulated that no performer be paid less than thirty-five dollars per week.[89]

For the 1909–1910 season only fifty-six members of the 102 musicians listed in one of the last concerts under Safonoff participated in Mahler's opening concert on November 4, 1909.[90] When examined more closely, however, twenty-six of the so-called new musicians represented musicians that already worked as extras for the Philharmonic during the 1908–1909 season.[91] As mentioned earlier, a number of long-time wind players and even some string, brass, and percussion players departed the society prior to the 1908–1909 season.

As the restructuring progressed, the Guarantor Committee gradually took over the daily operations and the administrative responsibilities of the orchestra. They changed the management by offering full-time salaries to Richard Arnold[92] as its vice president and Felix Leifels as secretary.[93] After Andrew Carnegie resigned from the Philharmonic's presidency in April 1909, the office remained vacant during 1910 and 1911. Finally, by 1912 all the officers and previous directors of the former New York Philharmonic Society were replaced.[94]

Notes

1. Paul Banks, "Mahler, Gustav," *The New Grove Dictionary of Music and Musicians*, ed. Stanley Sadie (London: Macmillan, 1980), 11:506.

2. Peter Franklin, "Mahler, Gustav," *The New Grove Dictionary of Music and Musicians*, ed. Stanley Sadie, 2d ed. (London: Macmillan, 2001), 15:604.

3. Banks, 507.

4. Franklin, 604.

5. Angelo Neumann (1838–1910) trained as a lyric tenor and sang throughout Europe and at the Vienna Court Opera (1862–1876). He then began managing opera, including the Bremen Opera (1882–1885) and the German opera in Prague at the Landestheater (1885–1910).

6. After studying at the Leipzig Conservatory, Anton Seidl (1850–1898) became chorusmaster of the Vienna Opera under Hans Richter and also worked with Wagner in Bayreuth until 1879. After conducting a tour of Wagner operas under Neumann, Seidl left for America in 1885 and conducted the German operas at the Metropolitan Opera House. In 1891, he became the permanent conductor of the New York Philharmonic Society and held the position until his death in 1898.

7. Arthur Nikisch (1855–1922) attended the Vienna Conservatory. After working as a violinist, he became second conductor for the Leipzig Theater. His career included a period at the Neues Stadttheater in Leipzig (1882–1889); then he joined the Boston Symphony Orchestra as conductor (1889–1893). After returning to Europe, he was director of the Royal Opera in Budapest (1893–1895) and then director of studies at the Leipzig Conservatory (1902–1907). Beginning in 1895 until his death Nikisch served as conductor of the Leipzig Gewandhaus Orchestra and conductor of the Berlin Philharmonic Orchestra. He also had an extensive career as a visiting conductor and led several tours, including one with the London Symphony Orchestra to America in 1912.

8. Banks, 508.

9. A more recent edition includes Gustav Mahler, *Die drei Pintos: Based on Sketches and Original Music of Carl Maria von Weber*, ed. James L. Zychowicz (Madison, WI: A-R Editions, 2000).

10. *Die drei Pintos: Based on Sketches and Original Music of Carl Maria von Weber*.

11. Norman Lebrecht, *The Maestro Myth*, revised ed. (New York: Citadel Press, 2001), 46.

12. Pollini (1838–1897), whose real name was Baruch Pohl, began his career as a tenor and also sang baritone roles. Beginning in 1874 he leased the Hamburg Stadttheater and turned it into one of the leading opera houses in Germany.

13. Franklin, 607.

14. Richter (1843–1916) became first Kapellmeister at the Imperial Opera, Vienna in 1893. From 1875 to 1897, he conducted opera and concerts of the Vienna Philharmonic Society. In 1897 Richter moved to Manchester and served as conductor of the Hallé Orchestra. Upon retiring in 1912, he spent his final years in Bayreuth.

15. Banks, 510.

16. Lebrecht, 48.

17. Lebrecht, 49.

18. Henry-Louis de La Grange, *Mahler*, vol. 3, *Triumph and Disillusion (1904–1907)* (Oxford: Oxford University Press, 1999), 670.

19. Anna von Mildenburg (1879–1947) was a dramatic soprano. She sang at Bayreuth and joined the Vienna Opera in 1898. She retired from singing in 1917 and taught voice at the State Academy in Munich.

20. Erik Schmedes (1866–1931) became known as a famous Danish tenor. Schmedes studied voice in Paris and in 1898 appeared as Siegfried at the Vienna Opera. He performed with the Vienna Opera until 1924 and during the 1908–1909 season was a member of the Metropolitan Opera Company.

21. La Grange, 3:654.

22. *Wiener Allgemeine Zeitung*, 22 May 1907 in La Grange, 3:645n102.

23. La Grange, 3:790.

24. La Grange, 3:739.

25. *Illustrites Wiener Extrablatt*, 7 June 1907 in La Grange, 3:674.

26. Heinrich Conried (1848–1909) started his career as an actor in Vienna and in 1878 arrived in New York and managed the Germania Theater. After running various theatrical organizations and serving as director of the Irving Place Theater (1892–1903), Conried became manager of the Metropolitan Opera (1903–1908).

27. John Dizikes, *Opera in America: A Cultural History* (New Haven: Yale University Press, 1993), 323.

28. "Conried Opera Co. to be Reorganized," *New York Times*, 16 October 1907, 1.

29. "Conried Opera Co. to be Reorganized," 1.

30. "Conried Opera Co. to be Reorganized," 1.

31. *New York World*, 29 March 1908, Metropolitan sec., 1; quoted in Zoltan Roman, *Gustav Mahler's American Years: 1907–1911* (Stuyvesant, NY: Pendragon Press, 1989), 119.

32. La Grange, 3:787.

33. Montrose Moses, *The Life of Heinrich Conried* (New York: Arno Press, 1977), 322.

34. Giulio Gatti-Casazza (1868–1940) abandoned his first career as an engineer when he became director of the Municipal Theater in Ferrara in 1893. He then progressed to director of La Scala (1898–1908) before becoming general manager of the Metropolitan Opera (1908–1935). Gatti-Casazza brought several conductors to America from Italy, including Arturo Toscanini. Upon resigning in 1935, he retired to Italy.

35. Andreas Dippel (1866–1932) first worked for a banking house in Kassel. After studying voice, he embarked on a career as a dramatic tenor and sang numerous roles at the Bremen Stadttheater, the Metropolitan Opera, and Covent Garden. He became administrative manager at the Metropolitan Opera House in 1908, and from 1910 until 1913 managed the Chicago Opera Company. He later formed his own opera company.

36. Roman, 16. Otto Herman Kahn (1867–1934) first worked in the banking profession in London (1888–1893) before arriving in New York and joining the Kuhn, Loeb, and Company. From 1907 to 1934 he was on the board of the Metropolitan Opera Company and also served as vice president of the New York Philharmonic.

37. Richard Aldrich, "Tristan und Isolde at the Metropolitan," *New York Times*, 2 January 1908, 9.

38. On February 18, 1908, Mahler conducted Mozart's *Don Giovanni* in Philadelphia. On April 8, 1908, Mahler conducted Wagner's *Die Walküre* in Boston. During the same week he also conducted Mozart's *Don Giovanni* on April 9, 1908, and Wagner's *Tristan und Isolde* on April 11, 1908, in Boston.

39. Marvin L. Von Deck, "Gustav Mahler in New York: His Conducting Activities in New York City, 1908–1911" (Ph.D. diss., New York University, 1973), 288.

40. Von Deck, 119.

41. Von Deck, 170.

42. Toscanini conducted *Die Götterdämmerung* on December 10, 1908.

43. "Reflections," *Musical Courier* 57, no. 14 (September 30, 1908): 22.

44. *New York Sun*, 21 February 1909, 7.

45. Philip Hart, *Orpheus in the New World: The Symphony Orchestra as an American Cultural Institution* (New York: W. W. Norton, 1973), 3.

46. Irving Kolodin, Francis D. Perkins, and Susan Thiemann Sommer, "New York," *The New Grove Dictionary of Music and Musicians*, 2d ed, 17:827.

47. John H. Mueller, *The American Symphony Orchestra: A Social History of Music Taste* (Bloomington: Indiana University Press, 1951), 88.

48. Kolodin et al., "New York," *New Grove Dictionary* 17:827.

49. The Russian Symphony Orchestra existed from 1904 to 1918 under the direction of Modest Altschuler (1873–1963). Born in Russia, Altschuler studied cello at the Warsaw Conservatory and immigrated to America. He later settled in Los Angeles as a teacher and completed his memoirs.

50. Walter Damrosch (1862–1950), the younger son of Leopold Damrosch, conducted several ensembles throughout his career, including the New York Oratorio Society (1885–1898, 1917), the New York Symphony Society (1885–1902, 1903–1927), and the New York Philharmonic Society (1902–1903). He also served as assistant conductor of the Metropolitan Opera House (1885–1891), led the Damrosch Opera Company (1894–1899), and conducted the NBC Symphony Orchestra in a weekly series of music appreciation concerts (1928–1942).

51. Frank Damrosch (1859–1937), the elder son of Leopold Damrosch, began these concerts in 1898. In 1893, he organized the Musical Art Society, which performed a cappella music until 1920. He held a number of positions throughout his life as chorusmaster and assistant conductor at the Metropolitan Opera House (1885–1891), supervisor of music in New York City public schools (1897–1905), and conductor of the choral group Musurgia (1891–1900), Oratorio Society (1898–1912), and Mendelssohn Glee Club (1904–1909). In 1905 he founded the Institute of Musical Art, which in 1926 became affiliated with the Juilliard School.

52. Carl Van Vechten, "The Coming New York Season," *New Music Review and Church Music Review* 9, no. 97 (December 1909): 19. Fiedler (1859–1939) was a guest conductor of the New York Philharmonic (1905–1907) and later served as conductor of the Boston Symphony Orchestra (1908–1912). After returning to Germany, he conducted the Symphony Orchestra at Essen (1916–1934) and guest conducted in Stockholm (1935). The Boston Symphony Orchestra offered one program each month performed on a Thursday evening and repeated on Saturday.

53. Howard Shanet, *Philharmonic: A History of New York's Orchestra* (Garden City, NY: Doubleday and Company, 1975), 202.

54. Shanet, 201.

55. Damrosch married Margaret Blaine in 1890. Her father was James Gillespie Blaine. He served as a member of Congress from 1863 through 1876 and as the speaker of the House of Representatives from the forty-first through forty-third Congresses. He served as a United States senator from 1876–1880, secretary of state in the cabinet of President Harrison from 1889–1892, and sought nomination for president three times (1876, 1880, and 1884).

56. Walter Damrosch, *My Musical Life* (New York: Charles Scribner's Sons, 1923), 207.

57. Damrosch, 208.

58. "Philharmonic Society Plan," *New York Times*, 19 February 1903, 3.

59. Franz Kaltenborn, Gustav Dannreuther, and Sam Franko all led their own orchestras and also played in the Philharmonic.

60. Mueller, 47.

61. "Damrosch May Quit the Philharmonic," *New York Times*, 2 March 1903, 7.

62. Damrosch, 209.

63. Shanet, 193.

64. Shanet, 195.

65. Mueller, 56.

66. Damrosch, 330.

67. Samuel O. Dunn, *Current Railway Problems* (New York: Railway Age Gazette, 1911), 35.

68. "Demands of Opera Deplete Orchestras," *New York Times*, 8 September 1908, 9.

69. "Demands of Opera Deplete Orchestras," 9.

70. Mueller, 36.

71. George R. Sheldon also served on the board of directors for Cincinnati Northern Railway Company, Detroit Edison Company, Electrical Securities Company, the Laclede Gas Light Company, Montreal Locomotive Works, Locomotive Securities Company, Metropolitan Trust Company, Milwaukee Light, Heat, and Traction Company, National Copper Bank, North American Company, New Jersey Terminal Dock and Improvement Company, Republic Iron and Steel Company, Rogers Locomotive Works, and St. Louis Transit Company.

72. "Safonoff to Return," *New York Times*, 26 July 1908, C3.

73. "New York to Have Notable Orchestra," *New York Times*, 23 August 1908, C1.

74. "New York to Have Notable Orchestra," C1.

75. "New York to Have Notable Orchestra," C1.

76. "To Form a New Orchestra," *New York Times*, 17 August 1908, 7.

77. "Mrs. Sheldon Explains Proposal for Its Reorganization," *New York Times*, 13 December 1908, 12.

78. Shanet, 207.

79. *New York Times*, 28 March 1909, sec. 4, 7. The other members included: Mrs. William Jay, Mrs. Douglas Robinson, Mrs. William P. Douglas, Henry Lane Eno, Mrs. C. B. Alexander, James Gayley, Mrs. Elbridge Gerry, Francis Lynde Stetson, Alexander S. Cochran, Mrs. Harry Payne Whitney, Mrs. E. H. Harriman, E. C. Converse, Mrs. Maurice Loeb, and E. J. de Coppet.

80. Shanet, 208. Vassily Ilyich Safonoff (1852–1918) first guest conducted the New York Philharmonic on March 4, 1904. He was appointed the regular Philharmonic conductor for three seasons (1906–1909) and at the same time served as director of the National Conservatory in New York. He studied at the Conservatory of St. Petersburg and later taught piano there (1881–1885). Before coming to America he also taught at the Moscow Conservatory (1885–1889) and became its director (1889–1905). Safonoff returned to Russia and was appointed conductor of the Imperial Russian Music Society (1909–1911).

81. *New York Sun*, 7 March 1909, sec. 3, 10.

82. Roman, 137.

83. Roman, 138. The Committee of Guarantors formally approved the contract at a meeting on March 30, 1909.

84. Jonathon Carr, *Mahler: A Biography* (Woodstock, NY: Overlook Press, 1999), 88.

85. Values were calculated using a historical CPI (Consumer Price Index) model. Calculations were made with the Consumer Price Index Calculator at the Federal

Reserve Bank of Minneapolis. For more information refer to minneapolisfed.org/Research/data/us/calc.

86. Theodore Spiering (1871–1925) was born in St. Louis and studied at the Cincinnati College of Music and at the Hochschule für Musik in Berlin. From 1909 to 1911 he served as concertmaster of the Philharmonic. During his career he organized a string quartet and also toured as a soloist in the U.S., Canada, and Germany.

87. *New York Daily Tribune*, 17 October 1909, sec. 4, 2.

88. Henry Finck, "A Musical Season with Novelties, *New York Evening Post*, 6 November 1909, Saturday Supplement, 2.

89. Shanet, 207 ff.

90. Roman, 248. Roman notes that the "overall turnover was in the range of 40–55%; 43 of the 58 (roughly 74%) string players were members of the old ensemble, 5 of the 14 second violins were new members." As Roman further points out on page 251, "Only 11 of Safonoff's 29 wind players appeared in Mahler's orchestra; all but three of them had been demoted. While two out of the three former trumpet players were retained, not a single one of the four flutes and piccolo players survived the reorganization."

91. Shanet, 220.

92. Richard Arnold (1845–1918) emigrated from Prussia to the United States in 1853 and later studied violin in Leipzig. He was a violinist in the Theodore Thomas Orchestra (1869–1876), concertmaster of the New York Philharmonic (1880–1909), and vice president of the New York Philharmonic (1909–1918).

93. Shanet, 209.

94. Shanet, 209.

~

CHAPTER TWO

Touring throughout America

Mahler's reign with the New York Philharmonic marked the first time that the orchestra performed beyond the New York area in an effort to supplement their season financially.[1] Management aimed for a season without a deficit, and the railroads provided transportation for the orchestra to perform in many locations with limited rehearsals, thus increasing the orchestra's revenue. Other ensembles, such as the New York Symphony, the Theodore Thomas Orchestra, and even the John Philip Sousa Band, already augmented their livelihood by touring America's prosperous cities. Moreover, touring extended the concert season and filled the gaps in the New York performance schedule. The idea proved so successful, with five concerts on tour during the 1909–1910 season, that the tours expanded to fourteen concerts for the 1910–1911 season.[2] When Josef Stransky took the reign as conductor in 1911, he practically doubled the number of touring concerts to thirty-one for the 1911–1912 season. During his twelve years as conductor, touring became a standard as the Philharmonic offered between nineteen and ninety-four concerts annually outside New York City.[3] In the brief window of the twentieth century that preceded the two world wars, the railroads dominated the transportation industry and allowed touring ensembles to thrive and earn profits.

Many musicians toured to increase their income and expand their audience base. By the end of the nineteenth century, soloists, orchestras, opera companies, and smaller ensembles, such as string quartets, scheduled touring as part of their season. For larger organizations with a home base, such as the

Boston Symphony Orchestra or the Metropolitan Opera, touring provided additional income for the organization, kept artists committed, and extended compensation beyond the New York engagements. These groups usually toured when they had no commitments at their home location, and before or after a season. However, some organizations, such as the Theodore Thomas Orchestra and the New York Symphony Orchestra, relied on touring as their primary source of income.

In 1884, the opportunity for touring exploded with the advent of America's transcontinental railroad. This modern transportation network connected small towns to large cities in a matter of hours. Moreover, the railroad proved to be cost effective, efficient, and convenient, by providing transportation and sleeping accommodations. By the peak of the rail industry in 1916, its gross revenue reached $3.5 billion with a total capitalization of $21 billion.[4] At the turn of the twentieth century, the railroads provided the primary mode of transportation, with trains averaging speeds between fifty and sixty miles per hour. By 1910 passengers also enjoyed savings, as fares dropped from three cents to roughly two cents a mile.[5] The price for overnight accommodations on a train competed with hotels and offered the advantage of passengers' waking up in their desired destination, thus saving time and money. During 1910, sleeping accommodations were available for $1.50 for the upper berth, and $2.00 for the lower berth.[6] The price for accommodations in New York City ranged between $1 and $3.[7] The availability of Pullman cars, drawing rooms, and dining cars provided luxury accommodations to satisfy any customer. The railroads continued to expand their territory and by 1916, the railroads reached their peak in America with over 254,037 miles of trackage.[8]

The Soloist on Tour

Soloists touring America at the turn of the twentieth century claimed the largest profits. European virtuosos typically drew lucrative incomes and performed during the concert season, which ran from fall until spring. A lengthy article from The New Times in 1907 estimated that "six millions dollars would be paid to European musicians" performing in America during the season.[9] Although musicians earned various amounts per concert, famous soloists such as Enrico Caruso, Ignace Paderewski, and Marcella Sembrich typically charged a minimum concert fee of $2,000. Other contracts called for the soloist to receive a guaranteed minimum amount and sometimes an additional percentage of ticket sales. For example, Paderewski agreed to appear for eighty concerts for a minimum of $1,500 per performance and often received between 75 and 80 percent of the ticket sales. Soloists earned supplemental income through contracts with piano manufacturers, which added another $40,000 to Paderewski's wallet, and through contracts with "gramophone people," which added another $40,000 to Caruso's wallet. Even less prominent pianists earned roughly $400 to $500 per performance and quickly booked concerts throughout the East Coast and Midwest.[10]

Soloists routinely appeared with orchestras, which lured concertgoers to the hall and impacted the potential profit and break-even point for the event. For example, when the New York Philharmonic and German soprano Johanna Gadski performed three concerts in New England in 1911, Gadski's contract called for 40 percent of the Philharmonic's share of the gross receipts.[11] Later, when the orchestra performed on tour with American soprano Lillian Nordica, her contract called for 50 percent of the net receipts after expenses.[12]

Although many large cities provided better quality accommodations than first-rate musicians expected, many smaller towns along tour routes offered dismal conditions. Therefore, a number of top musicians, especially opera singers, bought their own train cars and decorated them in a luxurious manner. For example, opera star Aldelina Patti's $65,000 train car of 1884 included heavy damask silk curtains, gilded leather tapestry on the walls and ceiling, a grand piano, valuable Italian pictures, a bathroom, and appliances for cooking and eating.[13]

Opera on Tour

Established in 1883, the Metropolitan Opera Company represented one of the oldest surviving performance organizations in America. The same year, the Metropolitan toured via train and continued with this mode of transportation until 1968. With the exception of the Great Depression and some war years, the Met usually toured in the autumn and spring. By the 1970s, the Metropolitan annually played to approximately 700,000 people at the Lincoln Center and another 250,000 people on the tours, resulting in 26 percent of the audience based from touring.[14]

The Met began touring out of necessity when Manager Henry Abbey quickly depleted the $1,000 per performance that stockholders provided for the first season. Expensive sets, high-salaried singers, and costumes soon ran Abbey into debt. In an effort to save the organization, Abbey took to the railroad for the Met's first tour to Boston on December 26, 1883.

Compared with a touring orchestra, opera companies needed to travel with many more people and much more baggage. Embarking on tour meant several cars for baggage, a diner, Pullmans, tourist sleepers, several coaches, and individual cars for various opera stars. Accommodations were also required for the orchestra. Moreover, opera companies usually took along costumes, props, scenery for multiple operas, technical staff, and administration. By the middle of the twentieth century a Met tour required two special trains, with a total of eighteen sleeping cars and twenty-two baggage cars.[15]

By the time Mahler arrived in America the Met had been touring for more than twenty years. During the 1907–1908 season the Met presented approximately forty-four operas on tour and traveled to six cities, including Philadelphia, Boston, Baltimore, Washington, D.C., Chicago, and Pittsburgh. Of these engagements Mahler conducted only performances of *Don Giovanni* and *Die Walküre* in both Boston and Philadelphia.[16]

Orchestras on Tour

Theodore Thomas pioneered orchestral touring throughout America. What began in 1864 as a New York ensemble performing an evening concert series soon evolved into the Theodore Thomas Orchestra. His orchestra began touring to survive, to increase revenue, and to keep the players together as a cohesive unit.[17] Although Thomas offered a variety of musical venues, there were a finite number of popular concerts that New Yorkers would support. Nevertheless, Thomas desired to make the orchestra a permanent, full-time organization. To increase his profit and maintain demand in New York, he decided touring would expand his market. Thomas had traveled with orchestras and solo artists during the 1850s and found touring a profitable enterprise. With an improved railroad system and more developed cities throughout the country, Thomas began touring in 1869 with a concert in Poughkeepsie, New York. He coordinated the tours, hired soloists, and made all the financial decisions. Without a middle man, Thomas was autonomous and increased his revenues but he also remained liable for losses.

To make the most of each tour, Thomas offered concerts at cities along train routes. For example, if the ultimate destination was Chicago, the orchestra performed at least twenty concerts between New York and Chicago. Thomas usually selected an alternate return route that allowed the orchestra to perform in more cities. The touring routes acquired the nickname of the "Thomas Highway."[18]

As other orchestras and conductors would soon discover, however, touring presented several challenges. To begin with, tours provided little time for musicians to practice individually or to attend extensive rehearsals.[19] Another major disadvantage proved to be inclement weather, especially in win-

ter months. Since orchestras usually scheduled only one evening for a concert in each city, they could not guarantee that the trains would arrive
promptly on a stormy night. At times rehearsals were missed, soloists failed
to arrive, concerts started several hours late, or a concert was cancelled. In
spite of these conditions, patrons at the turn of the twentieth century appeared tolerant and even waited several hours past the scheduled time for an
event to begin. Lastly, although the rail system proved efficient and economical, coal-burning locomotives were frequently dirty. In close living conditions and without proper ventilation, musicians seemed to contract more
illnesses when traveling.

As years passed, the Thomas Orchestra maintained full-time status while
gaining national recognition for fine programming and high quality orchestral playing. When visiting cities, Thomas considered the cultural level of
each community and provided a program oriented toward their taste. In the
initial visit to a city the orchestra frequently provided "light" music, and
upon subsequent visits Thomas programmed more serious works. Since cities
outside of New York and Boston had only part-time or amateur ensembles,
Thomas's orchestra exemplified "outstanding tone quality, precision, and ensemble technique," and soon became known as one of the finest orchestras
in the United States.[20]

When touring the country Thomas also limited his program selection. For
example, in 1889 when he presented twenty-five concerts in twenty-two
cities, he offered local managers three different programs that represented
American popular taste.[21] By limiting the choice of programs, Thomas minimized the orchestra's rehearsal time. Rather than scheduling a separate rehearsal, the orchestra could meet briefly before the concert to review specific
sections of music. This idea turned into a major cost-saving maneuver for
many touring orchestras, since it eliminated or largely reduced rehearsal
time. Most professional orchestras usually required a minimum of three to
four rehearsals before each concert. Thomas reduced or eliminated these
costs, and in their place provided concerts that generated revenue.

Walter Damrosch toured extensively with the New York Symphony Orchestra. An economical touring plan involved three-day festivals in one location. These festivals made use of local talent and often incorporated a local chorus to augment the orchestral offerings. Over the course of three days
the orchestra usually gave five concerts. The local committees tended to
group concerts together to increase their revenue and minimize their expenses. In this way a hall could be used multiple times in one day. Furthermore, the inclusion of local musicians encouraged patronage by their family
and friends and strong support for Damrosch and the orchestra in subsequent

years. To make the most of touring, Damrosch often booked a grueling schedule of two festivals within the same week, spending three days in each location.[22]

Touring also minimized hall rental expenses. Orchestras made contracts with local managers, who usually negotiated the hall rental and coordinated arrangements. By the turn of the twentieth century, however, many orchestras needed to rent a rehearsal and performance space. The cost of hall rental also ate into profits. For example, spaces such as Carnegie Hall charged orchestras for every rehearsal and performance, which ran as high as four hundred dollars per night.[23] One of the exceptions was the Boston Symphony Orchestra, which began performing in their own Symphony Hall in 1900. As the century progressed more orchestras owned halls and gained revenue by renting their facilities. This step also offset fixed costs such as heating, security, and routine maintenance.

In addition to orchestras earning a profit through touring, local managers usually benefited financially, and audiences enjoyed music at reasonable prices. With the affordability of rail travel, the price to attend a New York Philharmonic or Boston Symphony Orchestra concert remained comparable or even less expensive than a ticket to a local orchestra concert. Although touring allowed audiences to enjoy music by the best orchestras or opera companies, it also delayed the development and shortened the longevity of some regional orchestras.

To develop an orchestra in a new area required many start-up and ongoing expenses, such as rehearsal space, music, rehearsal pay, advertising, marketing, personnel, and a solid group of volunteers to serve on a board of directors. These factors comprised a portion of the ticket price to a concert by a local orchestra but played a minor role in the ticket price to a concert by a touring orchestra. The concert series also represented a good value. For example, in Cleveland critics believed imported music offered the best value in music as "nothing in the musical season of Cleveland compares in value for music-lovers, and music students of all classes."[24] In addition, touring orchestras frequently included a renowned soloist as part of the program, which attracted a larger audience. Other than a local impresario taking a financial risk by engaging a touring orchestra, the liability remained limited. Several reporters even admitted that the possibility of losing money on a local orchestra appeared to be an unattractive and unnecessary risk if a prestigious orchestra could be imported for concerts.[25]

This idea of imported music took shape in the Cleveland Orchestra Concert Series organized by Adella Prentiss Hughes. From 1901 until 1920 Hughes single-handedly managed 162 concerts by eleven touring orchestras under twenty-one conductors.[26] These series of concerts featured orchestras from cities such as Boston, New York, Philadelphia, Chicago, Minneapolis, and Pittsburgh. From 1902 until 1918 three local orchestras formed in Cleveland and developed a following.[27] However, these local orchestras could not compete with the touring ensembles that attracted Cleveland's wealthy and elite. Although Cleveland earned the recognition of having the fifth largest population in America at the turn of the twentieth century, it took almost another two decades to form a sustainable orchestra. Finally in 1918, Nikolai Sokoloff convinced Hughes to focus on developing a local orchestra. With major funding from wealthy individuals such as John L. Severance, Samuel Mather, and David Z. Norton, the Cleveland Orchestra formed, and the number of concerts offered by touring orchestras leveled off and eventually declined.

Touring orchestras could also spark support for local interest in the arts. Citizens might believe their city deserved the quality of a touring orchestra and might choose to form an ensemble. The visiting orchestra might be seen as a goal for a local community and an example of what could happen in the future.

Conversely, a touring orchestra sometimes contributed to the downfall of a local orchestra. Touring orchestras produced concerts more cost-effectively than a local orchestra, creating harmful competition. Rivalries resulted when cities imported music from one or more sources. Visiting orchestras eventually contributed to the downfall of the Pittsburgh Symphony Orchestra in 1910. When the orchestra was struggling for support, out-of-town orchestras compounded the problem.

Formed in 1898, the Pittsburgh Orchestra enjoyed several seasons of local support, and in 1904 even offered a concert with Richard Strauss as guest conductor. As orchestras from the East Coast began touring more regularly, however, the Pittsburgh Orchestra could not offer tickets at the same price as touring orchestras. Furthermore, touring orchestras would often appear in the city on an evening close to a concert date for the local orchestra. Potential concertgoers began choosing the more exclusive East Coast orchestral concerts rather than the local concerts. When Mahler arrived in Pittsburgh to conduct the New York Philharmonic on December 5, 1910, the concert marked a pivotal turn in the orchestra's collapse. Local supporters believed the event would rally concertgoers to contribute more money to the struggling Pittsburgh Orchestra. The plan backfired, however, and resulted in an immediate disbandment of the Pittsburgh Orchestra. In subsequent years, touring orchestras continued to expand their offerings and to schedule more concerts in Pittsburgh. It took sixteen more years for Pittsburgh to organize a professional self-sustaining orchestra. Finally, in 1926 today's Pittsburgh Symphony Orchestra formed.

Financing the Season

Few records exist detailing the expenses of each Philharmonic concert during the 1910s, but several memos and copies of contracts have survived. Based on a contract with Adella Prentiss Hughes, the Philharmonic received $2,000 for the December 1910 concert in Cleveland.[28] Contracts for other concerts stated varying amounts. For example, a 1911 memo indicated that the Philharmonic would receive 75 percent of the gross receipts for a Toronto concert with a minimum guarantee of $1,250 and a maximum of $2,000.[29]

Minutes from a December 1911 board of directors meeting revealed the orchestra's financial status during the 1909–1910 and 1910–1911 seasons. A financial statement for the 1909–1910 season presented the touring receipts averaging $674 versus $1,003 per New York concert and $528 for those in Greater New York. The gap soon narrowed as 1910–1911 tour values increased to $1,059 versus $1,120 for concerts in New York and only $486 for concerts in Greater New York, namely the Academy of Music in Brooklyn.[30] A complete summary of these values is presented below.

Unfortunately, the expenditures documented in the minutes fail to differentiate costs associated with concerts and rehearsals in New York versus costs incurred on tours. In addition, the expenditures grouped together fees and amounts paid to soloists, which significantly affected the receipts per concert. The report divided expenditures among all concerts and then sub-

Table 2.1.   Financial Analysis of the New York Philharmonic, 1909–1911

	Season	Per Concert	Season	Per Concert
Revenue and Costs	1909/10	1909/10	1910/11	1910/11
Total Expenditures	183,136.41	3,981.23	189,691.74	2,918.33
Total Concert Receipts	63,323.90	1,376.61	91,640.35	1,409.86
Deficiency	118,566.66	2,577.54	98,006.16	1,507.78
Receipts in More Detail				
From Subscriptions	$38,149.00	$1,003.92	$50,426.75	1,120.59
Box Office (Greater New York)	21,130.50	528.26	24,321.80	488.44
From Concerts on Tour	4,044.40	674.07	15,891.80	1,059.46
Accounting of Deficiencies				
Covered by Guarantee Fund	$86,391.66		$82,841.66	
Donations	23,675.00		15,374.95	
Interest	0		0	
Loans[a]	8,500.00		0	
Total:	$118,566.66		$98,216.61	

[a] Indicated that Advance of Payments made by Guarantors
Source: Minutes of the Meetings, 1911, New York Philharmonic Archives

tracted an average expenditure amount from concert revenue. However, the report clearly demonstrated that the receipts per concert in Greater New York declined while the receipts per tour concert increased almost 40 percent over the course of two seasons. The statement concluded that the numbers overall "indicate the financial progress in the right direction."[31] In the following years, concerts on tour continued to increase, with thirty-one concerts for the 1911–1912 season, thirty-two concerts for the 1912–1913 season, nineteen concerts for the 1913–1914 season, and twenty-six concerts for the 1914–1915 season.[32] Planning proved to be an essential step in offering successful tours to the public. The number of concerts during this period of transition is outlined in table 2.2.

Some tour receipts from subsequent years survive and document a snapshot of the financial conditions. For instance, for a November 1911 tour to Springfield, Massachusetts, and Providence, Rhode Island, the Philharmonic received between 75 to 80 percent of the gross receipts from tickets. Johanna Gadski, a premiere soloist, demanded 40 percent of the Philharmonic's gross receipts and others requested a flat fee. For example, Ernest Hutcheson requested $250 and Josef Lhévine demanded $300.[33] Sometimes the Philharmonic took 100 percent of the gross receipts from a concert and in return agreed to pay all the expenses, including advertising, ticket processing, and ticket distribution. This arrangement occurred more frequently in locations closer to New York, as in a November 1911 Philadelphia concert.

A note in the concert program from January 22, 1914, indicated that even if every ticket were sold for every concert in New York and Brooklyn, the deficit per year could not be less than $80,000.[34] From this document it remains clear that without individual donations, guarantors, and an endowment, the Philharmonic would not have survived. The overall operating budget for the new season was estimated at around $230,000. The salaries for the eighty-seven society members represented $118,685, the largest expenditure. (For other annual expenses projected in the report, see table 2.3.)

Table 2.2. Number of Philharmonic Concerts, 1908–1913

	Season	Season	Season	Season	Season
Type of Concert	1908/09	1909/10	1910/11	1911/12	1912/13
Greater New York Concerts	16	40	50	49	51
Concerts on Tour	0	6	15	31	32
Total	16	46	65	80	83

Source: Philharmonic Receipts, New York Philharmonic Archives

Table 2.3. New York Philharmonic Expenses, 1909–1913

Type of Expense	Minimum	Maximum
Rent of Hall	$23,000	$25,000
Soloists	20,000	25,000
Traveling Expenses	15,000	24,000
Management Expenses	16,000	18,000
Printing	8,000	11,000
Music	1,000	3,000
Advertising	8,000	10,000
Extra Musicians	1,000	2,000

Source: January 22, 1914, Program, New York Philharmonic Archives

Train Route, Times, Schedules, Costs

When the Philharmonic began touring, the railroads provided a critical link to communities beyond New York City. For these engagements the orchestra usually required three train cars, two coach cars for the musicians and a baggage car for the instruments and baggage. Each coach car could usually accommodate eighty passengers, which was the maximum number of musicians that usually toured with Boston Symphony Orchestra and the New York Symphony. When the New York Philharmonic traveled with almost one hundred musicians on the Great Lakes Tour in December 1910, however, they needed two coach cars, which significantly increased their expenses.

During the nineteenth century, hundreds of small railroad companies blossomed throughout the country. As the population in America tripled between 1865 and 1917, the rail network increased sevenfold, from 35,085 to 254,037 miles.[35] By the turn of the twentieth century, a number of mergers and conglomerates reduced the system to several dozen railroad companies. These mergers also made traveling convenient for passengers and groups, since it linked centers of business and commerce, and by 1916 the railroads provided 98 percent of the intercity passenger business.[36] For tours covering Massachusetts, Rhode Island, and Connecticut, the orchestra traveled via the line called the New York, New Haven, and Hartford Railroad. For cities such as Philadelphia, Washington, D.C., and Princeton, New Jersey, the Philharmonic had the option of traveling the Baltimore and Ohio Railroad or the Pennsylvania Railroad. When the Philharmonic toured the Great Lakes, they traveled via the Pennsylvania Railroad to Pittsburgh and Cleveland and switched to the New York Central Railroad for the remainder of the tour covering upstate New York.

Unfortunately, records regarding the cost of train travel are not available. During this period potential passengers inquired about ticket prices only at the train station and the railroads did not print these prices in newspapers or magazines. In addition, the railroads charged the Philharmonic a per diem for each reserved train car. For example, records from 1949 documented that the per diem for a Pennsylvania Railroad P-30 coach car cost approximately $13.50 and roughly $7.00 for a steel under-frame baggage car.[37] Since the orchestra transported delicate instruments, management probably chose the more durable steel baggage car, since it was subject to less motion from the tracks and was less likely to damage the instruments. In addition, by 1906 the Pennsylvania Railroad offered all-steel passenger coaches as part of their regular service.[38] Even though the railroad company likely provided a group discount to the orchestra, the passenger cost per musician contributed toward the overall expense.

During this period the railroad attached reserved cars to secondary trains rather than to the fast express trains. The railroads prided themselves on their punctual schedules, but since the weight of a reserved car would delay primary express trains, they were typically assigned to secondary trains. These trains still ran efficiently, offered sleeper cars, and transported the U.S. mail throughout the country. Although these trains would not stop at every station, they would stop at more stations than the express trains.

Once the Philharmonic reached its destination, the train detached the reserved cars. Musicians or contracted agents typically unloaded the baggage and the reserved car remained in the train yard until the orchestra left for the next destination. Since the detached cars provided no heat, musicians typically stayed in a local hotel following each concert. In many cases the orchestra traveled using one railroad line per tour, since each railroad company provided proprietary cars. When traveling from Cleveland to Buffalo, however, the Philharmonic switched from the Pennsylvania Railroad to the New York Central Railroad line.

Although specific railroad costs were not available for Mahler's tours, Loudon Charlton reported a railroad expense of $3,000 for a 1904 six-day/five-city East Coast tour that featured Lillian Nordica accompanied by Walter Damrosch and a fifty-five-member New York Symphony Orchestra.[39]

As the railroads expanded, the competition and economies of scale significantly reduced passenger rates, and by January 1911 a passenger could purchase a second-class ticket from Chicago to New York for six dollars or a first-class ticket for eight dollars, a reduction from roughly nineteen dollars.[40] Furthermore, with the opening of New York's Pennsylvania Station on November 27, 1910, an additional sixty-one through westbound and fifty-five through eastbound trains stopped daily in New York City.[41] This expansion broke the dependency on the New York Central Depot as the primary train station in Manhattan and made it more convenient and economical for passengers, baggage, and orchestras to travel throughout the country.

The Role of Concert Manager

A successful tour also depended on a competent orchestra manager. During Mahler's period, Felix Leifels served as business manager for the 1909–1910 season and Loudon Charlton took over the role for the 1910–1912 seasons. The orchestra manager forwarded biographical profiles, program notes, and materials to the local correspondent. A local contact then coordinated rehearsal space, ticket sales, local media, and accommodations. The manager disseminated similar information to each local contact and sometimes attached more extensive material describing the soloist.

Felix Leifels
Although Felix F. Leifels began his tenure with the Philharmonic as a bass player in 1890, he originally planned to become a lawyer and graduated from the De La Salle Institute. Born and raised in New York, he received music lessons from his father, Felix B. Leifels, also a member of the Philharmonic, and for a time both Leifelses played in the same orchestra. Leifels' education prepared him for the position of orchestra secretary from 1903 to 1909, and as business manager and secretary between 1909–1910 and 1912–1921. For Mahler's first season, Leifels received a salary of $2,000. In the next season the board offered Leifels $7,000 and expanded his responsibilities to include office administration, including hiring office personnel and rent. The board's offer of $7,000 was intended to cover Leifel's salary and those he hired for administrative functions. After accepting the position, however, Leifels shortly thereafter cancelled the contract, and the board agreed to accept Loudon Charlton as business manager. Leifels continued to function as personnel manager and secretary to the orchestra during this time.[42] He also provided an important connection as the orchestra transitioned to the guarantor plan with a new administration.

Loudon Charlton
Charlton, who conveniently located his office in Carnegie Hall, already had earned a reputation in the music business as manager of famous soloists such as Johanna Gadski, Marcella Sembrich, and David Bispham. In an article in *Musical America* Charlton described the three objectives of the concert manager: "1. To build up box office receipts. 2. To develop new territory, and thus extend the field of operation and profit, and to stimulate interest in good mu-

sic in every nook and corner of the land. 3. To secure as good a living as possible for oneself."[43] Charlton avoided saying that a manager makes an artist financially successful but expressed the idea that "good management increases many fold the value of an artist and that no artist can succeed without good management."[44] Furthermore, he noted that most successful artists were those who knew "the country best by personal contact."[45] With Charlton's insight, artists could "adapt themselves to local conditions," would not place "arbitrary or fictitious values upon their services," and never expected undeveloped locations to adapt to the artist.[46]

In another interview with *Musical America*, Charlton laid out a long-term plan for the New York Philharmonic to eventually offer roughly fifty concerts in New York and a touring scheme of thirty concerts that would not interfere with or lengthen the season. Charlton predicted that without increasing the cost to the organization the numbers of concerts would increase 80 percent and the deficit would decrease approximately 35 percent within two years.[47] After Charlton's first season with the Philharmonic, he believed that within two years the touring policy "would bring a net return of $25,000 above expenses."[48]

Although records in the Philharmonic do not verify Charlton's salary, he typically earned a commission of 10 percent when working with artists and other orchestras, calculated after subtracting expenses from the tour revenue. Compared with Leifels, Charlton's expertise assisted the Philharmonic in completing a more successful season. As manager, he knew how to create a profitable tour and which cities would support a visiting orchestra. Given his previous experience, he easily coordinated soloists for various concerts. During the 1909–1910 season, Charlton launched a series of orchestral concerts in New York and other large cities.[49] He also had experience working with the railroads, local managers, and the media to coordinate and promote each concert.

When Charlton managed Mahler's tours, he made several improvements. He minimized the use of soloists during the tour to reduce expenses. If the Philharmonic could fill a house without hiring a soloist, the orchestra achieved a larger profit. Charlton carefully selected soloists to join the orchestra in locations where they performed more than once, namely Philadelphia and Washington, D.C. Although soloists, such as Johanna Gadski, could quickly fill a house, they usually requested 50 percent or more of the concert revenue or an expensive flat rate. Charlton likely also encouraged Mahler to repeat one program throughout a tour to keep rehearsal time to a minimum.

Unfortunately Charlton's position with the Philharmonic included only two concert seasons, 1910–1911 and 1911–1912. Several articles indicate

Charlton encountered frustrations with the guarantors similar to those Mahler experienced. In a *Musical America* article, however, Charlton noted no friction in public with the committee throughout the season; they demonstrated a "lack of unity in their ideas for the proper conduct of the society's activities."[50] Charlton believed the committee failed to understand and agree with policies outlined for the orchestra's direction, which he based on a study of other successful orchestras. Moreover, he regretted the inability to carry out his plans and direction for the organization. Similar to Mahler's frustrations, Charlton noted, "There have been so many persons to please—and, as somebody said, some time ago, when any organization has forty or more heads, and they are nearly all women, it is hard for a man to work satisfactorily."[51] Even though Charlton wanted to raise the orchestra's status, the committee failed to agree with him on many important issues. After Charlton departed the Philharmonic he returned to managing other organizations and artists. In his thirty-year career he spent twenty-five years managing the Flonzaley String Quartet and later coordinated the American tour of Toscanini and La Scala in 1921.

City Selection

Charlton's experience selecting locations for tours benefited the orchestra's planning and scheduling. He chose cities based on their cultural sophistication, population, accessibility, availability, and previous success with other musical events. Many of the tours traced the paths of the Boston Symphony Orchestra and the New York Symphony Society tours. Today some cities represented in the tours have encountered difficult financial times and have experienced declining populations, but these cities thrived at the turn of the century. All of the cities where Mahler conducted on tour ranked among the largest seventy-five cities in the nation based on the 1900 U.S. Census report. At least 50 percent of the cities ranked among the twenty most populated cities and six of the cities ranked among the twelve most populated cities.

Beyond examining the reviews and attendance to gauge the level of support, it is important to look at the percentage of the local population that the audience represents. An audience of a hundred in a city such as Utica may constitute the same percentage as two hundred people in Syracuse or three hundred in Pittsburgh. By understanding the population size in each city, Charlton and Leifels could forecast the potential revenue per location. Based on arrangements with local impresarios, the Philharmonic could engage in a contract for a set amount per concert, a percentage of the ticket sales, or a combination of both.

Table 2.4. Population of Cities, 1900

Rank	City	1900 Population
1	New York City, NY	3,437,202
3	Philadelphia, PA	1,293,697
5	Boston, MA	560,892
7	Cleveland, OH	381,768
8	Buffalo, NY	352,387
11	Pittsburgh, PA	321,616
15	Washington, DC	278,718
20	Providence, RI	175,597
24	Rochester, NY	162,608
30	Syracuse, NY	108,374
31	New Haven, CT	108,027
49	Hartford, CT	79,850
60	Springfield, MA	62,059
66	Utica, NY	56,383

Source: U.S. Census Bureau, *Statistical Abstracts of the United States:* 1999

Planning the Tours

Well before Mahler arrived in the fall of 1910 as director of the Philharmonic, planning and touring arrangements were under way. Early planning proved necessary not only from the Philharmonic's point of view but also from a local one. Managers in several cities packaged the Philharmonic concerts into a group of subscription concerts in Cleveland, Washington, D.C., Syracuse, and Rochester. Rather than promote the concert as a single event, the local contact hoped to raise enough funds prior to all concerts to offset advertisements, hall rental, tickets, and administrative duties. By September or early October, extensive articles would have appeared describing the upcoming musical season. As with orchestras today, a large percentage of tickets sold through a subscription process rather than as single tickets.

Advertising

Many advertisements ran in local newspapers between two and three weeks before the performance. Most often feature stories ran in a Sunday edition and articles continued throughout the week in an arts or metropolitan section. Similar strategies were used in the tour promotional materials. When introducing the New York Philharmonic to a new community, most articles devoted at least half the space in an article to Mahler and the remainder discussed the program and the history of the Philharmonic.

All feature articles highlighted Mahler's experience as a European conductor and minimized his achievements as a composer. Writers focused on
Mahler's conducting experience in Vienna and his conducting style. Furthermore, stories of rehearsals with Mahler keeping "up a running fire of
comment and instruction, addressing the men in German"[52] seemed to be a
favorite among writers. Readers learned that Mahler's conducting style appeared more reserved than other conductors and that he used gestures for a
purpose rather than for show. Moreover, Mahler received enthusiastic re-
sponses from the musicians. Each feature article incorporated at least one
head shot of Mahler from 1907. These images highlighted his physical features and his mannerisms. Writers paid particular attention to his head size
and even described him as an "odd looking, nervous little man."[53]

Articles documented Mahler's work as a conductor and, when appropriate, addressed two compositions, his Eighth Symphony and his newly
arranged Bach Suites. Mahler recently had completed the Eighth Symphony
and news about its premiere and reception often accompanied each article.

Entertainment or amusement sections of newspapers contained advertisements for the Philharmonic concerts and other music venues. The management marketed the orchestra using various themes, emphasizing orchestra
size, first appearances, Mahler, or musical programming. Since other orchestras toured, the Philharmonic attempted to expand the audience base supporting the event. One of the favorite phrases that appeared in the ads emphasized the enormous number of musicians, often described as an
"Orchestra of 100,"[54] "99 Players,"[55] or "Ninety-Eight Performers."[56] These
slogans usually appeared during Mahler's first season. During the second season when the orchestra traveled with roughly eighty-five musicians, fewer
ads emphasized the size of the orchestra.

Another popular theme designed to make the Philharmonic stand out
promoted the concert with slogans such as the "Greatest Symphony Concert
Ever Given Here,"[57] "Symphonic Event of the Season,"[58] "Musical Event of
the Season,"[59] "Greatest Musical Event in Years,"[60] and "Engagement Extraordinary."[61] Boston, however, appeared to be one location where advertising
was more conservative; therefore the Philharmonic management hesitated to
declare the orchestra as the "Greatest" or to declare Mahler a superior conductor. Instead, ads for the Boston appearance stressed the concert as the
Philharmonic's "first time in Boston."[62]

Advertisements also highlighted the New York Philharmonic as the oldest orchestra in America and promoted the concert as worthy of attendance.
In Cleveland these ads declared "Oldest in America"[63] and in Providence ex-
tolled "Oldest Symphony Orchestra in the country founded in 1842."[64]

Some advertisements actually printed the upcoming Philharmonic program. A more substantial article in the music section of the paper usually addressed the program. One piece of music routinely appeared in the media, namely Mahler's Bach Suite. Remarks about the composition and Mahler's role as a performer, conductor, and composer followed as ads and articles promoted "Mahler to Play Bach Cycle on Harpsichord,"[65] "Steinway Piano Used,"[66] and "Mr. Mahler will also appear as soloist playing the Harpsichord."[67]

Phrases portraying Mahler as the best conductor in the country, or even the world, also dominated the Hartford and Springfield advertisement sections, which referred to Mahler as "A Great Man with a Great Big Orchestra"[68] and the "World's Greatest Symphony Conductor."[69] Mahler's name usually appeared just as large in print as the Philharmonic's name. Only when Johanna Gadski joined the Philharmonic for an all-Wagner concert in Philadelphia and Washington did Gadski upstage Mahler's name and the Philharmonic's name.

In addition, the term "first" became a favorite in each city where the Philharmonic appeared. Often the phrase mentioned that the concert would be the "First and Only Appearance,"[70] a "First Concert,"[71] or a "First Time in . . ."[72]

Subscription Tickets

When local impresarios packaged a New York Philharmonic concert with other concerts as part of a subscription series, they used several marketing strategies. In Pittsburgh, Cleveland, Buffalo, Rochester, and Syracuse, local managers sold subscription series tickets by early September and even offered subscription renewals before the final concert of each season. These series included concerts by other orchestras such as the Boston Symphony Orchestra, Theodore Thomas Orchestra, and New York Symphony, and even featured artists such as Mme. Schumann-Heink, Johanna Gadski, and Herbert Witherspoon.

Overall, the cities where the Philharmonic concerts became a subscription series enjoyed larger audiences than locations where individual tickets were sold for a single concert. Thus, the success of each Philharmonic concert depended not only on Mahler and the orchestra but also on the effectiveness of local promotion. In some cities a concert series had been in place for several years and had cultivated an audience base. In Rochester for example, Walter Bentley Ball placed the Philharmonic concert in a series of "Seven Concerts at Popular Prices" and by the middle of October had sold over two thousand season tickets.[73] In this way, Ball guaranteed a substantial amount of funding prior to the first concert.

Money collected from subscriptions assisted with early advertising, securing the hall, paying administrative staff throughout the year, and making arrangements for each concert. When the sale of season tickets closed in Pittsburgh several weeks prior to the first concert, the *Pittsburgh Leader* noted that it assured "a financial as well as an artistic success of this worthy undertaking to provide the best in the way of orchestral music."[74]

Furthermore, subscription sales gave local impresarios an idea of the number of additional tickets needed to be sold for the event. This aided managers in determining the necessity of additional advertisements, the possibility of discounting tickets, and the opportunity to reach potential concertgoers through other media. Rather than relying on slogans to promote just the Philharmonic concert, advertisements focused on the value and quality of all the orchestras, as the *Cleveland Leader* promoted the series as "Seven Magnificent Concerts."[75] Pictures of conductors and soloists often appeared together in newspapers and mailings. These promotional mailings often included a booklet with "interesting information regarding the orchestras and artists" accompanied by attractive portraits and "well chosen comments from the pens of the famous eastern and European critics" to provide an idea of the upcoming season.[76]

Instead of comparing orchestras with one another, managers promoted the concerts to complement one another with a variety of music and soloists. With this type of packaging, managers attempted to elevate the cultural level of their city. As the *Rochester Union and Advertiser* declared, "The time is fast approaching when Rochester must be classed with Boston and New York as one of the cosmopolitan centers of musical activity in this country. No other city in the world has the privilege of hearing a wonderful violinist like Macmilla[e]n or a great orchestra of 100 players like the Philharmonic for the sum of twenty-one cents."[77] The formation of a concert series also allowed cities to rise above one another. As the *Syracuse Herald* stated, "Syracuse is forging ahead among cities of its class as a patron of musical art in its grandest form of instrumental interpretation—the orchestra."[78]

Local managers sold the concept of value to promote subscription ticket sales. In Rochester, one dollar could buy a ticket to the six concerts in the series, averaging seventeen cents a concert. Otherwise, concertgoers paid a minimum of seventy-five cents for one ticket. Impresario Mai Davis Smith of Buffalo used the same tactic of value to sell subscription tickets, as an article reminded readers that the cost for all six concerts in the subscription series would amount to less than the amount to purchase tickets to four concerts.

A final promotional tactic focused on civic duty. Readers were encouraged for the sake of civic duty to purchase a season ticket, regardless of if they enjoyed classical music. Walter Bentley Ball promoted the concerts in Rochester using the slogan "Do It for Musical Rochester"[79] in the season brochure. In Syracuse readers felt obligated to purchase tickets as they read, "For the sake of music culture in Syracuse, we trust that the patronage of each of these noble concerts will justify and requite the enterprise of local promoters. In no other way can the city maintain the standard now happily set."[80] In addition to enjoying the best seats in the house, season subscribers often had their names in the concert program. Music supporters were even acknowledged in the newspapers and society periodicals. Surprisingly, the New York Philharmonic first began using this type of acknowledgment after their reorganization in 1909. It not only promoted the name of subscribers, but encouraged their friends and other socialites to rise to the same level of patronage.

The Program

Another aspect of tour preparation included the program notes. Throughout the program local businesses placed advertisements. A common advertisement focused on the Steinway and Sons Company. As the designer of the reconfigured piano, Steinway played an important position in advertising the tours. Mahler soon endorsed the Steinway piano, and full-page advertisements promoting the Steinway Company appeared in prominent locations, such as the back cover. Each program emphasized that Mahler traveled with and performed with only a Steinway piano. In addition to printing the piano manufacturer's name underneath the Bach selection in the program, full-page advertisements encouraged readers to purchase a Steinway from the local dealer. The ads were often altered to include the name and the location of the local dealer.

Throughout the tours the New York Philharmonic provided the program notes. Although the concert programs were usually printed in each location along the way, the Philharmonic forwarded the program and the program notes for each concert. When tour concerts were duplicated, the same notes accompanied multiple concerts. Henry Edward Krehbiel wrote the program notes for the orchestra during this period. He also wrote for the New York Symphony and the *New York Tribune*.[81] Krehbiel eventually became one of the critics that opposed Mahler as director of the Philharmonic and the changes Mahler imposed on the music. Overall, the notes are fairly extensive for this period, and only the writer of the *Buffalo Express* took time to critique them. This critic noted several inaccuracies in the program and notes. In his review of the Philharmonic program he criticized Krehbiel for inaccurately noting 1871 as the year that Wagner completed *Siegfried Idyll* and the year Wagner's son Siegfried was born. If Krehbiel had completed his research he would have realized that June 6, 1869,[82] marked the day of Siegfried's birth and that Wagner completed *Siegfried Idyll* in 1870.[83] Furthermore, the critic emphasized additional inaccuracies in the program and believed these mistakes distracted readers from fully appreciating and learning about the music.[84]

Income and Pricing

Before examining entertainment costs and expenses in detail, it is essential to consider the cost of living during this time. An ounce of first-class mail cost two cents, a pound of coffee fourteen cents, a loaf of bread five cents, a quart of milk six cents, and public transportation was almost universally a five-cent fare.[85] When comparing the cost for concert tickets, salaries, and traveling, however, it is helpful to use the Consumer Price Index to create a more realistic present-day value.

Each city created a pricing strategy for selling tickets. Individual ticket prices ranged between $.50 and $2.50 with most cities offering tickets in the $.75 to $2.00 range. In 2005 terms, values would range between $10.41 and $52.05.[86] Prices for attending opera appeared comparable to a symphony concert; however, tickets for other forms of entertainment were significantly less expensive. For example, tickets to attend a Sousa concert in Buffalo during the same period ranged from $.75 to $1.00 while tickets for a matinee reached only $.50 for adults and $.25 for children.[87] Pricing for Philharmonic tour tickets remained comparable to those for the Russian Symphony Orchestra. When the Boston Symphony Orchestra toured through the New England area, however, they offered less expensive tickets from $1.00 to $1.50 for a concert in Providence. Even when the Boston Orchestra offered a concert with Olga Samaroff in Springfield, Massachusetts, the tickets ranged between $.50 and $1.50. A difference in fifty cents for the most expensive seat to attend a concert in 1910 may seem insignificant, but in terms of 2005 values an increase of $.50 equaled $10.41.

At the turn of the twentieth century, vaudeville and talking pictures, later known as the movies, competed with live entertainment. Tickets for a talking picture ranged between five and ten cents and often included a double feature. An evening of vaudeville entertainment cost less than half the cheapest concert ticket and could be purchased for ten, fifteen, or twenty cents. Although Sousa, vaudeville, and the talking pictures offered a reduced rate for matinees or early shows, the Philharmonic maintained the same pricing structure for afternoon concerts in New York, Philadelphia, and Washington, D.C. In fact, Washington, D.C., afternoon concerts offered one of the most expensive prices with tickets selling as high as $2.50.

The Next Step

With the conditions set for touring and audiences interested in hearing top-class orchestras, it seemed an appropriate time for the New York Philharmonic to test the waters beyond New York City. Before traveling throughout the country, however, the orchestra tested their reception on audiences in New York, Brooklyn, and Philadelphia. These concerts prepared them for tours that extended several days and gave the orchestra recognition in other locations. To finish the preparations for touring, Mahler carefully selected music that would appeal to a wide variety of listeners and would demonstrate the refinement of the Philharmonic and himself. Programming proved to be an important component for a successful tour.

Notes

1. The orchestra traveled once to Rochester, New York, for the "First Annual Thomas Music Festival" on November 27 and 28, 1888, at the Lyceum Theatre. Refer to Ezra Schabas, *Theodore Thomas: America's Conductor and Builder of Orchestras, 1835–1905* (Urbana: University of Illinois Press, 1989), 170. Schabas notes that the New York Philharmonic performed at the festival. However, an article from the *New York Times*, "The Thomas Music Festival," dated November 28, 1888, called the orchestra the Thomas Orchestra. Since the Thomas Orchestra dissolved in the summer of 1888, it appears most likely that the orchestra at the festival was the New York Philharmonic.

2. Mahler became too ill to conduct the remaining concerts on tour in Princeton, New Jersey, on February 27, 1911, and March 27, 1911; and Washington, D.C., on February 28, and March 28, 1911.

3. Howard Shanet, *Philharmonic: A History of New York's Orchestra* (Garden City, NY: Doubleday and Company, 1975), 222. During the 1919–1920 season the Philharmonic embarked on a coast-to-coast tour encompassing ninety-four concerts.

4. John F. Stover, *American Railroads*, 2d ed. (Chicago: University of Chicago Press, 1997), 161.

5. Stover, 160.

6. *New York, New Haven and Hartford Railroad: Schedule of Through Trains* (New Haven: New York, New Haven and Hartford Railroad, 1910) n.p. These rates were

specifically for the New York, New Haven, and Hartford lines. Overnight accommodations for staterooms were available for $4.00 and $5.00, and $6.50 for a drawing room.

7. Ernest Ingersoll, *Rand McNally and Company's Handy Guide to New York City* (New York: Rand McNally and Company, 1912), 196. This guide provided the minimum rates to more than sixty New York hotels. Many of the cheapest rooms did not provide private baths during this time.

8. Stover, 96.

9. "Fortunes Made Every Season by Singers, Pianists, and Violinists Visiting This Country," *New York Times*, November 10, 1907, Magazine Section, 3.

10. "Fortunes Made Every Season by Singers, Pianists, and Violinists Visiting This Country," 3.

11. Felix Leifels, New York, to R. E. F. Flinsch, New York, n.d., TL File 008-01-13, "Papers of Leifels, Felix, 1903–1921," New York Philharmonic Archives, New York. Gadski's schedule called for performances with the New York Philharmonic in Springfield, Massachusetts, on November 8, 1911; in Providence, Rhode Island, on November 9, 1911; and in Boston, Massachusetts, on November 10, 1911.

12. Leifels to Flinsch. Nordica's schedule called for performances with the New York Philharmonic in Baltimore, Maryland, on November 27, 1911; in Washington, D.C., on November 28, 1911; and in Philadelphia on November 29, 1911.

13. Quaintance Eaton, *Opera Caravan: Adventures of the Metropolitan Company on Tour* (New York: Metropolitan Opera Guild, 1957), 41.

14. Francis Robinson, *Celebration: The Metropolitan Opera* (Garden City, NY: Doubleday and Company, 1979), 226.

15. Robinson, 229.

16. Robinson, 246–248. In Boston, Mahler conducted *Die Walküre* on February 11, 1908, and *Don Giovanni* on February 18, 1908. In Philadelphia, he conducted *Die Walküre* on April 8, 1908, and *Don Giovanni* on April 9, 1908.

17. Theodore Thomas, *Theodore Thomas: A Musical Autobiography*, ed. George P. Upton (New York: Da Capo Press, 1964), 66.

18. Schabas, 41.

19. Schabas, 41.

20. Schabas, 40.

21. Schabas, 176.

22. Walter Damrosch, *My Musical Life* (New York: Charles Scribner's Sons, 1923), 189.

23. "Gift Won't Provide Philharmonic Home," *Musical America* 15, no. 4 (11 December 1911): 21.

24. Alice Bradley, "Music and Musicians," *Cleveland Leader*, 23 October 1910, sec. 5, 5.

25. Bradley, sec. 5, 5.

26. Donald Rosenberg, *The Cleveland Orchestra Story: Second to None* (Cleveland: Gray and Company, 2000), 36.

27. For more information refer to Mary Wagner, "Early Orchestras in Cleveland" (Master's thesis, Kent State University, 1998).

28. Agreement from the Office of Loudon Charlton, in MAA Board of Trustees Contracts Series, Symphony Orchestra Series 1909–1910, Cleveland Orchestra Association, Cleveland.

29. Leifels to Flinsch, undated. File 025-02-12, "Itinerary and Expenses from 1911 Tour," Archives of the New York Philharmonic, New York.

30. Report to the Guarantors of the Fund for the Permanent Orchestra of the Philharmonic Society of New York, December 7, 1911, Minutes of the Meetings of the Board of Directors of the Philharmonic Society from 1903–1912, Archives of the New York Philharmonic, New York.

31. Report to the Guarantors, December 7, 1911.

32. Report to the Guarantors, December 7, 1911.

33. Leifels to Flinsch, undated. File 025-02-12, "Itinerary and Expenses from 1911 Tour," Archives of the New York Philharmonic, New York.

34. Concert Program of the New York Philharmonic, January 22, 1914, Archives of the New York Philharmonic, New York, np.

35. Stover, 96.

36. Stover, 160. This figure was reported by the Interstate Commerce Commission. The remaining 2 percent of non-railroad travel was on the Great Lakes.

37. *The Official Register of Passenger Train Equipment* (New York: Railway Equipment and Publication Company, 1949), 53–54.

38. Stover, 154.

39. Loudon G. Charlton, New York, to George H. Wilson, London, July 1, 1904, Pittsburgh Orchestra Correspondence, Vol. 4, Part 2, Music Division, Carnegie Library, Pittsburgh. Cities along the tour included five cities: Springfield, Massachusetts; Providence, Rhode Island; Worcester, Massachusetts; Portland, ME; and Boston.

40. "Railroads Slash New York–Chicago Passenger Rate," *The Buffalo Courier*, 1 December 1910, 1.

41. "Open Pennsylvania Station Tonight," *New York Times*, 26 November 1910, 5.

42. Shanet, 445n134. Leifels' proposed position of manager also included the duties of employing and paying "a competent and efficient deputy and assistant, and all necessary stenographers and office boys, hire and pay the rent of a suitable office for the Society, and supply all necessary articles and things connected with or used in and about said office except a telephone and stationery."

43. J. B. C., "The Concert Manager—His Duties and His Influence" *Musical America* 11, no. 6 (27 February 1909): 5.

44. "America's Most Notable Music Season, Say New York Managers," *Musical America* 16, no. 22 (12 October 1912): 13.

45. "America's Most Notable Music Season," 13.

46. "America's Most Notable Music Season," 13

47. "Mr. Charlton Quits the Philharmonic," *Musical America* 15, no. 19 (16 March 1912): 1.

48. "Gift Won't Provide Philharmonic Home," 21.

49. "What the New York Managers Have to Say about the Season," *Musical America* 10, no. 23 (16 October 1909): 14.

50. "Mr. Charlton Quits the Philharmonic," 1.

51. "Mr. Charlton Quits the Philharmonic," 1.

52. "Characteristic Poses of Gustav Mahler of the New York Symphony," *Pittsburgh Leader*, 27 November 1911, 25. This particular article incorrectly associates Mahler with the New York Symphony rather than the New York Philharmonic.

53. "Characteristic Poses of Gustav Mahler," 25.

54. "Amusements," *Syracuse Herald*, 4 December 1910, sec 4, 6.

55. "Amusements," *Washington Times*, 26 February 1911, 14.

56. "Amusements," *Boston Sunday Herald*, 13 February 1910, sec. 3, 7.

57. "Amusements, Meetings, etc.," *Springfield Daily Republican*, 20 February 1910, 23.

58. "Entertainments," *Hartford Daily Courant*, 15 February 1911, 7.

59. "Advertisements," *Rochester Democrat and Chronicle*, 9 December 1910, 20.

60. "Advertisements," *Rochester Herald*, 4 December 1910, 22.

61. "Amusements," *Buffalo Evening Times*, 6 December 1910, 3.

62. "Amusements," *Boston Globe*, 6 February 1910, 30.

63. (Advertisement), *Cleveland Town Topics*, 26 November 1910, 2.

64. "Amusements, Excursions, etc.," *Providence Journal*, 24 February 1910, 5.

65. Wilson G. Smith, "Mahler to Play Bach Cycle on Harpsichord," *Cleveland Press*, 29 October 1910, 7.

66. "Amusements," *Syracuse Herald*, 4 December 1910, sec 4, 6.

67. (Advertisement), *Cleveland Town Topics*, 26 November 1910, 2.

68. "Advertisements," *Hartford Daily Times*, 15 February 1911, 7.

69. *Springfield Daily News*, 17 February 1910, 2.

70. *Providence Evening Tribune*, 13 February 1910, sec. 2, 10.

71. "Amusements," *Philadelphia Press*, 16 January 1910, 13.

72. "Amusements," *Washington Post*, 15 January 1911, 3.

73. "Mr. Ball's Concert Series," *Rochester Democrat and Chronicle*, 16 October 1910, 24.

74. "Characteristic Poses of Gustav Mahler," 25.

75. "Amusements," *Cleveland Leader*, 23 October 1910, sec. 6, 2.

76. "In Musical Circles," *Cleveland Town Topics*, 8 October 1910, 15.

77. "That City Is Rochester," *Rochester Union and Advertiser*, 5 November 1910, 15.

78. "Three Great Concerts," *Syracuse Herald*, 5 December 1910, 8.

79. Walter Bentley Ball, *The Popular Concert Series* (Rochester: Walter Bentley Ball, 1910), np.

80. "Wieting—The New York Philharmonic Orchestra," *The Syracuse Herald*, 4 December 1910, 6.

81. Henry Edward Krehbiel (1854–1923) was music critic for the *New York Tribune* from 1880 until his death.

82. Horst Leuchtmann, "Siegfried Wagner," *The New Grove Dictionary of Music and Musicians*, 20:146.

83. Barry Millington, ed., *The Wagner Compendium: A Guide to Wagner's Life and Music* (London: Thames and Hudson, 1992), 311. Wagner completed the work in November/December 1870 and presented the work in their house at Tribschen on Christmas Day 1870.

84. M. M. H., "Music Hath Its Charms," *Buffalo Express*, 8 December 1910, 5.

85. These values appeared in *The 18th Annual Report of the U.S. Commissioner of Labor* under the portion of 1900 Chicago food prices.

86. Values were calculated using a historical CPI (Consumer Price Index) model. The values were entered for the CPI base year of 1910 and calculated in terms of 2005 values. Fifty cents in 1910 increased to $10.41 in 2005; $2.50 in 1910 increased to $52.05 in 2005; $1.00 in 1910 increased to $20.82 in 2005; $1.50 in 1910 increased to $31.23 in 2005. Calculations were made with the Consumer Price Index Calculator at the Federal Reserve Bank of Minneapolis. For more information refer to minneapolisfed.org/Research/data/us/calc.

87. "Amusements," *Buffalo Evening News*, 21 November 1910, 2.

~

CHAPTER THREE

Programming the Music

While Mahler served as conductor at the Metropolitan Opera he studied the patronage to orchestral concerts, reviewed concert programs, read newspaper articles, and followed the concert trends. Some of these programming themes included subscriptions series related to a specific composer, historically themed concerts, and Sunday "popular" concerts. Usually orchestral programs in America at this time included heavy emphasis on Romantic music and at least one selection that featured a soloist. Wagner and Beethoven led in popularity among composers selected for programs.

Carnegie Hall served as the Philharmonic's home in New York until the 1960s. Beginning in May 1891, the hall became the focal point of concert life, welcoming international artists from Tchaikovsky to Caruso. Carnegie Hall provided a home to thriving and competing orchestras, namely the New York Symphony, the Russian Symphony, and the Volpe Symphony Orchestra. It also served as the guest home for touring orchestras, including the Theodore Thomas Orchestra, the Philadelphia Orchestra, and also the Boston Symphony Orchestra, who began visiting New York in 1885, and by 1908 offered a series of ten concerts per season at the hall. Moreover, throughout the 1909–1910 season the "Calendar of Concerts" in the *New York Times* announced at least thirty concerts a month in the city with usually eighteen or more of these events scheduled for Carnegie Hall.[1]

A New Philharmonic

In a sense Mahler helped to transform the Philharmonic from a quasi-permanent orchestra to one with a board of directors, full-time employees, and a regular concert season. Compared with the era before 1909, Mahler nearly tripled the number of Philharmonic concerts to forty-six in his first season. If he had completed the second season, Mahler would have quadrupled the number of the concerts to sixty-five. Furthermore, the number of concerts extended the season to twenty-three consecutive weeks.

Mahler's primary objective as director focused on raising the popular musical standards and making the New York Philharmonic "the best in this country and the equal of any in the world."[2] In addition, the board encouraged concertgoers to support an expanded season. To meet these goals Mahler designed several series for his first season, including a traditionally classical series, a historical series, a Beethoven series, and a Sunday afternoon "popular series." Along these lines he hoped to gradually educate the public and to introduce more modern compositions into the programs.

One of the cycles focused on Beethoven's music, of which Mahler planned to perform seven of the eleven overtures and all the symphonies, with the exception of the first. Mahler programmed the Beethoven series for two-thirty or three o'clock on Friday afternoons. In general, Mahler envisioned two symphonies for each concert, separated by an overture from the same period.[3] Although this series may have been noted as "innovative" by some writers, other conductors, in particular Walter Damrosch, had already implemented this idea during the prior two seasons. Called perhaps the "most interesting programs to audiences in these two years,"[4] the New York Symphony offered a six-concert cycle featuring Beethoven's symphonies during March and April 1908, and based on this success, scheduled another Beethoven cycle for February and March 1909.

As somewhat of a novelty and as a method of educating listeners, Mahler designed a second series that focused on the history of orchestral music from Bach to the present. He programmed six consecutive historical concerts for Wednesday evenings, with each concert chronologically connecting the development of orchestral music.

In an effort to develop audiences, the Philharmonic also offered Sunday afternoon concerts intended to be popular concerts at affordable prices. This series had already proved successful with the New York Symphony, who had offered this format since 1903. Their series grew to more than twenty Sunday afternoon concerts by the fall of 1907, with most concerts offered at Carnegie Hall and some at the New Theatre.[5] As Andrew Carnegie finished his term as president of the Philharmonic in the spring of 1909, the Philharmonic Women's Committee inquired about renting Carnegie Hall for Sunday afternoons the following season, evidently for Mahler to conduct popular concerts. Carnegie's acceptance of this proposal heightened the competition between the Philharmonic and the New York Symphony. Carnegie informed the hall's manager to decline rental to the New York Symphony for Sunday afternoons, forcing Damrosch to seek a less desirable location.[6]

Mahler maintained the traditional classical series as part of the orchestra's core business. These concerts usually included at least one symphony, and a concerto or second symphony. The programs sometimes included an overture, incidental music, or orchestral music from various operas. The Philharmonic offered this series on Thursday evenings and repeated them on Friday afternoons at two thirty.

Finally, as part of the overall plan, the Philharmonic started touring. Compared with the other programs, these concerts featured more of a potpourri of music that demonstrated the versatility of the orchestra and Mahler's ability as a conductor and performer.

Mahler avoided a number of approaches found in the programming of other orchestras. Compared with Damrosch, Mahler sparingly included local choruses in his Philharmonic programs. Damrosch, however, viewed the inclusion of local choruses and volunteers as a way to develop a larger audience base and musical offerings. Although not always regarded as an exceptional conductor, Damrosch developed a strong following in and out of New York City as concertgoers and critics praised his work with local groups, youngsters, and amateurs.

Orchestras learned not to compete with the opera season. During this period opera attracted far greater support than orchestral concerts. Therefore, orchestra schedules became subservient to opera premieres and productions that featured world-renowned artists. On December 10, 1910, *The Girl of the Golden West* premiered to a full house at the Met with nineteen curtain calls and in the presence of Puccini.[7] Meanwhile, the Philharmonic performed on tour in Utica, New York. Not only did this tour engage the musicians for a week of performing, but it also eliminated the risk of offering concerts in New York that would attract a small audience and accrue a large deficit.

Another popular trend in American programming involved the inclusion of a vocal or instrumental soloist on part of the program. Although this equated to a greater number of concertgoers and higher revenue, soloists typically received a large percentage of the receipts. Soloists usually guaranteed a large crowd and even convinced individuals to attend their concert rather than another cultural event. Mahler believed, however, that the orchestra alone could attract a large crowd, so much so that he opened his first Philharmonic concert on November 4, 1909, without a soloist.[8] Although he engaged soloists, Mahler frequently also featured musicians from the orchestra, including himself.

Throughout the spring and summer of 1909 other orchestras finalized their upcoming seasons. The New York Symphony planned to continue their symphony concerts for young people and a series of concerts grouped by nationalities. In addition, the Russian Symphony Orchestra offered a series focusing on Slavic composers. Overall, New York boasted nearly a hundred symphony concerts for the 1909–1910 season. As the *New York Tribune* pointed out, it was more than double the number offered in either Berlin or Vienna.[9]

Unfortunately, none of the touring or local orchestras clearly communicated their programs with other ensembles, which resulted in the duplication of works. The Philharmonic received criticism on this point after a concert on December 12, 1909. Several critics remarked that all the selections had been heard in New York since the start of the season. The Symphony Society performed the Beethoven Symphony No. 5 in C Major on November 14, 1909; the Boston Symphony Orchestra previously performed Richard Strauss's *Till Eulenspiegels lustige Streiche* on November 11, 1909,[10] and Yolando Mérö repeated the Pianoforte Concerto No. 2 in A major by Liszt, just as she performed on November 3, 1909, as part of her premiere at Carnegie Hall with the Russian Symphony Orchestra.[11]

Program Order

One of the recent programming styles in America at the turn of the twentieth century that Theodore Thomas first instituted with the Philharmonic involved placing an overture as the opening piece on a concert. This order allowed latecomers to be seated after the overture. The break was less disruptive to the continuity of a program than taking a long pause between symphony movements to accommodate latecomers. Furthermore, for conductors who refused seating to latecomers this approach permitted them to hear the bulk of the program.

Some of Mahler's programming experience from his era as director of the Vienna Philharmonic is reflected in his first season of programming at the New York Philharmonic. His Viennese programs from 1898–1900 focused on orchestral music and at times even included multiple symphonies on a program. Beethoven and Wagner rated among the most popular composers on these programs, while other favorites included Brahms, Mozart, and several performances of Berlioz's *Symphonie Fantastique*. It was quite standard for Mahler to open a program in Vienna with a symphony. He also limited the use of solo vocalists on these orchestral programs.

When applied to Philharmonic programs, Mahler's decision to open with a symphony appeared unusual; the *Philadelphia Record* critic referred to the program as "peculiar in form" and found it quite "unusual for an orchestral concert to begin with a symphony."[12] Luckily Mahler's rendition of the opening piece, Beethoven's Symphony No. 5, still pleased the writer and received a favorable review.

In the twenty-first century conductors frequently perform works in chronological order, but Mahler appeared more willing to place the works out of chronological order. For example, during the first year of tours, the Berlioz *Symphonie Fantastique* often opened the program with the Bach Suite as the second selection. Mahler may have chosen this order to impress audiences with the sheer volume and size of the orchestra, which consisted of one hundred musicians. During the second season when Mahler toured with a somewhat smaller orchestra of usually eighty-seven musicians, he removed the Berlioz work and frequently opened with the Bach Suite. Furthermore, he chose Beethoven over Berlioz for these programs.

Few articles mention the concert atmosphere between selections, but a *Musical Courier* review addresses differences between Mahler and other conductors. At the first Brooklyn concert Mahler offered no intermission and did not "allow enough time between the numbers for conversation, or making 'calls' upon friends."[13] No matter what the reasoning, the timing had interrupted the social custom and led the writer to conclude that "Mahler's scholarly and rigid musicianship and discipline is puzzling the fashionable element."[14]

Compared with previous New York Philharmonic conductors, Mahler shortened the overall program length. He achieved this with briefer pauses between selections, trimming or eliminating the intermission, and fewer or briefer selections. This reduction encouraged concertgoers to remain for the entire program rather than "rushing away thirty or forty minutes" before the concert's conclusion, which had become a problem.[15] The *Musical America* critic even applauded Mahler's programming, because in less than an hour and a half, he heard three masterworks.[16]

In addition to expanding the number of performances, Mahler demanded regular rehearsals and required attendance at rehearsals and performances. In the past, the Philharmonic prepared concerts haphazardly. Even Walter Damrosch complained that during the 1902–1903 season an average of only fifty-nine out of seventy society members appeared for concerts that required a hundred musicians, forcing the society to hire substitutes and extras on a regular basis and furthermore not developing a cohesive ensemble.[17] With regular rehearsals the Philharmonic took on greater works and soon made inroads to achieving a quality closer to the Boston Symphony Orchestra. Recognition of a proper and systematic method of rehearsing drew the attention of the *Musical Courier* editor, who applauded Mahler's efforts and believed that until his reign the "Philharmonic could not consider itself capable of producing great works unless thoroughly rehearsed for each performance."[18]

Based on the union guidelines with a maximum rehearsal length of three and a half hours, Mahler also carefully organized rehearsals. A number of sources recalled his desire for precision and a willingness to repeat a section until it met his satisfaction. Theodore Spiering, concertmaster, recalled Mahler's rehearsal style, stating, "Mahler always worked flat out. Every minute counted. There were no breaks. We almost never just played anything through."[19]

The Tour Schedule

During Mahler's two seasons with the Philharmonic the tours covered 2,814 miles, with sixteen concerts presented beyond Greater New York. These tour routes are outlined in the table below.

During Mahler's first season with the Philharmonic from 1909 to 1910, he conducted forty-six concerts, of which thirty-two were in New York, five in Brooklyn, two in Philadelphia, and four in New England. None of the concerts outside New York interfered with the subscription concerts series, and they offered the Philharmonic an opportunity to perform while other ensembles, such as the Boston Symphony Orchestra, seized the spotlight in New York City. On average Mahler conducted three concerts a week during his first season with the New York Philharmonic. Philadelphia marked the first location Mahler conducted the Philharmonic outside New York, when he appeared at the Academy of Music on Monday, January 17, 1910. This concert broadened Mahler's reputation, and allowed management to refine their preparations before more extensive touring.

Roughly a month later, Mahler and the Philharmonic embarked on a tour in New England starting with New Haven, Connecticut, on February 23; Springfield, Massachusetts, on February 24; Providence, Rhode Island, on February 25; and finally Boston on February 26. Since each location offered a slightly different program and sometimes featured a soloist, Mahler usually conducted an afternoon rehearsal in each location. In several cases this

Table 3.1. Miles of Tours, 1909–1911

Arrival Date	City/ST	Point of Depart	Miles	Tour Miles
January 17, 1910	Philadelphia	New York	91.70	
January 18, 1910	New York	Philadelphia	91.70	
				183.40
February 23, 1910	New Haven, CT	New York	72.28	
February 24, 1910	Springfield, MA	New Haven, CT	61.98	
February 25, 1910	Providence, RI	Springfield, MA	121.60	
February 26, 1910	Boston, MA	Providence, RI	44.86[a]	
February 27, 1910	New York	Boston, MA	212.27	
				512.99
March 14, 1910	Philadelphia	New York	91.70	
March 15, 1910	New York	Philadelphia	91.70	
				183.40
December 5, 1910	Pittsburgh, PA	New York	440.50[b]	
December 6, 1910	Cleveland, OH	Pittsburgh, PA	148.30	
December 7, 1910	Buffalo, NY	Cleveland, OH	183.00	
December 8, 1910	Rochester, NY	Buffalo, NY	68.38	
December 9, 1910	Syracuse, NY	Rochester, NY	80.43	
December 10, 1910	Utica, NY	Syracuse, NY	53.12	
December 11, 1910	New York	Utica, NY	236.79	
				1,210.52
January 23, 1911	Philadelphia	New York	91.70	
January 24, 1911	Washington, DC	Philadelphia	135.80	
January 24, 1911	New York	Washington, DC	227.50	
				455.00
February 15, 1911	Springfield, MA	New York	134.26	
February 16, 1911	Hartford, CT	Springfield, MA	30.24	
February 17, 1911	New York	Hartford, CT	104.02	
				268.52
Total Tour Miles:				2,813.83

Source: The Official Guide of the Railways (New York: National Railway Publication, 1916). This table was formed through mileage documenting the distance between train stations.
[a] To travel from Springfield to Providence on the New York Central Railroad passengers had to travel back to Hartford and switch trains to travel from Hartford to Providence.
[b] All trains headed to Pittsburgh from New York on the Pennsylvania Railroad first traveled through Philadelphia.

marked the only time Mahler rehearsed with the soloist and the orchestra. Following each tour, the musicians usually received just one day of rest before resuming rehearsals and their performance schedule.

Although March marked the final month of concerts for the Philharmonic, Mahler's schedule became extremely busy as he prepared and conducted the American premiere of Tchaikovsky's *Pique Dame* at the Metropolitan Opera. The first performance took place on March 5, 1910, and was soon followed with three additional performances on March 9, March 17, and March 21. In between these events Mahler conducted the last concerts of the regular Philharmonic season on March 10 and March 11. Several days later, on Monday, March 14, 1910, the Philharmonic made a second trip to Philadelphia and performed once again at the Academy of Music. With this concert the Philharmonic hoped to lay a foundation for an ongoing concert series in Philadelphia.

Even though Mahler offered the most concerts in any one season of the Philharmonic's history, not everyone appeared satisfied with the repertoire. Throughout the year Mahler conducted roughly ninety-seven different works representing thirty-three composers.[20] Although Mahler probably did not know the program schedule of the other orchestras in New York, critics declared that the Philharmonic offered too much repetition and too much Beethoven. As a result, the guarantors designated a program committee to oversee the selection of music for the Philharmonic's next season. Mahler decided to drop the Beethoven and the historical cycle of concerts.[21]

Overall, the first season's tour results sparked management to engage more audiences beyond New York. Leifels reported that the orchestra's services were in high demand and stated, "In consequence, the directors of the Philharmonic have decided to widen the scope of operations beginning next fall, and it is the present intention of giving several times the number of concerts out of the city than were held this year."[22]

Programming for the tours during the first season offered a variety of music, but usually at least 50 percent of the program consisted of romantic music. Several favorites appeared on the programs for the first tours, including Berlioz's *Symphony Fantastique* and Mahler's arrangement of Bach's Orchestral Suites. Both pieces worked especially well as "selling points" for the concerts. The *Symphonie Fantastique* allowed audiences to hear the dynamic contrasts possible with a larger orchestra. Furthermore, the work had never been heard before in some cities such as Providence, Rhode Island. Although Walter Damrosch had performed the work with roughly fifty-five musicians in the previous season, Mahler toured New England with an orchestra almost twice as large. Not to be outdone by Mahler, the managers of the New York

Symphony Orchestra soon announced that to celebrate Damrosch's twenty-fifth year as conductor he would also tour with one hundred players through the East and Midwest for two weeks beginning in January 1910.[23]

With such a large number of musicians performing on the Philharmonic tour, stage accommodations were needed in certain cities. In Providence local management built the stage out to accommodate the musicians and the additional percussion including six tympani, a bass drum, and a chime piano.[24]

Mahler arranged the Bach work prior to beginning his first Philharmonic season, and it soon became the "trademark" of his Philharmonic era as he performed it at least twenty-three times between 1909 and 1911.

Mahler's Bach

Mahler's arrangement of the Bach Orchestral Suites combined the Overture and Rondeau from Bach's Orchestral Suite No. 2 followed by the Air and Gavotte from the Orchestral Suite No. 3.[25] To create a baroque setting, Mahler conducted from, and also played, the keyboard for this selection. Although noted as a harpsichord in the programs and reviews, Mahler played a Steinway baby grand piano. To produce a sound similar to a harpsichord, the Steinway Company placed tacks on the hammer portion of the keys. Since an authentic harpsichord could not produce enough sound for a standard American concert hall, the sound of a reconstructed piano with the strength of modern metal strings could adequately fill the larger halls. Some people believe Mahler asked the Steinway Company to create such an instrument, but this noted "harpsichord" had become part of the New York music scene several years earlier.

At the turn of the twentieth century several collectors imported harpsichords to America and the Dolmetsch-Chickering Company of Boston briefly produced harpsichords.[26] Performers such as Arthur Whiting offered chamber concerts and solo recitals in New York on a Dolmetsch-Chickering harpsichord and elevated interest in early music throughout the city.[27] At the same time, musical directors began to reevaluate performance practices for baroque and classical music.

Prior to Mahler's arrival, conductor Nahan Franko of the Metropolitan Opera engaged a modified Steinway piano to accompany the recitatives in a production of *Don Giovanni* in January 1906. The performance commemorated Mozart's 150th birthday and the *New York Times* noted, "The long successions of recitative with accompaniment for the pianoforte, representing the old harpsichord, jar upon modern ears."[28]

When Mahler arrived at the Metropolitan Opera to produce *Don Giovanni* in January 1908, he decided to use the same Steinway instrument to accompany the recitatives. As in Mozart's time, the conductor played the accompaniments. Although the sound seemed overstated, the critics now approved and such an exaggeration was deemed necessary in a house the size of the Metropolitan.[29]

Other conductors throughout New York City also became interested in the instrument, and less than two months later it appeared in a Musical Art Society concert at Carnegie Hall on March 11, 1908. Several days later, on March 15, 1908, Walter Damrosch incorporated the so-called harpsichord in a New York Symphony performance. In a concert designed to be part of a Beethoven series, Damrosch played the harpsichord in Beethoven's Trio in G Major for Piano, Flute, and Bassoon.[30] Although Damrosch was criticized for placing too much emphasis on the harpsichord, the audience reacted with enthusiasm.[31] A few weeks later at Carnegie Hall, Frank Damrosch (Walter's brother) conducted the New York Oratorio Society in a production of Bach's *St. Matthew Passion* on April 16, 1908, and again used the instrument. Critics commended the conductor's attempt to reproduce "significant features of the work that are today to a greater or less extent obsolete or neglected."[32]

Mahler continued to make use of the instrument, and the following year it again appeared at the Metropolitan Opera on January 13, 1909, in a production of Mozart's *The Marriage of Figaro*. Based on Mozart's specification he designated the secco recitatives to be accompanied by the modified piano to suggest the sound of a harpsichord.[33]

Thus, by the time that Mahler agreed to direct the Philharmonic he realized the capabilities of the Steinway reconfigured instrument. Compared with a traditional harpsichord, the modified Steinway piano would balance with the size of the orchestra, the modern instruments, and the size of the larger halls.

Mahler decided that just as Damrosch played the harpsichord in the New York Symphony concert, he would demonstrate his keyboard and conducting skills simultaneously in a new arrangement of the Bach Orchestral Suites. To accomplish this task Mahler insisted the harpsichord be placed on a platform constructed of three blocks, to give him full view of the orchestra. Although the platform may not have seemed essential for performance spaces such as Carnegie Hall, in other locations along the tour, such as Infantry Hall in Providence, Rhode Island, the audience watched the concert from one flat level. Thus, the platform permitted the audience to view Mahler as a conductor and soloist.

Furthermore, the instrument also proved durable in strenuous winter conditions. A traditional harpsichord would quickly become out of tune without proper heating and temperature control, but a piano could maintain its pitch with more variant temperature. Today pianos are shipped in specific crates, but the moving conditions at the turn of the twentieth century were much more primitive. For example, a memo from the Philharmonic's archives details the delivery of the keyboard instrument to Boston. The letter mentions that a sled transported the piano from the Steinway Company to the train station in New York for the Philharmonic tour.[34] Based on Steinway's records this sled consisted of a wooden board on wheels with two straps that secured the instrument on its side. The sled could then be attached to a carriage and taken to the Grand Central Depot.[35]

Programs on Tours

Although some writers criticized Mahler's era at the Philharmonic as one where concerts had the smallest audiences, one must take into account the drastic organizational changes and the expansion of the season. In fact, concerts during the opening month of the season in November 1909 had record attendance, as confirmed by *Musical Courier*, which noted that "so far the paid attendance at the Mahler appearance has been far in excess of that of any other Carnegie Hall orchestral concerts of this season or the past season."[36]

However, the season's artistic accomplishments became dampened by the accruing deficit, which by the end of March 1910 approached $75,000. This amount was significantly less than the reported $750,000 deficit the Metropolitan Opera reported for the same season. No expense seemed to be spared to gain control of New York's musical life as more musical organizations formed or reorganized. Yet changes at the Met and the Philharmonic, such as the hiring of full-time employees, drastically affected the bottom line. The new expenses quickly changed their financial bottom line, and critics often blamed the conductor or director. New Yorkers were reminded that progress could not happen overnight and that the Philharmonic needed several years to accomplish the level of quality and the financial stability of the Boston Symphony Orchestra. The writer for the *Musical Courier* emphasized that it took roughly twenty years for the Boston Symphony Orchestra to develop patronage for concerts in Brooklyn and even when Nikisch conducted the Boston Symphony Orchestra the house remained far from sold out.[37]

Mahler's Second Season with the Philharmonic

As the season ended, Arnold discontinued his position as business manager, and the orchestra quickly hired Loudon Charlton as its new manager. Well before Mahler settled into his summer home in Toblach, Charlton began signing contracts and making arrangements for the 1910–1911 season. In retrospect, some admonished Charlton for scheduling too many tours for a man in Mahler's condition, which had been diagnosed in 1907.[38] Charlton, on the other hand, designed a touring schedule for the Philharmonic on the same caliber as that of the New York Symphony, the Philadelphia Orchestra, and the Boston Symphony Orchestra.

This plan developed into fourteen concerts on tour, more than double the number of performances outside New York during the previous year. Charlton organized the first tour of the 1910–1911 season for the week of December 5, 1910. This series began on Monday evening in Pittsburgh and continued onward to Cleveland, Buffalo, Rochester, Syracuse, and ended in Utica, New York, on Saturday, December 10, 1910. For this tour the Philharmonic provided the same program in each city, which reduced the rehearsal time and simplified the production of programs and promotional materials. Visits also continued throughout the season to Philadelphia and Washington, D.C., and the Philharmonic offered three concerts in a series in Washington, D.C. Mahler, however, managed to conduct only the first concert of this series in Philadelphia on January 23, 1911, and made his first Washington appearance on Tuesday afternoon, January 24, 1911. Once again the orchestra performed the same program in each location and featured the renowned lyric soprano Johanna Gadski.

In the middle of February, Mahler completed a final tour to New England encompassing Springfield, Massachusetts, and Hartford, Connecticut, on February 15 and 16, 1911. For the second time Mahler conducted in Springfield and repeated his arranged Bach Suite. Concertgoers in the nearby city of Hartford experienced one of Mahler's last moments at the podium and the final time he performed at the harpsichord. Although less publicized than previous tours, this set of concerts occurred only one week before Mahler's final appearance at Carnegie Hall with the New York Philharmonic on February 21, 1911.

Programming

As Mahler outlined the second season, he believed that a symphony concert should continue to be the backbone of music development in a community and also knew that it would be essential to consider the view of the guarantors, press, and the audience. For even during the first season, Mahler noted, he would study the audience and take into consideration public opinion: "I intend to let my public and the music critics of the press help me in picking out the musical way we should go."[39]

As a result, the eleven concerts that constituted the Beethoven series and the historical series of concerts were eliminated. The regular series of Friday afternoon concerts increased from eight to sixteen, with seven Sunday afternoon concerts and eight Tuesday evening performances. Friday afternoon concerts offered the most consistent time and location. The programs for Fridays were most often performed several days earlier on a Tuesday evening program and subsequently on a Sunday afternoon program in either Brooklyn or at Carnegie Hall. Other repetitions of the music occurred on tour. Mahler repeated programs an average of three times rather than the average of two times as in the previous season. Furthermore, out-of-town concerts for the 1910–1911 season more than doubled from six to fourteen concerts (not including the Brooklyn concerts) and encompassed a broader territory covering 1,933 miles of rail.[40]

Mahler's programming plan for the second season divided the music "more or less evenly between the classic and the modern schools."[41] In addition he planned to play music from many nations and emphasized that a conductor should have no preferences.[42] Mahler's repertoire for the second season highlighted works by more contemporary composers such as Enrico Bossi, Henry Hadley, Edward MacDowell, and George Chadwick. Compared with the programming from the first season, this music offered Mahler an opportunity to explore new repertoire and marked the first time he conducted many of these modern works.

Mahler's second season reflected a huge contrast in programming. During this season an unprecedented amount of twentieth-century music appeared on programs, including compositions by American and European composers. This contrast may be reflected in Mahler's desire to conduct new music and another trend in New York to include more contemporary music. Mahler's interest in modern music is mentioned in several letters and remarks. As he wrote to Bruno Walter, "My only pleasure is rehearsing works that are new to me. And I still derive immense pleasure from making music. If only the musicians themselves were a little better."[43]

During Mahler's final season he conducted ninety-four works by thirty-eight composers.[44] Compared with the previous season, "no fewer than seventy-three works by seventeen composers were new" to Mahler's final schedule.[45] Furthermore, by the end of Mahler's second season the Philharmonic managed to achieve a 50 percent increase in subscriptions and box office sales.[46]

Repetition of selected works in the programs also helped to reduce the rising costs of paying musicians. Although the musicians supposedly signed their yearly contracts prior to the rise in musician union rates, it is significant to note that the cost per musician rose from two to four dollars per rehearsal and the cost for a concert increased from seven to eight dollars per musician. With a union limit of three and a half hours per rehearsal, Mahler made the most of each minute to learn the new repertoire.

Programming for the tour also changed for the 1910–1911 season. When on tour in December 1910, the Philharmonic offered the identical program in six cities on six consecutive evenings. Compared with the first season this strategy reduced the rehearsal time. With greater territory to cover on this tour, along with the time required to set up the orchestra, reducing rehearsal time also helped the Philharmonic's pocketbook. The Philharmonic further minimized costs by not programming soloists and traveling with fewer musicians. Traveling with a smaller orchestra of perhaps eighty-five to eighty-seven required only one passenger railway car instead of two, which reduced expenses.

Wagner

A new strategy for the 1910–1911 season focused on the music of Richard Wagner for the month of January 1911. Wagner's music seemed to always draw a large audience, and this proved a pivotal move in gaining more concertgoers. To complement the orchestral music Mahler hired the famous soprano Johanna Gadski. Gadski made her American debut with the Damrosch Opera Company in 1895.[47] She appeared in numerous operas at Covent Garden, Bayreuth, and at the Metropolitan Opera House. During Mahler's period at the Met, Gadski sang a number of roles for Wagner and Mozart productions. Gadski also toured extensively throughout America, and in January 1910, she appeared with Toscanini at Philadelphia's Academy of Music in the role of Isolde.[48] An article in the *Philadelphia Press* noted Gadski's approaching appearance as "one of the most important events in the musical season."[49] Announcements proclaimed Gadski to be in glorious voice and introduced the diva as a German singer who made six successful tours in America. Although she enjoyed spending summers at home in Berlin, her friends regarded her as being as much American as German.[50] Gadski often contracted with an opera house for a complete season, but this period marked a time of transition in her career when she was available to sing with ensembles. As a result, some of the largest audiences of the season attended these concerts, and even after overwhelming applause followed each number, the audience recalled Gadski at least a dozen times.[51] After hearing her sing four Wagnerian programs, the New York audience still demanded Gadski return to the stage. Therefore, the Philharmonic scheduled another concert with Gadski as the soloist on Friday afternoon, January 27, marking Gadski's sixth appearance with the Philharmonic during January 1911.

Perseverance and careful programming paid off as support grew for the Philharmonic. On Sunday afternoon, January 22, 1911, the day before the tour to Philadelphia, Mahler's popularity continued to grow as the largest crowd of the season filled Carnegie Hall to capacity.[52] Even the reporter for the *New York Post* now admired Mahler's gift of "making all music entertaining, and the best of it of thrilling interest," and believed the New York public enjoyed "one of the best orchestras in the world."[53]

Beethoven's Symphony No. 6

In addition to Wagner, Beethoven's music dominated the repertoire of symphonic music Mahler performed throughout his career. Although Mahler regularly conducted orchestral and operatic scenes from Wagner operas, he performed Beethoven orchestral music roughly 150 times throughout his career.[54] Compared with other conductors, Mahler made discretionary changes to keep Beethoven's music contemporary and accessible to modern audiences accustomed to the richness of music by Strauss and Wagner. Mahler's liberties in updating the works drew praise as well as criticism. On the whole, critics outside of New York City offered more favorable reviews of Mahler's alterations. Yet, one must remember that during this period conductors often reworked pieces for a more modern orchestra and larger performance spaces.

During the tour season Mahler performed Beethoven Symphony No. 6 in eight out of ten cities. In various sections throughout the work, such as the duple part of the Scherzo, Mahler added trumpet parts in unison with the strings, and at other climactic moments he added trombones to the trumpet line. The most notable change occurred when he included more kettledrums during the storm at the end of the Scherzo.[55] Some critics raved about Mahler's retouching and believed the "new" symphony made the symphony no longer "archeology, but music in which the spirit of the master lives and rejoices."[56]

Mahler's reception throughout America is more clearly revealed when examining the planning and reviews of concerts outside New York. The

Table 3.2. New York Philharmonic Tours, 1909–1911

Date	Day	City/ST	Place	Seats
New England Tour 1910				
February 23, 1910	Wednesday	New Haven, CT	Woolsey Hall	2,683
February 24, 1910	Thursday	Springfield, MA	Court Square Theater	1,860
February 25, 1910	Friday	Providence, RI	Infantry Hall	NA
February 26, 1910	Saturday	Boston, MA	Symphony Hall	2,625
Great Lakes Tour 1910				
December 5, 1910	Monday	Pittsburgh, PA	Soldiers and Sailors Memorial Hall	2,378
December 6, 1910	Tuesday	Cleveland, OH	Grays Armory	5,000
December 7, 1910	Wednesday	Buffalo, NY	Convention Hall	5,000
December 8, 1910	Thursday	Rochester, NY	Convention Hall	3,000
December 9, 1910	Friday	Syracuse, NY	New Wieting Opera House	2,140
December 10, 1910	Saturday	Utica, NY	Majestic Theater	1,345
Philadelphia and Washington, D.C. Tours				
January 17, 1910	Monday	Philadelphia, PA	Academy of Music	2,897
March 14, 1910	Monday	Philadelphia, PA	Academy of Music	2,897
January 23, 1911	Monday	Philadelphia, PA	Academy of Music	2,897
January 24, 1911	Tuesday	Washington, DC	New National Theatre	1,676
New England Tour 1911				
February 15, 1911	Wednesday	Springfield, MA	Court Square Theater	1,860
February 16, 1911	Thursday	Hartford, CT	Parsons' Theater	1,700

following chapters on Mahler's era in America help to complete the perspective of his Philharmonic career. The concerts to be explored include the following, listed in Table 3.2.

Notes

1. For more information refer to the "Calendar of Event" articles in the *New York Times*. For example, the report for the "Calendar of Concerts," 26 December 1909, Metropolitan sec., 13, indicated thirty-four concerts for January 1910; of these nineteen were offered at Carnegie Hall. The report for the "Calendar of Concerts," 30 January 1910, Metropolitan sec., 15, indicated thirty-nine concerts for February 1910, of which nineteen were offered at Carnegie Hall.

2. "Nation's Best Orchestra, Mahler's," *Musical America* 10, no. 25 (30 October 1909): 31.

3. "Beethoven Series Begun by Mahler," *Musical America* 11, no. 3 (27 November 1909): 13.

4. George Martin, *The Damrosch Dynasty* (Boston: Houghton Mifflin, 1983), 193.

5. Martin, 188.

6. Martin, 196.

7. For more information, refer to "Great Welcome for New Opera," *New York Times*, December 11, 1910, 1.

8. This program included Beethoven's Overture "Die Weihe des Hauses" and his Symphony No. 3, *Eroica*, followed by the Liszt *Mazeppa*, and concluded with *Till Eulenspiegels lustige Streiche* by Strauss.

9. "Music," *New York Tribune*, 18 November 1909, np.

10. Reginald de Koven, "Philharmonic Again in a Sunday Concert," *New York World*, 13 December 1909, np.

11. "Yolando Mero's Concert," *New York Times*, 4 November 1909, 9.

12. "Under Mahler Baton," *Philadelphia Record*, 18 January 1910, 6.

13. "Brooklyn: Tilly Koenen Charms Brooklyn," *Musical Courier* 60, no. 7 (16 February 1910): 51.

14. "Brooklyn: Tilly Koenen Charms Brooklyn," 51.

15. "Maud Powell with N.Y. Philharmonic," *Musical America* 11, no. 9 (8 January 1910): 19.

16. "Maud Powell with N.Y. Philharmonic," np. The writer is referring to the concert on December 29, 1909, that included the Schubert Symphony No. 8 *Unfinished*, Mendelssohn's Violin Concerto Op. 64, and the Schumann Symphony No. 4.

17. Martin, 170.

18. "Reflections by the Editor," *Musical Courier* 59, no. 19 (10 November 1909): 21.

19. Theodore Spiering, "Zwei Jahre mit Gustav Mahler in New York," *Vossische Zeitung*, evening ed., Berlin, 21 May 1911, np; quoted in Kurt Blaukopf and Herta Blaukopf, ed., *Mahler: His Life Work, and World* (New York: Thames and Hudson, 2000), 227.

20. Zoltan Roman, *Gustav Mahler's American Years 1907–1911* (Stuyvesant, NY: Pendragon Press, 1989), 380.

21. Howard Shanet, *Philharmonic: A History of New York's Orchestra* (Garden City, NY: Doubleday and Company, 1975), 215.

22. *New York World*, 3 April 1910, Metropolitan sec., 5; quoted in Roman, 368.

23. "Notes of the Musical World," *New York Times*, 26 September 1909, Fashion and Society Section, 6.

24. "Philharmonic Tomorrow," *Providence Evening Tribune*, 24 February 1910, 12.

25. Gustav Mahler, *Suite aus den Orchesterwerken von Johann Sebastian Bach*, "Suite from the Orchestral Works of Johann Sebastian Bach," (New York: Schirmer, 1910). This work included an arrangement of the Overture and Rondeau from Bach's Orchestral Suite No. 2 in B Minor, BWV 1067, followed by the Air and Gavotte from the Orchestral Suite No. 3 in D Major, BWV 1068. Throughout this book the work will be referred to as the Bach Suite.

26. From 1905–1911 Arnold Dolmetsch worked with Chickering and Sons to manufacture harpsichords, spinets, clavichords, viols, and lutes. During this period

roughly thirty-three clavichords, thirteen two-manual harpsichords, and a few virginals and spinets were produced. For more information see Larry Palmer, *Harpsichord in America: A Twentieth-Century Revival* (Bloomington: Indiana University Press, 1989), 20.

27. Palmer, 34.

28. "Mozart's Masterpiece on his 150th Birthday," *New York Times*, 28 January 1906, 7. The opera took place on January 27, 1906.

29. "*Don Giovanni* given at the Metropolitan," *New York Times*, 24 January 1908, 7. Mahler conducted the opera on January 23, 1908.

30. Beethoven, Trio in G Major for Piano, Flute, and Bassoon, WoO37. Damrosch thought the harpsichord served as an appropriate instrument for the work since the Beethoven work called for a clavicembalo instead of a piano. Although written during the 1786–1790 period in Bonn, the work was not published until 1888.

31. "Beethoven Novelty Heard," *New York Times*, 16 March 1908, 7.

32. "Bach's 'Matthew Passion,'" *New York Times*, 17 April 1908, 6.

33. Richard Aldrich, "A Triumph in Italian Grand Opera: Revival of Mozart's 'Marriage of Figaro' at the Metropolitan Wins the Public," *The New York Times*, 17 January 1909, Fashions and Automobile Section, 7. This article refers to the production on Wednesday, January 16, 1909.

34. Albert Steinert, Providence, to Felix Leifels, New York, 19 February 1910, Papers of Felix Leifels, Archives of the New York Philharmonic.

35. Henry Steinway, interviewed by author, 28 February 2001, Steinway Hall, New York.

36. "Mahler and the Philharmonic," *Musical Courier* 59, no. 21 (19 November 1909): 53.

37. "Brooklyn: Tilly Koenen Charms Brooklyn," 51.

38. Professor Kovacs diagnosed Mahler with the heart condition of mitral incompetence and stenosis. Although most people with this condition live a fairly normal life, Mahler was devastated psychologically from the diagnosis and Kovac recommended Mahler reduce his active lifestyle. For more details refer to Henry-Louis de La Grange, *Mahler*, vol. 3, *Triumph and Disillusion (1904–1907)* (Oxford: Oxford University Press, 1999), 694.

39. "Mahler and the Philharmonic," 53.

40. For more details refer to table 3.1.

41. Emilie Frances Bauer, "Music in New York," *Musical Leader*, 7 April 1910, no. 14, 3.

42. Bauer, 3.

43. Gustav Mahler, *Letters to his Wife*, ed. Henry-Louis de La Grange and Günther Weiss, in collaboration with Knud Martner, trans. Antony Beaumont, 2d ed. (Ithaca, NY: Cornell University Press, 2004), 351.

44. Roman, 380.

45. Roman, 380.

46. "Philharmonic Society Plans Greatest Season," *Musical America* 14, no. 2 (20 May 1911): 32.

47. "A Glance at the Weeks Amusements: Gadski Concert Tuesday," *Washington Herald*, 22 January 1911, sec. 2, 6.

48. "News of the Musical Season," *Philadelphia Inquirer*, 2 January 1910, sec. 2, 11. Johanna Gadski (1872–1932) was born in Prussia and married Captain Hans Tauscher, a former German Army officer. During World War I she was forced to return to Europe. After the war, Gadski continued to perform, formed her own opera company, and visited the United States.

49. "Music," *Philadelphia Press*, 15 January 1911, sec. 2, 11.

50. "Music," 11.

51. "Music and Drama," *New York Evening Post*, 11 January 1911.

52. *New York Daily Tribune*, 23 January 1911, 7.

53. *New York Evening Post*, 23 January 1911, 9.

54. Knud Martner, *Gustav Mahler im Konzertsaal* (Kopenhagen: Martner, 1985), 181.

55. Alice Bradley, "Concert Delight to Big Audience," *Cleveland Leader*, 8 December 1910, 9.

56. "Music and Drama: Convention Hall," *Rochester Post Express*, 9 December 1910, 11.

CHAPTER FOUR

~

The New England
Tour—February 1910

The New York Philharmonic's inaugural tour encompassed four New England cities: New Haven, Connecticut; Springfield, Massachusetts; Providence, Rhode Island; and Boston, Massachusetts. Because of the close proximity of the cities and the convenient train routes, the Philharmonic completed the tour in only five days. Beginning on February 23, 1910, Mahler conducted the first concert in New Haven at Yale University's Woolsey Hall. After a short ride north the following morning, the Philharmonic played in Springfield on the evening of February 24, 1910, at the Court Square Theater. Heading southeast through Massachusetts on February 25, 1910, the orchestra reached Providence in the afternoon and gave an evening concert in Infantry Hall. The climax of the week occurred on Saturday evening, February 26, 1910, when the Philharmonic performed in Symphony Hall, the home of the Boston Symphony Orchestra. For the first time, audiences throughout New England heard the Philharmonic and "one of the first four orchestral leaders in the world,"[1] Gustav Mahler.

· In contrast to the usual critics in New York City, numerous writers offered fresh perspectives on Mahler and the New York Philharmonic. Although New England citizens supported other visiting orchestras, for the first time concertgoers witnessed a larger ensemble of one hundred musicians rather than the standard fifty to seventy members seen with a typical touring orchestra. With this expanded size, the Philharmonic performed romantic works by Berlioz, Strauss, and Wagner. With the exception of Providence, the concerts in New Haven, Springfield, and Boston included selections from the Bach Suite, thus highlighting Mahler as the arranger, soloist, and conductor. Articles encouraged readers to attend this rare event and witness Mahler performing the same Bach work that New Yorkers praised.

The New Haven Concert on Wednesday, February 23, 1910

By the beginning of February 1910, reports of the Philharmonic's visit to New Haven circulated in the local papers. Feature articles and advertisements ran in the *Yale Daily News*, *New Haven Evening Register*, *New Haven Union*, *New Haven Times Leader*, *New Haven Palladium*, and the *New Haven Morning Journal-Courier*.[2] New Haven took pride in being the initial city along the tour and the spot that gave "the orchestra the first greeting it has ever had from an audience outside of New York."[3] The *New Haven Morning Journal-Courier* reported, however, that "the society's distinguished leader," rather than the business manager, "expressed a desire to play in Woolsey Hall."[4]

New Haven provided several advantages as a concert location. First of all, the concert took place in Woolsey Hall, a building on the prestigious campus of Yale University. Woolsey Hall, still functioning today as a performance site, honors Theodore Dwight Woolsey, president of Yale from 1846 to 1871. The hall also offered the Newberry Memorial Organ, which Professor Harry Jepson agreed to play during Mahler's arrangement of the Bach Suite. Furthermore, Woolsey Hall offered familiar territory to several Philharmonic Society musicians who performed there as members of the New Haven Symphony Orchestra.

Preparations began on March 11, 1909, almost a year prior to concert, when Felix Leifels wrote a letter to Horatio Parker asking if the Philharmonic could give a concert in Woolsey Hall during the week beginning February 21, 1910.[5] In addition to serving as conductor of the New Haven Symphony Orchestra (1895–1919), Horatio Parker served as dean of the Yale University Department of Music[6] (1904–1919)[7] and the local coordinator of the New York Philharmonic concert. At the time of the letter Leifels anticipated that the orchestra would play in Boston and possibly Springfield or Hartford. Leifels requested a meeting with Parker in New Haven during the following week to gain his "view regarding the advisability of giving such a concert."[8] Leifels gained Parker's cooperation and soon investigated other cities for the tour. In a second letter to Parker, dated May 5, 1909, he mentioned the potential for concerts in Providence and Boston and requested a change in the New Haven date from February 23 to February 24 to accommodate a concert in Springfield, Massachusetts, on February 23. Fortunately, the manager of the Parsons' Theater in Springfield later offered Leifels the date of February 24, preserving the original date of February 23, 1910, for the New Haven concert.[9]

Articles during the tour recognized the Philharmonic Society as "not only the oldest, but in the first rank of symphony orchestras of the world."[10] Unlike musicians in local orchestras, the members of the Philharmonic "have played all over the world."[11] With a promise of a hundred musicians, New Haven advertisements guaranteed a program of unusual excellence rather than the traditional "hackneyed compositions routinely offered by smaller touring orchestras."[12]

While numerous advertisements promoted Mahler and the Philharmonic as the main attraction, many concertgoers believed Olga Samaroff offered "the event of the evening."[13] As a featured soloist for the concert, Samaroff planned to perform the Grieg Concerto in A Minor, op. 16. Samaroff first met Mahler at a dinner party hosted by Mr. and Mrs. Charles Herman Steinway in New York City. During the evening Samaroff managed to ignite a conversation with Mahler and generate a long discussion over Dostoevsky's *The Brothers Karamazoff*.[14]

Surprisingly, even though Olga was born in San Antonio, Texas, and named Lucie Hickenlooper, she changed her name to create the persona of a Russian pianist and promoted herself as such in New Haven advertisements.[15] Samaroff became the first American woman to win a scholarship to the Paris Conservatoire. In 1900, she returned to the United States to work with Ernest Hutcheson and later completed studies with Ernst Jedliczka in Berlin. Samaroff made her New York debut in 1905 with Walter Damrosch and the New York Symphony and toured extensively with major orchestras throughout the country. From 1911 to 1923 she was married to Leopold Stokowski, director of the Philadelphia Orchestra. After retiring because of an arm injury in 1925, she taught at the Philadelphia Conservatory and later at the Juilliard School.[16]

To further heighten public interest in the concert, several articles detailed the exceptional conducting, composing, and performance abilities of Mahler and proclaimed him an ideal leader. Several commentaries defined Mahler as a conductor "to whom art is the highest and first consideration"[17] and as a "musical hero of the day."[18] Reports further portrayed Mahler as a crusader of music[19] and a "fearless man who is great enough to do what he feels,"[20] yet, "as all great artists and geniuses, sensitive and easily affected by the atmosphere of his surroundings."[21]

Journalists also believed Mahler possessed the power to transform baroque music into modern popular music. Mahler "placed his personality" into a new arrangement of Bach's Orchestral Suites and suddenly "all the musical world finds new beauties in a composition it has listened to with complacency for generations."[22]

As early as February 9, 1910, the *New Haven Morning Journal-Courier* assured that a "large and representative audience" would attend the concert.[23] Interest in the upcoming event flourished, and by February 17, 1910, an article in the *Journal-Courier* concluded, "There is little doubt now that the concert on Wednesday night will largely be attended."[24] Subsequent articles promoted the concert as an unparalleled occasion and expected it to be "the most notable musical event New Haven has had in many years."[25]

Ticket prices ranged from $1.00 to $2.50. Parker received mail orders for the higher priced tickets, and on February 19, 1910, the regular sale of tickets opened at Woolsey Hall.[26] This event attracted many music lovers beyond the Yale campus and New Haven community. Prior to the general ticket sales, Parker received orders for tickets from Hartford, Winsted, and Litchfield.[27] Additional parties of considerable size from Bridgeport, Waterbury, and Meriden also ordered tickets for the concert.[28]

The Day of the Concert

On February 23, 1910, the orchestra left New York City at 7:30 in the morning on the New Haven Express and arrived in New Haven at 2:54.[29] Samaroff arrived at the train station from Boston where she had assisted the Kneisel Quartet the previous evening.[30] Scarcely an hour after the train's arrival from New York, the rehearsal began in Woolsey Hall. This meeting provided the only time for Samaroff and the orchestra to coordinate the Grieg work, and also gave Professor Jepson, a professor of music at Yale University, a chance to work with Mahler on the Bach piece.

While the orchestra rehearsed the music, numerous concertgoers began their journey to New Haven, and some local socialites prepared their homes for dinner parties. The society pages of the *Journal-Courier* and the *Evening Register* documented a number of festivities planned for the evening.[31] After these parties, guests and hostesses headed to Woolsey Hall where the concert commenced at 8:15 in the evening.[32]

The Philharmonic opened the concert with the *Symphonie Fantastique*, op. 14, and followed with Mahler's Bach Suite. The next selection featured Samaroff as soloist in the Grieg Concerto in A Minor for Piano, op. 16. The evening concluded with Richard Strauss' *Till Eulenspiegels lustige Streiche*.

Reviews of the New Haven Concert

Selecting New Haven as the first city for the Philharmonic's tour proved advantageous, as positive reviews filled the newspapers on the morning of February 24, 1910. The *Palladium* favorably reported:

> Unsurpassable music, illustrating all the stations of passion, sentiment and fancy, from the widest convulsions of jealousy to the wildest caprices of roguery; an orchestra whose perfection was unwavering, a conductor whose harmonic strategy was equal to all the myriad difficulties of his program, and a pianist for whose silvery touch no fortissimo was too great, no pianissimo too delicate, no intermediate nuance too subtle—these four elements constitute the recital of the Philharmonic Society of New York, conducted by Gustav Mahler, "the little giant," with Olga Samaroff as soloist, the crowning event of the musical season at Woolsey Hall.[33]

The performance surpassed the expectations of listeners and created a "tremendous"[34] and "notable event in the music history of New Haven."[35] Overall, the evening offered "a very high class program" as the Philharmonic "produced with perfect artistic finish."[36] With the exception of the Grieg Concerto in A Minor, the concert marked the premiere of the Berlioz, Bach, and Strauss selections in New Haven. The musical forces required for these works achieved success as the large orchestra created a "richness and breadth of tone with the large number of strings."[37]

Viewpoints differed drastically on who was the star performer of the night. Some reviewers credited Samaroff's performance as the "climax of the evening,"[38] while other critics believed Mahler captured the spotlight as conductor and performer. The *Times Leader* concluded, however, that "people go to the Philharmonic concerts to hear the wonderfully perfectly drilled orchestra, not to see Mahler conduct."[39]

New Haven articles focused on Mahler's conducting technique. The *Evening Register* printed the most favorable review and reported that the orchestra's "playing was finished and thorough under the dominance of Mr. Gustav Mahler's baton."[40] The *Morning Journal-Courier* concluded that even though Mahler was "not a revolutionist" in the matter of readings, he "seeks sincerely the spirit of the composer and aims to express his ideas. Mr. Mahler's vision is clear and his music ideas are the same and vigorous."[41] The *Times Leader* recorded that "Conductor Mahler has no personal magnetism, but he has marvelous musical ability."[42] This critic also complimented Mahler on refraining from making unnecessary gestures or poses found in dramatic conductors such as Walter Damrosch, Anton Seidl, and Theodore Thomas. The article praised Mahler as one of the world's best conductors "because of very unusual artistic talent and the ability to train expert musicians to do the best of which they are capable."[43] Moreover, the *Palladium* viewed Mahler in more authoritative terms and observed, "Mahler directs his orchestra like a general. He is a commander."[44]

Berlioz

When the concert opened with the Berlioz *Symphonie Fantastique*, listeners immediately realized the dynamic contrasts possible with a large orchestra. The writer of the *Journal-Courier* stated, "In the matter of minute detail, delicacy in the pastoral scenes, sonorous vigor in tumultuous phrases and a skillful adjustment of instrumental values in the orchestration, the orchestra displayed the splendid grasp of Mr. Mahler."[45] The critic compared Mahler's reading of the score with a recent New York performance by Walter Damrosch. He concluded that Mahler's reading of the score "differed somewhat and on the whole to its advantage."[46]

Bach

With Jepson doubling the keyboard part on the organ, Mahler conducted and performed the Bach Suite. Even though the work appeared as a novelty with a "made-over piano," the piece was "thoroughly enjoyable."[47] Critics also recognized that some purists might be offended by Mahler's tampering with the score of a sacred composer. Yet both the *Times Leader* and the *Journal-Courier* believed the work "better than anything else shows Mr. Mahler's genius and originality."[48] As a keyboardist, Mahler received praise for his "fine sympathy and rhythmic precision."[49]

The only suggestion, or possible criticism, came from the reviewer of the *Evening Register*, who advised Mahler to reduce the size of the orchestra. Although no documents verified the number of musicians performing this work, the reviewer recommended "that a better result might have been obtained by using only a few strings and a clavichord with less tone so that more transparency might have been gained."[50] On the whole, Mahler created a renewed interest in Bach, and several articles applauded his efforts. The *Times Leader* and the *Courier-Journal* concluded, "We doff our hat to the man who can make Bach interesting even if he has to tamper a little with the score to do it."[51]

Olga Samaroff

After the stage was rearranged, Olga Samaroff captured the audience's attention with her performance of Grieg's Concerto in A Minor as she skillfully mastered the technical difficulties with "absolute ease, accuracy and finish"[52] and fused long runs into "single continuous cascades of crystal sound."[53] Samaroff also demonstrated "invariable ease and repose even at the crises of the piece" and created an "instantaneous response to the various moods of the music."[54] By the close of the third movement the hall filled with a thunder of enthusiasm, and the "queenly Russian was compelled to appear seven times before the clamor subsided."[55] Even though the audience demanded more, Samaroff just "graciously smiled, gracefully bowed and nothing more."[56] The orchestra's role also added to Samaroff's performance, as the *Times Leader* acknowledged the accompaniment as "a delight and revelation to New Haven."[57]

Strauss

The evening concluded with Strauss' *Till Eulenspiegels lustige Streiche*. As a popular composer among American audiences, Strauss offered eccentricities to please the listeners. With an orchestra, Mahler created "ornate splendor in the larger proportions and taste and orchestral beauty in every line."[58] Mahler's interpretation pleased the crowd and critics alike. While the *New Haven Palladium* recognized Mahler's most successful conducting in the fourth and fifth movements of the Berlioz *Symphonie Fantastique*, the reviewer and many listeners preferred the Strauss piece with its "madcap collection of colorful narrative and commentary."[59]

By the end of the evening, New Haveners demonstrated their enthusiasm for the music with great applause and requested repeated encores. The reviews unfortunately failed to document the number and selection of encores. Mahler showed his appreciation of the musicians when in "bowing his acknowledgements, graciously indicated that the men of the orchestra deserved an equal share in the honors of the evening, and they did."[60] Critics generally refrained from comparing the Philharmonic to other orchestras, such as the Boston Symphony Orchestra, but in a closing remark the *Times Leader* concluded, "We all enjoyed the concert as we never before enjoyed the work of any orchestra."[61]

A Post-Concert Snack

As concertgoers traveled home, Mahler invited Samaroff and her traveling companion Miss Dehon to join him for dinner. Even though Miss Dehon declined, Samaroff and Mahler searched the area unsuccessfully for a restaurant. Unfortunately, most businesses closed earlier in the evening, leaving Mahler to mutter, "Was für eine Stadt! What kind of students do they have here? No wine, no songs, and not yet midnight."[62] After returning to the sitting room of Samaroff and Dehon, Mahler enjoyed their conversation to the "wee small hours" of the morning as they "feasted on milk and crackers."[63]

During the following week Samaroff prepared to perform the Piano Concerto No. 4 in G Major, op. 58, by Beethoven with Mahler and the Philharmonic at Carnegie Hall on Friday, March 4, 1910.[64] However, several days prior to the concert Samaroff suffered acute appendicitis, and Yolanda Mérö substituted as the soloist.[65] During the next year Samaroff remained in contact with Mahler, and during his final weeks in New York, Dehon and Samaroff constantly sent him soup and other "dainty dishes" to sustain him until he left for Europe.[66]

The Springfield Concert on Thursday, February 24, 1910

The next stop along the tour, Springfield, Massachusetts, was only a short train ride of sixty-six miles north from New Haven. Along the way the train passed through Hartford, Connecticut. The Philharmonic scheduled no concert in this city because the Boston Symphony Orchestra planned a performance on Monday, February 28, 1910. Originally, the Boston Symphony Orchestra also arranged to stop in Springfield, Massachusetts, during February, but the orchestra canceled the appearance to increase their revenue and exposure by covering more territory in Philadelphia, Baltimore, and Washington, D.C. In previous years, the Boston Symphony Orchestra had offered several performances each season in Springfield, but during 1910, they held only one concert on March 27.[67] Since these concerts had become a tradition in Springfield, some supporters and even reporters felt slighted by the Boston Symphony Orchestra. The public eagerly awaited the New York Philharmonic event that appeared to compensate for the disappointment that the Boston Symphony Orchestra generated and perhaps created an even more receptive audience. As the *Springfield Daily Republican* reported, "The opportunity for so superb a performance to fill the gap thus made [by the Boston Symphony Orchestra] is the more welcome."[68]

As the second largest city in Massachusetts, Springfield boasted several active theaters and five major newspapers including the *Springfield Daily Republican*, *Springfield Union*, *Springfield Daily News*, *Springfield Weekly Republican*, and the *Springfield Homestead*.[69] Compared with other stops on the 1910 New England tour, more promotional articles, advertisements, and reviews filled the pages of these newspapers than in any other city. Notices in Springfield went as far as to recognize Mahler as the "World's Greatest Symphony Conductor" and proclaimed the event to be the "Greatest Symphonic Concert Ever Given Here."[70] The portrayal of the concert as a spectacular occasion lured readers to purchase tickets during the first weeks of February. The coming of Mahler and the Philharmonic promised to "cause a thrill of anticipated pleasure"[71] and present a man "who never fails to thrill and excite his audience."[72] The approaching evening created "almost sensational interest,"[73] and along with Mahler offered an organization that "will be as nearly perfect as possible."[74]

William F. A. Engel coordinated local arrangements and scheduled the concert at one of the most luxurious theaters, the Court Square Theater. Set in the center of Springfield along Main Street, the theater offered easy accessibility to hotels and transportation. Owned by Dwight O. Gilmore, the Court had 1,860 seats with a customary balcony and even featured boxed seats. Prices for tickets ranged between $.75 for family circle tickets to $2.50 for exclusive boxed seats.[75] Again the program featured the *Symphonie Fantastique* and Mahler's arranged Bach Suite. As a featured lyric soprano, Corrine Rider-Kelsey[76] prepared to sing "Quanto dolci" from Handel's *Flavio* and "Voi che sapete" from Mozart's *Le Nozze di Figaro*. For the second half of the evening Mahler planned to conduct *Till Eulenspiegels lustige Streiche* and Prelude to *Die Meistersinger von Nürnberg*.

Advertisements for the concert first appeared on February 7, 1910, and introduced Mahler to readers. Through a series of articles, writers proclaimed Mahler as a wonder in the field of conducting who reshaped the New York Philharmonic. The *Springfield Daily Republican* even reproduced portions of an article from the *New York Evening Post* written earlier by Henry T. Finck. In the article, Finck declared that Mahler worked a miracle on the orchestra and that within two months transformed the Philharmonic to the "equivalent of the Boston Symphony Orchestra, if not its superior."[77] Several days later the *Daily Republican* encouraged potential concertgoers to hear "the greatest of New York orchestras" and compare it with the Boston Symphony Orchestra to decide which organization should be declared superior.[78]

Overall, articles promoted Mahler and the Philharmonic and only briefly mentioned the soloist Corrine Rider-Kelsey. As the first opportunity to hear an orchestra of one hundred musicians, writers encouraged readers to witness

the historical event which promised to "be among the most notable ever offered to a Springfield audience."[79] Local advertisements proved beneficial as
readers purchased tickets for the event. The *Daily Republican* predicted that
the Court Square Theater would be crowded and that anyone who cared
even slightly for music would not stay away.[80]

In addition to the musicians and their usual instruments, the Philharmonic also transported the reconfigured Steinway piano for the Bach selection. The writer of the *Springfield Daily News*, however, referred to the instrument as a "Klavier" and emphasized that the instrument was "brought to
this city specially for this concert."[81]

Reviews of the Springfield Concert

Critics overwhelmingly praised Mahler and the Philharmonic for one of the
finest performances ever heard in Springfield.[82] The *Springfield Homestead* concluded that even without an understanding of the classical music, "the evening
could still be enjoyed as no other affair of the kind during this, or past seasons."[83]
At the Court Square Theater the audience generously filled the balconies and
offered a "fairly good representation of music lovers on the main floor."[84]

Reporters soon made comparisons to other events in Springfield's cultural
history. The *Homestead* declared the New York Philharmonic "indisputably
first, in the quality of the musicians it contains, in its willingness to adopt
modern musical ideas, powerfully indicated in its rendition of an unusual
program, in numbers, and in the man who guides the performances."[85] Even
though the renowned conductor Anton Seidl reigned as the leader of the
Philharmonic from 1891 to 1898, the critic of the *Homestead* viewed Mahler
as "a far more vigorous leader"[86] and even noted a "temptation" to declare
him a "greater" conductor than the esteemed Seidl.[87]

Other newspapers, such as the *Weekly Republican*, immediately realized listeners would compare the Philharmonic with the Boston Symphony Orchestra; yet critics believed this comparison was pointless since the Boston
orchestra had never appeared in concert with such a large ensemble. Therefore, writers withheld declaring either orchestra superior, commended the
outstanding performance, and concluded "seldom has an audience so obviously been impressed."[88]

Berlioz

Mahler opened the evening with a splendid rendition of the Berlioz *Symphonie Fantastique*. While many audiences along the tour rated *Till Eulenspiegels lustige Streiche* as the masterpiece of the evening, listeners in Spring-

field hailed the *Symphonie Fantastique* as the highlight of the concert. Critics alike rated the Berlioz as "superbly given," and as the *Homestead* noted, "Other composers represented on the program were made to take a secondary position."[89] Even though a Springfield audience usually refrained from going wild over entertainment, they demonstrated enthusiastic appreciation after each movement of the Berlioz work.[90] The *Daily Republican* reinforced this perspective in a review that ranked the *Symphonie Fantastique* in first place. Even as the program proceeded, listeners compared the remaining works to the Berlioz selection. By the time Mahler finished conducting the Strauss work, the critic of the *Daily Republican* remarked that *Till Eulenspiegels* was "a gorgeous divertimento, though it suffered beside the flaming enthusiasm of the youthful Berlioz."[91] The *Daily News* printed an extremely descriptive account of the Berlioz work, and, as noted below, commended Mahler's ability to meld the conductor and orchestra to create a brilliant rendition reflective of Berlioz's original intentions.

> Conductor and orchestra united in a performance of the Berlioz work that was tremendously fascinating in its effect. The ball movement was performed in exquisite style and in "the scene in the fields" the counterfeiting of the sound of the shepherd's pipe was a lovely piece of work. The thematic matter typifying the march of the murderer to the scaffold was brought out to the fullest and the orchestra played it with transcendently satisfying effect, making one instinctively feel the oppressive gloom of the occasion. The climax, the "dream of the night of the witches' sabbath," in conclusion was a striking exemplification of Mahler's proficiency, in the reading of the great Berlioz work, the orchestra's performance being faithful in all respects to the fantastic morbidness of the score.[92]

Bach

Mahler contrasted the romantic works with his arrangement of the Bach Suite. After concluding the Berlioz selection, the reconfigured piano was moved to the center of the stage[93] and placed on three blocks so Mahler could also conduct the orchestra.[94] The critic of the *Weekly Republican* regarded the performance of the Bach work as an "extremely interesting novelty," as the "wiry twang of the harpsichord added a quaint touch which transported one instantly into another century."[95] Mahler impressed critics as he gave another illustration of his remarkable ability to understand music from different periods, to arrange a composition, and to play the harpsichord. Although the review in the *Weekly Republican* commended Mahler on the work, the critic believed that while the violinists played admirably, they did not have the same brilliance as those in the Boston Symphony Orchestra.[96]

Corinne Rider-Kelsey

Baroque music continued to fill the program as Corinne Rider-Kelsey followed the Bach work with "Quanto dolci" from Handel's *Flavio* and "Voi che sapete" from Mozart's *Le Nozze di Figaro*. Less known to American audiences than Samaroff, Rider-Kelsey was born in Batavia, New York, in 1877. After attending Oberlin College, she continued to study voice in Chicago and New York.[97] In 1904, she made her professional debut in St. Louis, in Handel's *Messiah*. Beginning in 1905, she appeared with the New York Oratorio Society in their annual performance of the *Messiah*. In July 1908, she made her first operatic appearance at Covent Garden as Micaëla in Bizet's *Carmen*.[98] Several days prior to the concert on Tuesday, February 22, 1910, Rider-Kelsey joined the Boston Symphony Orchestra on their tour in Baltimore, Maryland. In their concert at the Lyric Theater, she successfully sang the soprano solo in Beethoven's Symphony No. 9 in D Major before departing for Springfield.[99]

Earlier in the season Rider-Kelsey appeared with Mahler in the first so-called historical concert of the New York Philharmonic at Carnegie Hall on November 9, 1909. Similar to the Springfield event, the November concert also included the selection from Handel's *Flavio* and Mahler's arrangement of the Bach Suite. As a featured soloist on the program, Rider-Kelsey quickly won overwhelming applause. The writer for the *Union* thought her appearance was too brief. Had the audience demonstrated more appreciation for this "exquisite artistry," her portion of the program might have been lengthened, he speculated.[100] Critics from other newspapers also raved over Rider-Kelsey's voice as "full, of excellent quality, and perfectly trained,"[101] and the *Daily News* noted her style, execution, and enunciation as flawless.[102] The critic of the *Weekly Republican* also admired Rider-Kelsey as "one of the very few who could carry the [Mozart] thing off."[103] Her rendition of "Quanto dolci" demonstrated "the lovely quality of her tone," but the second selection "Voi che sapete" proved her to be a singer of exceptional quality; "her liquid notes were as mellow as those of a flute" and her enunciation so clear and distinct that "one unversed in the language would have had little difficulty in following the words."[104]

Strauss and Wagner

The closing pieces on the program included Strauss' *Till Eulenspiegels lustige Streiche* followed by Wagner's Prelude to *Die Meistersinger von Nürnberg*. As late romantic compositions, these works employed a hundred musicians and gave the audience a taste of the musical potential of a large orchestra. In contrast to the wild enthusiasm for the *Symphonie Fantastique*, these remaining selections received minimal coverage in the reviews. Writers demonstrated high regard for Mahler's ability to extract various tonal effects from the orchestra and believed his reading of the scores "in the interpretation of Berlioz and Strauss would do credit to any leader that ever lived."[105] Another review from the *Daily News* complimented the "sprightliness and abandon" in the Strauss work and the "truly captivated rendition" that followed in the Wagner selection.[106] As the final piece, the Prelude to *Die Meistersinger von Nürnberg* created "splendid sonorous effects" as it was superbly played under Mahler and thus created a "triumphal close to the evening."[107]

Mahler's Conducting

Of significant importance to the audience and critics of Springfield was the opportunity to witness Mahler as a conductor and director of the Philharmonic. From the reviews, Mahler surpassed the audience's expectation and proved himself an undisputed genius.[108] Rather than as a dictating maestro, Mahler was portrayed by local critics as a conductor who worked with the orchestra. As the *Daily News* observed, "He positively makes no attempt to separate himself from this orchestra or to make Mahler, and not the musicians, the attraction."[109] Using that "glorious black magic of his," Mahler achieved "wonderful stunts" as he conducted with "grace, energy and vigor always, but without appeal to the sensational, and without resort to the clamor that the over-temperamental conductor sometimes calls forth."[110] In conclusion, the *Daily Republican* regarded the event as a stimulating program that offered "a superb orchestra, a conductor of the 'first force,' as the fencing masters say, a delightful singer. . . . What more could be asked?"[111] The warm reception in Springfield broke ground for future concerts.

Mahler's Thoughts on Traveling

Unfortunately, Mahler did not always enjoy traveling from city to city. In a letter he wrote to Alma from Springfield on February 24, 1910, he reminisced about home at the Savoy Hotel in New York City as he reemphasized the drudgeries of traveling:

> Today I am in a hole (there is nothing else here), a roar of machinery, 'cars', and so on. My stomach is also no longer in order! Perhaps it is the butter again,

which I will cut out from now on. It is very cold, and everything is snowed in and icy![112]

He concluded that "New Haven is a nice little place with a bad hotel. Springfield is a wretched hole with an impossible hotel."[113] Nevertheless, the following year Springfield was the only city from the New England tour of 1910 that Mahler and the Philharmonic chose to include in a tour planned for February 1911.

Since Mahler did not require the transformed piano for the Providence concert, it was immediately shipped after the concert in Springfield to Boston in care of M. Steinert and Sons.[114] This allowed ample time to tune the instrument before the Philharmonic arrived in Boston on Saturday afternoon.

The Providence Concert on Friday, February 25, 1910

Providence, Rhode Island, offered the third stop along the Philharmonic's tour. At the beginning of the twentieth century, Providence stood as the leader in woolen production, third in the manufacture of machinery and machine tools, and the jewelry capital of the nation.[115] Although numerous ensembles and international musicians such as Richard Strauss, Victor Herbert, Fritz Kreisler, Ossip Gabrilowitsch, Serge Rachmaninoff, and Percy Grainger are documented as "famed personages" who appeared at Infantry Hall, Mahler's visit with the Philharmonic is not included.[116]

During the first week of February 1910, advertisements for the concert began running in local newspapers such as the *Providence Evening Tribune, Providence Sunday Tribune, Providence Journal, Providence Sunday Journal,* and the *Providence Evening Bulletin.*[117] Compared to the almost daily publicity for musical events in Springfield newspapers, local media in Providence provided sparse coverage, with only thirteen articles featuring the upcoming Philharmonic's visit. Of these few reports, however, only two appeared before February 20, 1910, leaving a mere five days for newspapers to print promotional notices and articles.

Entertainment in Providence

Unfortunately, a number of musical events surrounded the Philharmonic concert. On the same day as the scheduled Philharmonic concert, Fritz Kreisler also offered his final recital of the season at Memorial Hall,[118] which was sponsored by the Providence Musical Association.[119] On February 15,

1910, ten days prior to the Philharmonic concert, the Boston Symphony Orchestra presented its third seasonal concert in Providence to a large and enthusiastic audience. Although the concert ran longer than usual, "the audience was intensely interested until the final note, here and there applauding and showing its appreciation of the efforts of the musicians whenever opportunity offered."[120] Two days later on Thursday, February 17, 1910, the Russian Symphony Orchestra from New York City gave a concert in Providence. Local newspapers probably postponed giving coverage to the Philharmonic concert until these earlier musical events concluded.

The *Evening Tribune* first generated regional interest on February 13, 1910, when it advertised the event as the "First and Only Appearance in Rhode Island of the New York Philharmonic Society"[121] and as the "Largest Musical Organization ever to play in Providence."[122] A day before the event the *Evening Tribune* recommended the concert as an opportunity to hear an orchestra rated "one of the best in the world, conducted by Gustav Mahler, claimed to be the highest salaried conductor in symphony music."[123]

Featured articles filled the newspapers the week of the concert as the *Sunday Tribune* hailed Mahler as one of the first four orchestral leaders then living,[124] and the *Evening Bulletin* declared the event to be the "greatest symphony concert" ever to be given in Providence.[125] Likewise, the *Sunday Journal* assured listeners the evening would create a "memorable musical event" and an occasion "that will hardly be neglected by any music lover."[126]

Local Management

Albert M. Steinert, manager and head of the M. Steinert and Sons Company, coordinated local arrangements and sold tickets for the concert.[127] Ticket prices ranged from $.75 to $2.00 for the Philharmonic event and appeared comparable to prices touring ensembles offered such as the Russian Symphony Orchestra, which set ticket prices from $.75 to $2.50.[128] However, the Boston Symphony Orchestra offered considerably more affordable tickets ranging from $1.00 to $1.50 for their concert.[129]

Infantry Hall

Built in 1879, Infantry Hall served as the scene of Providence's musical, political, and sporting events until it closed in 1926.[130] Prior to the Philharmonic's debut in 1910, the orchestras previously heard in Providence numbered between fifty and seventy musicians. With the anticipation of the Philharmonic's arrival, however, Steinert enlarged the stage to accommodate one hundred musicians and the additional percussion including six tympani, a bass drum, and a chime piano.[131]

Lecture Series

To prepare listeners for the approaching concerts Hans Schneider, owner of the Hans Schneider Piano School in Providence, presented two free lecture recitals. During the first lecture on Wednesday, February 16, 1910, at four thirty in the afternoon in the Recital Hall of the Butler Exchange Building, Schneider discussed the changes in the form, harmony, and orchestration since Beethoven, and highlighted the efforts of Berlioz, Wagner, Liszt, and Strauss.[132] The *Evening Tribune* recorded that "beside the pupils of the schools, a large number of outside music lovers followed the exposition of the lecture with a great deal of interest."[133] The next Wednesday, February 23, 1910, at four thirty in the afternoon in the Recital Hall, Schneider addressed the Philharmonic's program with analyses and illustrations of the music. Since the concert marked the first time a Providence audience would hear Berlioz's *Symphonie Fantastique* and Richard Strauss' tone poem, Schneider prepared listeners to understand the music.

Reviews of the Providence Concert

On Friday evening, February 25, 1910, Mahler opened the concert in Infantry Hall with the *Symphonie Fantastique* by Hector Berlioz. Theodore Spiering, the concertmaster and "one of America's foremost violinists," followed as the soloist with the Violin Concerto No. 5 in A Minor, op. 37, by Henri Vieux-temps.[134] The symphonic poem *Till Eulenspiegels lustige Streiche* by Richard Strauss appeared as the third selection. Mahler concluded the evening with Wagner's Prelude to the opera *Die Meistersinger von Nürnberg*.[135] Compared to the other concerts on the tour this performance excluded Mahler's arrangement of the Bach Suite. He may have elected to omit the work because of the hall's acoustics and the absence of a permanent organ.

Even though Infantry Hall lacked a full house for the concert, critics rated the evening an overall success and condemned those who did not attend the event. A journalist with the *Evening Bulletin* remarked, "A good many people lost the opportunity to hear one of the best concerts of the kind, and certainly the most splendid orchestral programme, which has ever been given here."[136] A review in the *Evening Tribune* reinforced this superior rating and concluded, "There have been few concerts given in this city of the class of that last evening at Infantry Hall by the Philharmonic Society of New York."[137]

The opening *Symphonie Fantastique* soon captivated the audience and immediately became one of their favorite selections.[138] Concertmaster Theodore Spiering then gave a brilliant rendition of the Violin Concerto No. 5 by Vieuxtemps as the second selection. Spiering's mastery of the composition quickly won the audience's acclaim.[139] "As a virtuoso piece of the most pronounced character" and filled with "bristling technical difficulties," the composition was "surmounted" by Spiering "with convincing ease and skill."[140] Following the final note, the audience vigorously applauded Spiering and further expressed their approval with half a dozen recalls.[141]

Again the Strauss work earned the honor of "best selection of the evening."[142] The *Evening Tribune* commended Mahler on his ability to bring so many musicians "capable of properly rendering the most difficult classical music."[143] Although no reporter mentioned the Wagner work, the quality of the orchestra impressed listeners and the critic of the *Evening Bulletin* ranked the musicians as "a superb body of players, [who] under the inspiring leader of Conductor Gustav Mahler, made a magnificent showing."[144]

Society Attends

Local newspapers reserved substantial space on the society page to mention the full names of socialites who attended the concert. As in other cities throughout America during this period, society and even entertainment sections of newspapers routinely reported on the dress and attendance of the elite at social functions. In the society section of the *Evening Tribune* twenty-five names of affluent citizens present at the concert appeared.[145]

Beyond coverage by local media, the international musical periodical the *Musical Courier* critiqued the Philharmonic's concert in Providence as "one of the best orchestra programs that Providence has ever heard."[146] The article recognized that the evening marked the debut of the Strauss work in Providence and also documented the "hearty approval"[147] Theodore Spiering received from playing the Vieuxtemps concerto. In closing, the writer credited the success of the event to local impresario Albert Steinert.[148]

The Kreisler Concert

Across town the Kreisler concert enjoyed "a very large audience" filled with great enthusiasm for the artist.[149] Potential concertgoers in Providence had to decide between two events that offered remarkable music and outstanding violinists. While some patrons may have been curious to hear the Philharmonic's Theodore Spiering perform the Vieuxtemp's Concerto No. 5 in A

Minor, he did not evoke enough curiosity to lure people away from the Kreisler concert. In fact, Kreisler also included a work by Henri Vieuxtemps on his program, namely the Violin Concerto No. 2 in F-sharp Minor, op. 19. For lovers of violin music, Kreisler became the primary attraction for the evening. The *Evening Tribune* summarized: "The [Philharmonic] concert was one which deserved a large attendance, and it was unfortunate that many who have really enjoyed the offering had made previous arrangements to attend another musical recital on the same evening. If the Philharmonic gives another concert in this city, the hall will probably be filled."[150]

Music in Providence

Perhaps numerous conflicts hindered citizens from patronizing the Philharmonic event. Limited advertisements only a week before the concert, the Kreisler concert in Memorial Hall on the same evening, and strong loyalty to the Boston Symphony Orchestra affected attendance. Yet, the writer of the article concluded that those who turned out to see the Philharmonic "would take some trouble, if necessary to hear another like it."[151]

Subsequent articles reinforced the ineffectiveness of touring with a larger sized orchestra. When the Boston Symphony Orchestra traveled only fifty miles to Providence, they refrained from performing larger works in Providence because of the extra expense and the size of Infantry Hall.[152] Even with the Philharmonic's strategy of traveling with a large orchestra, the Boston Symphony Orchestra managed to maintain a larger market share of patrons with a smaller traveling orchestra.

The Boston Concert on Saturday, February 26, 1910

For over one hundred years Symphony Hall has served as the major music hall in Boston, home for the Boston Symphony Orchestra, and the location for the Philharmonic concert on February 26, 1910. With the availability of the hall's organ, built by George S. Hutching, Mahler included his Bach Suite in the program.

This concert would not be Mahler's first visit in Boston, but his second. On April 8, 1908, he had first appeared in Boston as an operatic conductor when the Metropolitan Opera House Company performed Wagner's *Die Walküre*. During the same week Mahler conducted Mozart's *Don Giovanni* on April 9, 1908, and Wagner's *Tristan und Isolde* on April 11, 1908, in Boston. With opera in the forefront of musical entertainment, Mahler and the Metropolitan Opera received mixed reviews. In a review of *Don Giovanni*, Henry

Taylor Parker of the *Boston Evening Transcript* expressed disappointment in the scenery, the replacement of original cast members, and the lack of "dramatizing voice that Mr. Mahler can give" to the "great airs," thus creating an opera that lacked excitement and thrill.[153] Yet, Philip Hale of the *Boston Sunday Herald* wrote approvingly of Mahler, stating, "His fine taste and poetic mind were at once recognized."[154]

Bostonians knew Mahler in several ways. When the Boston Symphony Orchestra discussed a possible successor for Max Fiedler in February 1910, they considered Mahler and several other conductors as possible replacements before renewing Fielder's contract.[155] Bostonians also recognized him as a modern composer. During February 1906, the Boston Symphony Orchestra performed Mahler's Fifth Symphony on two occasions.[156] While the work offered some listeners new sonorities, dissonant chords, and even chaotic sounds, the *Boston Evening Transcript* referred to Mahler as a twentieth-century Berlioz and concluded,

> Whether or not he realizes what he has conceived, he has filled his work with such powerful moments, such transporting beauty, developing and transforming his themes into such dramatically interesting variations, instrumenting so beautifully and powerfully, that he captivates and conquers his audiences.[157]

Advertisements for the New York Philharmonic concert began on January 29, 1910, and emphasized the upcoming event as the Philharmonic's first concert in Boston. During the following weeks promotional articles appeared in the *Boston Daily Advertiser*, *Boston Evening Transcript*, *Boston Evening Record*, *Boston Globe*, *Boston Sunday Globe*, *Boston Herald*, *Boston Sunday Herald*, *Boston Journal*, *Boston Post*, and the *Christian Science Monitor*.[158] Starting on February 13, 1910, Louis H. Mudgett, the manager of Symphony Hall, began accepting mail orders for the concert.[159] The public sale of tickets opened on Friday, February 18, 1910, and on the average they were more expensive in Boston than in any other city along the tour, with tickets priced from one to two dollars.[160]

The scheduling of the concert coordinated well with the Boston Symphony Orchestra's schedule for the winter of 1910. During the week the Philharmonic toured New England, the Boston orchestra toured through Washington, D.C., Baltimore, Philadelphia, New York City, Brooklyn, and Hartford, Connecticut.[161] Coincidentally, as the Boston Symphony Orchestra played in New York on Saturday afternoon, February 26, 1910, the Philharmonic prepared for an evening performance in Boston. While this date marked the debut of the New York Philharmonic in Boston, it also celebrated the twenty-fifth season that the Boston Symphony Orchestra performed in New York.[162] Even though no other major soloist or ensemble appeared in Boston during this weekend, a full operatic schedule competed with the Philharmonic's concert and forced music lovers to select only one event on Saturday evening. The busy weekend opened on Friday evening, February 25, 1910, with the French opera *Lakmé* by Delibes, continued on Saturday afternoon, February 26, 1910, with Boito's *Mefistofele*, and in the evening the Boston Opera Company presented Donizetti's *Lucia di Lammermoor*.[163] The weekend concluded with Puccini's *Madame Butterfly* on Sunday evening, February 27, 1910.[164]

Local promoters capitalized on the public's curiosity surrounding Mahler and his fame to increase attendance. The *Evening Transcript* emphasized that since Weingartner's visit four years ago, "no conductor of like distinction has come in such circumstances to Boston, and none that has come meanwhile has brought with him so interesting and able an orchestra as the new Philharmonic."[165] Articles in the *Sunday Herald* indicated the Philharmonic would offer an attractive program displaying "the ability of the leader and orchestra to full advantage."[166] As the article continued the writer predicted "curiosity alone should fill Symphony Hall to overflowing."[167]

As the concert date approached, more articles described the Philharmonic's transformation. Philip Hale of the *Sunday Herald* remarked that in the past the orchestra included excellent, mediocre, and even poor players, and, at times, the concerts ranged from brilliant to commonplace. Now, however, the new Philharmonic Society had become an "alert and puissant" orchestra whose playing demonstrated "power, expression, a vivid sense of contrast, a pervading warmth of tone, and a rare rhythmic accent."[168] With Mahler as conductor of the reorganized orchestra, "all things it does, it does largely, robustly, with force and with fire."[169]

Furthermore, promoters encouraged the public to demonstrate Boston's appreciation and admiration for the orchestra as a cultural asset. For a number of years, many New Yorkers attended Boston Symphony Orchestra concerts held in New York City and Brooklyn; now concertgoers in Boston were persuaded to reciprocate. In an article dated less than a week before the concert, the *Boston Daily Advertiser* pleaded: "It is hoped that Boston will welcome heartily the Philharmonic Society of New York next Saturday night, as New York has for many years welcomed the Boston Symphony Orchestra."[170] The *Evening Transcript* reinforced the sentiment as it printed, "We Bostonians almost owe it to our own orchestra to make Mr. Mahler and his men heartily welcome."[171] A third newspaper, the *Sunday Herald*, emphasized the same viewpoint as it appealed to readers, "Let not Boston be outdone by New York in hospitality."[172]

Reviews of the Boston Concert

While Bostonians managed to turn out in strong numbers for Boston Symphony concerts, visiting orchestras rarely drew large crowds in this city. Attracting audiences proved to be the greatest task for any manager since the public had "no curiosity over the conductors and orchestras of the big world outside."[173] In previous years, for example, when the New York Symphony Orchestra performed in Boston under the renowned Weingartner, they played to only a few hundred listeners.[174] At the turn of the twentieth century other groups such as the Pittsburgh Orchestra made a number of unrewarding ventures to Boston, and even the well-established Chicago Orchestra became wary of touring the Boston area.[175] Even a few days prior to the Philharmonic's debut, Fritz Kreisler gave a final concert to a warm and delighted but "relatively small" audience.[176] In spite of his position as one of the leading violinists in the world, Kreisler also encountered difficulty filling the seats in Jordan Hall.

News of the concert soon reached local and international media. The *Musical Courier* documented how Mahler and the Philharmonic "descended on the city," and in a style similar to Caesar "they came, they saw and they conquered."[177] Reviews of the concert also filled the pages of Boston newspapers. As in Providence, the citizens of Boston only filled a portion of the hall. In Boston, however, the competing event of the night, and even the entire musical season, appeared to be the opera. These same conditions prevailed in Boston and soon jeopardized other entertainment, as the *Evening Transcript* reported:

> The opera house has been filled; Symphony Hall has been filled with Symphony Concerts, but the season through, the public has been persistently indifferent to all else musical. The existence and the novelty of the opera is of course, the explanation of the mourning managers and the chagrined artists. It has taken too much of the money, the leisure, the interest and the musical ambition of the community to leave it with an eager mind to concerts.[178]

The Philharmonic concert also experienced a smaller crowd than anticipated, as the *Daily Advertiser* wrote: "The audience, although fairly large was by no means as vast as the occasion warranted."[179] Yet those present eagerly and intently absorbed the music as they "applauded spontaneously, heartily, and long at every opportunity."[180] Other critics expressed their disappointment in Bostonians as incapable of recognizing and supporting a notable musical event, as Louis C. Elson voiced in the *Daily Advertiser*: "There were a great many Boston music lovers who woke up on Sunday morning and found they had missed one of the greatest musical events of the season."[181] Philip

Hale of the *Sunday Herald* reflected a similar opinion as he commented, "The size of the audience did not reflect credit on the boast of Boston that she is a musical city."[182]

Three works on the program Mahler recently conducted on the tour in other cities. The evening again opened with the Berlioz *Symphonie Fantastique*, followed by Mahler playing harpsichord and conducting his arranged Bach Suite. Unique to the Boston concert, Mahler placed the Overture No. 3 to *Leonore*, op. 72, by Beethoven as the third selection. The event concluded with a crowd-pleasing rendition of the Strauss *Till Eulenspiegels lustige Streiche*.

Berlioz

While critics disagreed about Mahler's interpretation of some musical selections they unanimously approved his reading of the *Symphonie Fantastique*. After the audience greeted Mahler with thunderous applause, he sought to win their admiration, and by the end of the second movement, he "reawoke his listeners to their powers of appreciating symphonic pictures."[183] Critics raved over the Philharmonic's ability to faithfully reproduce the Berlioz work and to transport the audience into the realm of the supernatural. As the *Christian Science Monitor* reported, "Realism was kept in restraint in the thunderstorm at the close of the adagio and was allowed to assert itself only twice in the march of the allegretto."[184] Hale of the *Sunday Herald* also agreed that Mahler produced a valid rendering of the Berlioz work and preserved the composer's wish by keeping the image of distance present throughout the music.[185]

To create a successful interpretation of the composition, the critic of the *Evening Transcript* thought the conductor and musicians must "believe" in the music and "must play as though not only they saw and felt but as though they knew and believed."[186] With this, Mahler and the Philharmonic made the audience also believe and produced "the best interpretation that we have ever heard."[187] The *Daily Advertiser* recorded the crowd's enthusiasm over the work, documenting that "the audience went wild with delight and recall after recall ensued, both orchestra and conductor acknowledging the ovation."[188] The critic of the *Boston Globe* echoed similar approval, saying that Mahler infused the symphony with "an absorbing subtlety, and enkindling glow, a breadth and sweep of passion, which made them luminous with the poetry and terror of the work."[189] Even though the *Christian Science Monitor* printed a more conservative analysis of the crowd's response, it concluded that "there has not been such a picturesque reading of a piece of program music since Dr. Muck was in Boston."[190]

Bach

Conflicting accounts appeared regarding Mahler's interpretation and arrangement of the Bach Suite. Elson of the *Daily Advertiser* hesitated to proclaim Mahler a genius and remarked, "We did not see any especial advantage in Mahler's conducting at the piano except to give an object-lesson in the eighteenth century style of leadership. If any auditor thought that the result brought us nearer to the actual effect of Bach's performances he was mistaken."[191] Elson predicted his readers would not conclude that Mahler or the Philharmonic could surpass the Boston Symphony Orchestra's status as he wrote, "The Bach Suite was excellently done but not better than many performances that our orchestra has given."[192]

Reporters of the other major newspapers, however, formed more complimentary opinions, as the suite not only pleased the audience, but also sparked interest in the baroque period. Hale of the *Sunday Herald* believed Mahler succeeded in bringing to life the vitality of Bach and concluded, "The music that is sometimes merely dead as dry bones was last night living flesh radiant with beauty."[193] Hale was aware that some listeners or even perhaps critics, such as Elson, disapproved of Mahler's interpretation and the manner in which he used the harpsichord. Rather than dropping the matter, however, Hale addressed those opposing the arrangement and commented, "If they were asked what they would have [done] they would be at a loss for reply."[194] Mahler's skill as a conductor, arranger, and interpreter of Bach found favor in the column of the *Evening Transcript,* as the conductor created the "eloquence" of Bach "in the varying substance and color of the tonal mass, in the differing animations of diverse rhythms, in the contrasts and combinations of adroitly and modulated instrumental voice."[195] Another endorsement appeared in the *Christian Science Monitor,* which noted that every movement in the suite displayed "vigor and freshness."[196]

Although Elson voiced some negative comments about Mahler's interpretation, he spoke highly of two musicians. He first noted the fine playing of organist Arthur S. Hyde, who served as the organist of St. Bartholomew Church in New York. Bostonians remembered him best, however, as the previous organist from Emmanuel Church in Boston.[197] Unlike New Haven, where a local organist joined the Philharmonic for the Bach selection, Hyde traveled from New York for the concert. Elson also admired the upper register "splendid trumpet playing" of Mr. Carl Rodenkirchen.[198]

Rather than depend only on New York to depict Mahler's conducting technique, these Boston reviews offered insight on the conductor's position during the Bach selection. Instead of partially or completely facing the audience, Mahler looked upon the orchestra "with his back to the audience."[199] Readers might have assumed Mahler used a baton during this work, but a reporter from the *Boston Globe* confirmed the opposite as he documented "the precision of the playing last night without the accustomed baton," as the leader guided his men "by nod of head or movement of arm."[200]

Beethoven

The third piece on the program, the Overture No. 3 to *Leonore* by Beethoven, offered familiar music to Bostonians. Few critics documented whether the performance surpassed those the Boston Symphony Orchestra gave, but Elson attempted to draw a comparison. He offered a seemingly pessimistic view as he wrote, "The overture has had great performances in this city and here we feel that our recent conductors have given readings equally great and our own orchestra has achieved even more striking results."[201] Although the *Christian Science Monitor* resisted evaluating the Philharmonic's interpretation on the basis of the local orchestra, the writer believed the work did not make a lasting impression.[202]

Listeners were well aware of Mahler's reputation for reworking and arranging works as numerous articles reported Mahler's interpretation of Beethoven's works. Yet Mahler appeared to preserve and uphold Beethoven's specifications in this performance. The *Evening Transcript* remarked that even the "severest purist might not reproach Mr. Mahler with any 'liberties' with the *Leonore* overture. He did not once try to manipulate or in the smallest respect to re-fashion it."[203] The same article continued to explain "the music 'ran' as it ran from Beethoven's hand" and with the "power with which Beethoven propelled it."[204] Mahler accomplished this feat not with some calculated interpretation, but through passionate surrender to the music.[205]

Strauss

Mahler conducted *Till Eulenspiegels lustige Streiche* as the final selection on the program, leaving the audience with a memorable impression. Elson of the *Daily Advertiser* proclaimed that Boston possessed one of the best Strauss readers in the world, namely Max Fiedler, yet he admitted, "Somehow our orchestra has never displayed the virility that the New York orchestra displayed in this work."[206] The *Evening Transcript* commended Mahler on mastering every complicated strand of music.[207] In addition, Mahler depicted the adventures throughout the composition "of ironic humor, of huge improvisation, now amused, [and] now also cynical."[208] Hale's review in the *Sunday Herald* evoked a similar view that admired Mahler's "rare exhibition of clearness in exposition of the general structure" along with "rhetorical brilliance" and even an "ever pervasive sense of humor" throughout the performance.[209] The *Christian Science Monitor* believed that even though the performance reflected the Strauss spirit, the work did not create a lasting impression.[210] Before Mahler left the stage, he received a large laurel wreath from a local representative.[211]

Mahler as a Leader

Reporters remained loyal to the Boston Symphony Orchestra, but commended Mahler on the Philharmonic's progress. In the *Sunday Herald* Hale believed the ensemble was "probably artistically stronger than at any time in its history" and the changes in management and the discipline under Mahler were "brought to fruition during the concert."[212] The writer for the *Musical Courier* also cited several distinctions in Mahler's conducting and explained that these qualities

> lie primarily in his sane, wonderfully developed and highly poetic imagination, absolute musical knowledge, which makes for the highest authority, and a personality so extraordinarily vivid and full of concert energy as to make itself felt like an invisible thread to every man under his baton.[213]

Unlike the wild conducting caricatures of Mahler portrayed in newspapers and periodicals abroad, a more reserved commander appeared before the audience in Boston. He ruled with a decisive beat free from exaggeration or eccentricity.[214] Elson noticed that Mahler achieved the sound he desired from the orchestra with only a few mannerisms, and he displayed "a great fondness for staccato fortissimo effects up in the brass, and a desire for the sharpest contrast."[215] He further noted that Mahler "never dawdles his times" and "never indulges in sentimentality."[216] Hale also agreed that Mahler exemplified a great conductor in numerous ways: "in his choice of tempi; in his control of rhythm; in his indefinite wealth of dynamic graduations; in his sense of continuity; in his expression of detail without checking the melodic flow; in his obtaining powerful effects without sacrifice of tone."[217] Hale classified Mahler as a genius willing to convey and share his appreciation of the music with the audience.[218] On the whole, however, Mahler's reading was careful, but not meticulous, "overpowering in moments of wild fancy, charmingly poetic in its tenderness, and at all times superbly imaginative."[219] Recalling Mahler's days as a conductor of opera, the *Evening Transcript* depicted his conducting as follows:

> Though he stood as still, as he used to sit at the Metropolitan, and though his beat kept its old quiet clearness, he was prolific and animated of gesture; he summoned instruments and groups of instruments; and he sought by play of face and arm and hand not only to gain the pace, the rhythm and the emphasis that he desired, but also, and anxiously, to heighten the quality of the tone.[220]

The Orchestra

Beyond commenting on the music and Mahler's conducting technique, some critics also reported on the sound of specific musicians and various sections. The *Christian Science Monitor* critiqued the first violin tone as thin and a double bass tone that lacked limpidity. Mahler covered these sounds successfully "under a large volume of second violin and viola tone."[221]

Stunned by the sheer power of the contrabasses and bassoons, Elson wrote, "Cold type cannot impress upon the reader who was not there the portentous power of the pizzicato harmonies of the contrabasses, or the dreadful foreboding of the two bassoons, in the 'March to the Guillotine.'"[222] After hearing the end of this movement, Elson praised the orchestra's sound as "much more graphic and forceful than we have had it in some of the previous Boston performances."[223]

Elson described the "Dream of the Witches' Sabbath" from the *Symphonie Fantastique* as overwhelming when the piccolo and the E-flat clarinet "screamed out the love-theme with savage mockery."[224] Elson also remarked that the "piccolo fully earned his salary in this work." Compared to the local brass musicians Elson concluded, "The brasses seemed superior in quality to those out of our own orchestra."[225] At the end of the Berlioz selection even the cymbal player made his part important and gave the last note "in a manner that meant something."[226] During the Strauss composition Elson also admired the first horn Xaver Reiter "who perfectly played the extremely difficult sections."[227]

In the end, the Bostonians still believed the Boston Symphony Orchestra ranked superior. The critics, however, recognized the vast improvements of the Philharmonic and the ground gained with Mahler at the helm. Although Elson voiced negative comments regarding some portions of the performance and believed the Philharmonic might not offer the same finesse as the

Boston Symphony Orchestra, he acknowledged the orchestra "certainly achieved greater power and resonance."[228] Nevertheless, Elson paid homage to Mahler as a genius among conductors, and even though the details of technique were not as perfect as the Boston Symphony Orchestra, the Philharmonic offered "many points which we can study to great advantage."[229] The review of the concert in the *Musical Courier* also commended Mahler for his efforts in raising the quality of the Philharmonic through his splendid discipline.[230] Unfortunately, this was not only his second visit, but also the last time Bostonians saw Mahler conduct in their city.

The following day, February 27, 1910, Mahler and the Philharmonic departed Boston and returned to New York City. Sunday provided the only day of rest before the Philharmonic resumed rehearsals in Carnegie Hall on Monday, February 28.[231] Following a rehearsal on Tuesday, March 1, 1910, the Philharmonic played its fifth "historical concert" on March 2, 1910, which included works by Liszt and Wagner.[232]

Several years later, in 1916, when the New York Philharmonic first performed Mahler's Eighth Symphony, the Society of Friends of Music compiled a booklet in appreciation of Mahler. Arthur Foote recalled Mahler's visit to Boston in 1910 and remembered that the performance proved Mahler to be one of the greatest conductors of all time. Foote remarked, "Could he have lived, his 'passion for perfection' in orchestra playing would have been a constant object-lesson to us; with our easygoing way of never caring to do the thing just the way it should be done, we need such teaching."[233]

Notes

1. "Musical Notes," *Providence Sunday Times*, 20 February 1910, sec. 3, 24.

2. The *N. W. Ayer and Son's Newspaper Annual and Directory of 1910* (Philadelphia: N. W. Ayer and Son, 1910) printed the daily/weekly circulation of each paper as follows on page 104: *Yale Daily News*, 1,500; *New Haven Evening Register*, 17,007, Sunday edition 13,116; *New Haven Union*, 16,240, Sunday edition 9,599; *New Haven Times Leader*, 6,300, Sunday edition 7,200; *New Haven Palladium*, 5,500; *New Haven Morning Journal-Courier*, 7,439.

3. "First Concert by Philharmonic," *New Haven Morning Journal-Courier*, 21 February 1910, 10.

4. "Philharmonic Society," *New Haven Morning Journal-Courier*, 4 February 1910, 8.

5. Letter from Felix F. Leifels of Carnegie Hall, New York to Professor Horatio Parker, Yale University, New Haven, Connecticut, March 11, 1909. Horatio Parker Papers, School of Music Papers, MSS 3, Box 1, 1909 Folder, Series I, Yale University Library (hereafter cited as Parker TS).

6. Luther Noss, *The History of the Yale School of Music: A Condensed Chronological Summary, 1848–1970*, [photocopy] Yale University Library, Music Library, 1980. At the beginning of the 1914–1915 academic year, with a major reorganization of the University, the "Department of Music" was officially designated the "School of Music." Prior to this time some documents had referred to the department as the Yale School of Music.

7. Parker joined Yale as a professor of music theory in 1894. For more information on the music faculty during this time see Luther Noss's *Yale University: Faculty Appointment in Music*, 1890-1970, TS [photocopy] Yale University Library, Music Library, 1978, revised 1981.

8. Leifels to Parker, March 11, 1909.

9. Leifels to Parker, May 5, 1909, Parker TS, MSS 3, Box 1, 1909, Folder Series I.

10. "Philharmonic Society of New York to Give Concert at Woolsey Hall," *Yale Daily News*, 16 February 1910, 5.

11. "Mahler Will Get First Impression of His Tour," *New Haven Evening Register*, 21 February 1910, 7.

12. "Great Organ Used in the Bach Suite," *New Haven Evening Register*, 22 February 1910, 2.

13. "Great Concert on February 23," *New Haven Morning Journal-Courier*, 9 February 1910, 2.

14. Olga Samaroff Stokowski, *An American Musician's Story* (New York: W.W. Norton and Company, 1939), 159.

15. "Philharmonic Society," 8. Subsequent articles continued to refer to Samaroff as a Russian pianist including "Notable Concert Tonight," *New Haven Morning Journal-Courier*, 23 February 1910, 12.

16. John G. Doyle, "Samaroff, Olga," *The New Grove Dictionary of Music and Musicians*, ed. Stanley Sadie (London: Macmillan, 1980), 16:447. Stokowski (1882–1977) conducted the Philadelphia Orchestra from 1912 to 1938. The Juilliard School was founded in 1905 and was known as the Institute of Musical Art until 1923.

17. "Great Organ Used in the Bach Suite," 2.

18. "Bach Klavier," *New Haven Morning Journal-Courier*, 14 February 1910, 14. This article reprinted remarks from a New York critic. The comments were made following the Philharmonic concert on November 10, 1909.

19. "Bach Klavier," 14.

20. "A Very Notable Musical Event," *New Haven Morning Journal-Courier*, 19 February 1910, 6.

21. "First Concert by Philharmonic," *New Haven Morning Journal-Courier*, 21 February 1910, 10.

22. "A Very Notable Musical Event," 6.

23. "Great Concert on February 23," *New Haven Morning Journal-Courier*, 9 February 1910, 2.

24. "Philharmonic Seat Sale to Open Saturday," *New Haven Morning Journal-Courier*, 17 February 1910, 10.

25. "A Very Notable Musical Event," 6.

26. "Philharmonic Society of New York to Give Concert at Woolsey Hall," *Yale Daily News*, 16 February 1910, 5.

27. "Philharmonic Seat Sale to Open Saturday," 10.

28. "A Very Notable Musical Event," 6.

29. "Philharmonics and Mahler Here Tonight," *New Haven Evening Register*, 23 February 1910, 5. Rather than designating the orchestra as the New York Philharmonic, this article referred to the ensemble as the "Philharmonics."

30. The concert took place at Chickering Hall, Boston, on Tuesday, February 22, 1910, at 8:15 P.M.

31. "Society-Social-Personal," *New Haven Morning Journal-Courier*, 23 February 1910, 10.

32. "Society," *New Haven Evening Register*, 22 February 1910, 7.

33. Mason, "Philharmonic Society's Concert," *New Haven Palladium*, 24 February 1910, 5.

34. "Philharmonics and Mahler Here Tonight," 5.

35. "Superb Playing of Philharmonic," *New Haven Morning Journal-Courier*, 24 February 1910, 12.

36. "The Philharmonic Concert a Treat for Music Lovers," *New Haven Times Leader*, 24 February 1910, 4.

37. "Philharmonics and Mahler Here Tonight," 5.

38. Mason, 5.

39. "The Philharmonic Concert a Treat for Music Lovers," 4.

40. "Philharmonics and Mahler Here Tonight," 5.

41. "Superb Playing of Philharmonic," 12.

42. "The Philharmonic Concert a Treat for Music Lovers," 4.

43. "The Philharmonic Concert a Treat for Music Lovers," 4.

44. Mason, 5.

45. "Superb Playing of Philharmonic," 12.

46. "Superb Playing of Philharmonic," 12.

47. "Philharmonics and Mahler Here Tonight," 5.

48. "Superb Playing of Philharmonic," 12. This portion of the article also reported in "The Philharmonic Concert a Treat for Music Lovers," *New Haven Times Leader*, 24 February 1910, 4.

49. "Superb Playing of Philharmonic," 12.

50. "Philharmonics and Mahler Here Tonight," 5.

51. "Superb Playing of Philharmonic," 12.

52. "The Philharmonic Concert a Treat for Music Lovers," 4.

53. Mason, 5.

54. Mason, 5.

55. Mason, 5.

56. "The Philharmonic Concert a Treat for Music Lovers," 4.

57. "The Philharmonic Concert a Treat for Music Lovers," 4.

58. "The Philharmonic Concert a Treat for Music Lovers," 4.

59. Mason, 5.

60. "The Philharmonic Concert a Treat for Music Lovers," 4.

61. "The Philharmonic Concert a Treat for Music Lovers," 4.

62. Samaroff Stokowski, 161.

63. Samaroff Stokowski, 161.

64. "Concerts of the Week," *New York Times*, 27 February 1910, Metropolitan Sec., 15.

65. "Music and Drama: A Wagner-Liszt Philharmonic," *New York Post*, 3 March 1910, 9.

66. Samaroff Stokowski, 162.

67. Prior to March 1910, the Boston Symphony Orchestra offered a concert on November 12, 1909, which featured Max Fiedler as conductor and Olga Samaroff as the soloist. Samaroff performed the Piano Concerto No. 4 in D Minor by Anton Rubinstein.

68. "A Notable Concert," *Springfield Daily Republican*, 24 February 1910, 3.

69. The *N. W. Ayer and Son's Newspaper Annual and Directory of 1910* (Philadelphia: N. W. Ayer and Son, 1910) printed the daily/weekly circulation of each paper as follows on page 382: *Springfield Daily Republican*, 16,102; *Springfield Union*, 25,000; *Springfield Daily News*, 10,243; *Springfield Weekly Republican*, 17,415; and the *Springfield Homestead* (Monday, Wednesday, and Saturday), 5,000.

70. *Springfield Daily News*, 17 February 1910, 2.

71. "The Philharmonic Concert," *Springfield Daily Republican*, 20 February 1910, 9.

72. "Of Music and Musicians," *Springfield Weekly Republican*, 17 February 1910, 6.

73. "Of Music and Musicians," 6.

74. "Plays, Players and Coming Attractions: Great Musical Event," *Springfield Daily News*, 10 February 1910, 10.

75. "New York Philharmonic," *Springfield Daily Republican*, 7 February 1910, 11. Seats were priced as follows: Box seats $2.50, $2.00 and $1.00; orchestra chairs and three rows orchestra circle, $2.00; orchestra circle, seven rows, and three rows balcony $1.50; balcony, nine rows, $1.00; family circles, $.75

76. Philip Lieson Miller, "Rider-Kelsey, Corinne," *The New Grove Dictionary of American Music*, eds. H. Wiley Hitchcock and Stanley Sadie (New York: Macmillan, 1986) 4:42. Miller referred to Rider-Kelsey as a lyric soprano with a rich and well-rounded voice.

77. "Music and Drama: Busoni and the Philharmonic," *New York Post*, 7 January 1910, 9; quoted in "Philharmonic Concert," *Springfield Daily Republican*, 19 February 1910, 14.

78. "A Notable Concert," 3.

79. "The Philharmonic Concert," *Springfield Daily Republican*, 18 February 1910, 3.

80. "A Notable Concert," 3.

81. "Plays, Players, and Coming Attractions: New York Philharmonic," *Springfield Daily News*, 17 February 1910, 10.

82. "Of Music and Musicians: The Philharmonic Concert," *Springfield Weekly Republican*, 3 March 1910, 6.

83. "A Remarkable Concert," *Springfield Homestead*, 26 February 1910, 14.

84. "The Theaters: A Superb Orchestra," *Springfield Union*, 25 February 1910, 9.

85. "A Remarkable Concert," 14.

86. "A Remarkable Concert," 14.

87. "A Remarkable Concert," 14.

88. "Of Music and Musicians: The Philharmonic Concert," 6.

89. "A Remarkable Concert," 14.

90. "A Remarkable Concert," 14.

91. "The Philharmonic Concert," *Springfield Daily Republican*, 25 February 1910, 3.

92. "Gustav Mahler and Philharmonic Society," *Springfield Daily News*, 25 February 1910, 4.

93. "Gustav Mahler and Philharmonic Society," 4.

94. "Of Music and Musicians: The Philharmonic Concert," 6.

95. "Of Music and Musicians: The Philharmonic Concert," 6.

96. "Of Music and Musicians: The Philharmonic Concert," 6.

97. Nicolas Slonimsky, *Baker's Biographical Dictionary of Musicians*, 5th ed. (New York: Schirmer, 1958), 1,340.

98. In 1926, she married violinist Lynell Reed. She died on July 10, 1947, in Toledo, Ohio.

99. "In the Realms of Music: Symphony Trip," *Christian Science Monitor*, 17 February 1910, 6.

100. "The Theaters: A Superb Orchestra," 9.

101. "A Remarkable Concert," 14.

102. "Gustav Mahler and Philharmonic Society," 4.

103. "Of Music and Musicians: The Philharmonic Concert," 6.

104. "The Theaters: A Superb Orchestra," 9.

105. "A Remarkable Concert," 14.

106. "Gustav Mahler and Philharmonic Society," 4.

107. "The Philharmonic Concert," *Springfield Daily Republican*, 25 February 1910, 3.

108. "A Remarkable Concert," 14.

109. "Gustav Mahler and Philharmonic Society," 4.

110. "Gustav Mahler and Philharmonic Society," 4.

111. "The Philharmonic Concert," *Springfield Daily Republican*, 25 February 1910, 3.

112. Alma Mahler, "Ein Leben mit Gustav Mahler," TS, 908, The Charles Patterson Van Pelt Library, University of Pennsylvania, Philadelphia; quoted in Zoltan Roman, *Gustav Mahler's American Years 1907-1911: A Documentary History* (Stuyvesant, NY: Pendragon Press, 1989), 347.

113. Roman, 347.

114. Albert Steinert, Providence, to Felix Leifels, New York, 19 February 1910, TS, Papers of Felix Leifels, Archives of the New York Philharmonic.

115. Patrick T. Conley and Paul R. Campbell, *Providence: A Pictorial History* (Norfolk, VA: Donning, 1982), 144.

116. "Famed Personages of the World Once Seen in Infantry Hall," *Providence Journal*, 5 October 1942, 5.

117. The *N. W. Ayer and Son's Newspaper Annual and Directory of 1910* printed the daily/weekly circulation of each paper as follows on page 810: *Providence Evening Tribune*, 25,803; *Providence Sunday Tribune*, 16,487; *Providence Journal*, 21,683; *Providence Sunday Journal*, 27,825; and the *Providence Evening Bulletin*, 45,677.

118. Born in 1875, Fritz Kreisler attended the Vienna Conservatory and made several tours to the United States. In 1943, he became an American citizen and died in New York in 1962. For additional information see Boris Schwarz, "Kreisler, Fritz," *The New Grove Dictionary of Music and Musicians*, ed. Stanley Sadie, 2d ed. (London: Macmillan, 2001), 13:889–891.

119. "In Local Society," *Providence Evening News*, February 26, 1910, 8.

120. "Symphony Concert," *Providence Evening Tribune*, February 16, 1910, 5.

121. *Providence Evening Tribune*, 13 February 1910, sec. 2, 10.

122. *Providence Evening Tribune*, 13 February 1910, sec. 2, 10.

123. "Philharmonic Tomorrow," *The Providence Evening Tribune*, 24 February 1910, 12.

124. "Musical Notes," *Providence Sunday Tribune*, 20 February 1910, sec. 3, 24.

125. "Amusements, Excursions, Etc.," *Providence Evening Bulletin*, 25 February 1910, 5.

126. "Musical Notes: Philharmonic Orchestra Concert in Infantry Hall Next Friday," *Providence Sunday Journal*, 20 February 1910, sec. 3, 8.

127. The M. Steinert and Sons Company stood at 327 Westminster Street, Providence, Rhode Island.

128. *The Providence Sunday Journal*, 6 February 1910, sec. 3, 11. Tickets for the Russian Symphony Orchestra concert were available for $2.50, $2.00, $1.50, and $1.00.

129. "Amusements," *Providence Sunday Journal*, 13 February 1910, sec. 3, 9.

130. "Famed Personages of World Once Seen in Infantry Hall," *Providence Journal*, 5 October 1942, 5. On October 4, 1942, the Hall burned, and in its place the city erected an eight-level parking garage.

131. "Philharmonic Tomorrow," 12.

132. "Philharmonic Lecture," *Providence Evening Tribune*, 17 February 1910, 5.

133. "Philharmonic Lecture," 5.

134. "Philharmonic Tomorrow," 12.

135. "An Enjoyable Concert," *Providence Evening Tribune*, 26 February 1910, 12.

136. W.A.P., "N. Y. Philharmonic Players Give Fine Performance Here," *Providence Evening Bulletin*, 26 February 1910, sec. 2, 8.

137. "An Enjoyable Concert," 12.

138. "An Enjoyable Concert," 12.

139. "An Enjoyable Concert," 12.

140. W.A.P., "N. Y. Philharmonic Players Give Fine Performance Here," sec. 2, 8.

141. W.A.P., "N. Y. Philharmonic Players Give Fine Performance Here," sec. 2, 8.

142. "An Enjoyable Concert," 12.

143. "An Enjoyable Concert," 12.

144. W.A.P., "N. Y. Philharmonic Players Give Fine Performance Here," sec. 2, 8.

145. "Events in Local Society: Philharmonic Concert," *Providence Evening Tribune*, 26 February 1910, 4. These names included: Mrs. William B. Weeden, Mrs. Nathaniel W. Smith, Miss Mary Anthony, Miss Ellen Anthony, Miss Lorania Beckwith, Mrs. William Harkness Arnold, Mr. George A. Freeman, Mr. and Mrs. Dexter B. Potter, Mrs. Anne Gilbreth Cross, Miss Dorothy Seymour, Miss Olive Stafford, Miss Harriet E. Barrows, Mrs. Frank N. Sheldon, Miss Bertha Sheldon, Mr. and Mrs. Hans Schneider, Mrs. John R. Hess, Miss Clara Hess, Miss Caroline Keely, Dr. J. T. Lynch, Mr. and Mrs. Edward B. Lederer, Mrs. Charles B. Frye, Mr. William Frye.

146. "Music in Providence," *Musical Courier* 60, no. 11 (16 March 1910): 41.

147. "Music in Providence," 41.

148. "Music in Providence," 41.

149. "Events in Local Society," *Providence Evening Tribune*, 26 February 1910, 8.

150. "An Enjoyable Concert," 12.

151. "An Enjoyable Concert," 12.

152. W.A.P., "N. Y. Philharmonic Players Give Fine Performance Here," sec. 2, 8.

153. Henry Taylor Parker, "A Dull 'Don Giovanni,'" *Boston Evening Transcript*, 10 April 1908, 13.

154. Philip Hale, "Great Interest in Boston's Opera: News and Gossip of the Musical World," *Boston Sunday Herald*, 13 February 1910, sec. 3, 8.

155. "Mr. Fiedler Continues," *Boston Evening Transcript*, 5 February 1910, sec. 2, 6. The article also noted that Dr. Karl Muck, Felix Weingartner, Richard Strauss, and Ernst von Schuch were discussed as replacements.

156. The first performance took place on February 2 and 3, 1906. On February 23 and 24, the orchestra performed the work again before leaving on tour to New York and Philadelphia.

157. *Boston Evening Transcript*, n.d.; quoted in Henry-Louis de La Grange, *Gustav Mahler*, vol. 3, *Vienna: Triumph and Disillusion (1904–1907)* (Oxford: Oxford University Press, 1999), 313 n116. While no date is indicated for the original article, it most likely appeared in the newspaper on the morning following the concert, February 3, 1906.

158. The *N. W. Ayer and Son's Newspaper Annual and Directory of 1910* printed the daily/weekly circulation of each paper as follows on pages 362–367: *Boston Daily Advertiser*, 22,500; *Boston Evening Transcript*, (daily) 30,083, (Saturday edition) 42,500; *Boston Evening Record*, 85,000; *Boston Globe*, 178,334; *Boston Sunday Globe*, 321,671; *Boston Herald*, 75,000; *Boston Sunday Herald*, 90,000; *Boston Journal*,

100,000; *Boston Post*, 238,126, (Sunday edition) 215,947; and the *Christian Science Monitor* (circ. not available).

159. Mudgett introduced Sunday concerts in the concert hall. Mudgett managed the hall from its opening until 1922. For more information see H. Earle Johnson, *Symphony Hall, Boston* (Boston: Little, Brown and Company, 1950).

160. Tickets were available at $1.00, $1.50, and $2.00.

161. "In the Realms of Music: Symphony Trip," *Christian Science Monitor*, 17 February 1910, 6. The Boston Symphony played in Washington, D.C., at the New National Theater on Monday afternoon, February 21, 1910; in Baltimore, Maryland, at the Lyric Theater on Tuesday evening, February 22; in Philadelphia, Pennsylvania, at the Academy of Music on Wednesday evening, February 23; in New York City at Carnegie Hall on Thursday evening, February 24, and on Saturday afternoon, February 26; in Brooklyn, New York, at the Academy of Music on Friday evening, February 25; and in Hartford, Connecticut, at the Parsons' Theater on Monday evening, February 28, 1910.

162. "A Historic Orchestra," *New York Sun*, 25 September 1910, n.p., from "Press Clippings Collection," Pres 56, Archives of the Boston Symphony Orchestra.

163. *Lakmé* began at 7:45 p.m. on February 25, 1910. *Mefistofele* started at 1:30 p.m. on February 26, 1910, and *Lucia di Lammermoor* opened at 8 p.m. on February 26, 1910.

164. "In the Realms of Music: The Opera," *Christian Science Monitor*, 28 February 1910, 6. *Madame Butterfly* began at 8 p.m.

165. Henry Taylor Parker, "Music and Musicians: Mr. Mahler to Conduct Again in Boston," *Boston Evening Transcript*, 13 January 1910, 13.

166. Philip Hale, "Great Interest in Boston's Opera: News and Gossip of the Music World," *Boston Sunday Herald*, 13 February 1910, sec. 3, 8.

167. Hale, "Great Interest in Boston's Opera," sec. 3, 8.

168. Hale, "Great Interest in Boston's Opera," sec. 3, 8.

169. Hale, "Great Interest in Boston's Opera," sec. 3, 8.

170. "New York Philharmonic," *Boston Daily Advertiser*, 19 February 1910, 5.

171. Parker, "Music and Musicians: Mr. Mahler to Conduct Again in Boston," 13.

172. Hale, "Great Interest in Boston's Opera," sec. 3, 8.

173. "Music and Drama: Mr. Mahler as a Concert Conductor," *Boston Evening Transcript*, 28 February 1910, 18.

174. "Music and Drama: Mr. Mahler as a Concert Conductor," 18.

175. "Music and Drama: Mr. Mahler as a Concert Conductor," 18.

176. Henry Taylor Parker, "Music and Musicians: A Winter of Concerts without Audiences," *Boston Evening Transcript*, 25 February 1910, 14.

177. "Boston and New England," *Musical Courier*, 60, no. 9 (2 March 1910): 44.

178. Parker, "Music and Musicians," 14.

179. Louis C. Elson, "Symphony Concert was a Great One," *Boston Daily Advertiser*, 28 February 1910, 5.

180. "Music and Drama: Mr. Mahler as a Concert Conductor," 18.

181. Elson, "Symphony Concert was a Great One," 5.

182. Philip Hale, "Boston Premiere of Philharmonic," *Boston Sunday Herald*, 27 February 1910, 4.

183. "In the Realms of Music: Philharmonic Concert," *Christian Science Monitor*, 28 February 1910, 6.

184. "In the Realms of Music," 6.

185. Hale, "Boston Premiere of Philharmonic," 4.

186. "Music and Drama: Mr. Mahler as a Concert Conductor," 18.

187. "Music and Drama: Mr. Mahler as a Concert Conductor," 18.

188. Elson, "Symphony Concert was a Great One," 5.

189. "Magnetic Maestro," *Boston Globe*, 27 February 1910, 15.

190. "In the Realms of Music: Philharmonic Concert," 6. Dr. Carl Muck was director of the Boston Symphony Orchestra from 1906 to 1908 and from 1912 to 1917. In March 1918, he was arrested as an enemy alien and interned for the duration of the war.

191. Elson, "Symphony Concert was a Great One," 5.

192. Elson, "Symphony Concert was a Great One," 5.

193. Hale, "Boston Premiere of Philharmonic," 4.

194. Hale, "Boston Premiere of Philharmonic," 4.

195. "Music and Drama: Mr. Mahler as a Concert Conductor," 18.

196. "In the Realms of Music," 6.

197. "Notes and Comments Upon Musical Matters: New York Philharmonic," *Boston Sunday Post*, 20 February 1910, 37.

198. Elson, "Symphony Concert was a Great One," 5.

199. "Magnetic Maestro," 15.

200. "Magnetic Maestro," 15.

201. Elson, "Symphony Concert was a Great One," 5.

202. "In the Realms of Music: Philharmonic Concert," 6.

203. "Music and Drama: Mr. Mahler as a Concert Conductor," 18.

204. "Music and Drama: Mr. Mahler as a Concert Conductor," 18.

205. "Music and Drama: Mr. Mahler as a Concert Conductor," 18.

206. Elson, "Symphony Concert was a Great One," 5.

207. "Music and Drama: Mr. Mahler as a Concert Conductor," 18.

208. "Music and Drama: Mr. Mahler as a Concert Conductor," 18.

209. Hale, "Boston Premiere of Philharmonic," 4.

210. "In the Realms of Music: Philharmonic Concert," 6.

211. "Magnetic Maestro," 15.

212. Hale, "Boston Premiere of Philharmonic," 4.

213. "Boston and New England," *Musical Courier* 60, no. 9 (2 March 1910): 44.

214. Elson, "Symphony Concert was a Great One," 5.

215. Elson, "Symphony Concert was a Great One," 5.

216. Elson, "Symphony Concert was a Great One," 5.

217. Hale, "Boston Premiere of Philharmonic," 4.

218. Hale, "Boston Premiere of Philharmonic," 4.

219. Hale, "Boston Premiere of Philharmonic," 4.

220. "Music and Drama: Mr. Mahler as a Concert Conductor," 18.

221. "In the Realms of Music," 6.

222. Elson, "Symphony Concert was a Great One," 5. The "March to the Guillotine" is the fourth of five movements in *Symphonie Fantastique*. Listed under basses were August Kalkhof, Frank Ruhlender, H. Reinshagen, F. W. Daehne, H. Kissenberth, C. Beyer, E. Wallach, and W. F. Weber. Listed under bassoons and bass bassoons were P. Pieschel, B. Kohon, A. Weiss, and M. Kohon.

223. Elson, "Symphony Concert was a Great One," 5.

224. Elson, "Symphony Concert was a Great One," 5. Listed under flutes and piccolo were N. Laucella, D. Maquarre, M. Korslofsky, and U. Gingras. Listed under clarinets and bass clarinets were A. Selmer, H. Levy, P. Perrier, and G. Nevraumont.

225. Elson, "Symphony Concert was a Great One," 5.

226. Elson, "Symphony Concert was a Great One," 5. Listed under tympanis and percussion were A. Friese, G. Braun, Jr., H. A.Yerks, Wm. Brown, and Wm. Lowe.

227. Elson, "Symphony Concert was a Great One," 5.

228. Elson, "Symphony Concert was a Great One," 5.

229. Elson, "Symphony Concert was a Great One," 5.

230. "Boston and New England," 44.

231. *Carnegie Hall: Collection of Ledgers and Cash Book Covering the Period 1891–1925*, vol. 6, 175, Fine Arts Division of the New York Public Library.

232. *New York Sun*, 3 March 1910, 9; quoted in Roman, 350. The Philharmonic offered a series of five educational concerts during the season and labeled them as "historical concerts."

233. *Gustav Mahler: The Composer, the Conductor and the Man* (New York: Society of Friends of Music, 1916), 12. The New York Philharmonic first performed Mahler's Eighth Symphony in New York City on April 9, 1916.

Gustav Mahler, 1911, director of the New York Philharmonic. Courtesy of The Kaplan Foundation Collection, New York

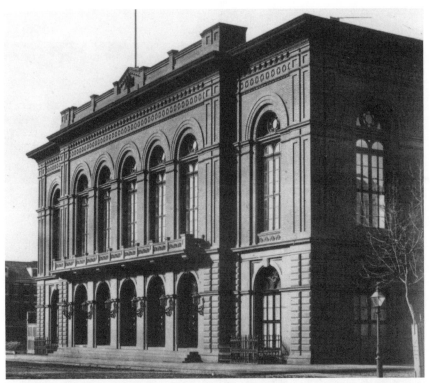

Academy of Music, Philadelphia. Site of January 17, 1910, March 14, 1910, and January 23, 1911, concerts. Photographer unknown. Courtesy of the Athenaeum of Philadelphia

Woolsey Hall, New Haven, circa. 1904. Site of February 23, 1910, concert. Photographer unknown. Published in Views of New Haven and Yale University *(New Haven: Howe and Stetson Company, 1905)*

New York Philharmonic Concert Program of February 23, 1910 (cover). Courtesy of the New York Philharmonic Archives

Programme

BERLIOZ. Symphony . . . . "Fantastic"

BACH. . . . . Suite for Orchestra

GRIEG. . . . . Concerto for Piano

STRAUSS. . . . . "Till Eulenspiegel"

SOLOIST
OLGA SAMAROFF
PIANO

PRINTED BY STYLES & CASH
NEW YORK.

*New York Philharmonic Concert Program of February 23, 1910 (inside). Courtesy of the
New York Philharmonic Archives*

Court Square Theater, Springfield. Site of February 24, 1910, and February 15, 1911, concerts. Photographer unknown. Courtesy of Connecticut Valley Historical Museum

Infantry Hall, Providence. Site of February 25, 1910, concert. Illustrated by H. S. Inman, 1886. Courtesy of Rhode Island Historical Society

Symphony Hall, Boston. Site of February 26, 1910, concert. From a vintage postcard owned by author, circa 1900, published by Hugh C. Leighton

Soldiers and Sailors Memorial Hall, Pittsburgh. Site of December 5, 1910, concert. From a vintage postcard owned by author, circa 1909, no publisher indicated

Grays Armory, Cleveland. Site of December 6, 1910, concert. From a vintage postcard owned by author, circa 1900, published by the Cleveland News

CONVENTION HALL, BUFFALO, N.Y.

10554

Convention Hall, Buffalo, circa 1918. Site of December 7, 1910, concert. From a vintage postcard owned by author, circa 1910, published by A. C. Bosselman

Convention Hall, Rochester. Site of December 8, 1910, concert. Photographer unknown. Courtesy of Rochester Democrat and Chronicle Archives, Rochester

New Wieting Opera House, circa 1897. Site of December 9, 1910, concert. Photographer unknown. Courtesy of Onondaga Historical Association, Syracuse

Majestic Theater, Utica, circa 1907. Site of December 10, 1910, concert. Photographer unknown. Published in 1907 Utica City Directory *(Utica: Utica Directory Publishing Company, 1907), 64*

New National Theatre, Washington, D.C. Site of January 24, 1911, concert. Photographer unknown. Published in Douglas Bennett Lee, Roger L. Meersman, and Donn B. Murphy, Stage for a Nation: The National Theatre, 150 Years (New York: University Press of America, 1985), 135

Parsons' Theater, Hartford. Site of February 16, 1911, concert. Photographer unknown. Courtesy of Connecticut Historical Society

The Philharmonic Society

of New York

1910... SIXTY-NINTH SEASON ...1911

Gustav Mahler ... Conductor

MANAGEMENT   LOUDON CHARLTON
LOCAL MANAGEMENT   WM. F. A. ENGEL

Parsons Theatre

THURSDAY EVENING, FEBRUARY 16

AT 8.15 O'CLOCK

Programme

1. **BACH-MAHLER**   -   -   -   Suite for Orchestra
   (MR. MAHLER AT THE HARPSICHORD)

2. **BEETHOVEN**   Symphony VI, Pastoral, F major, op. 68
   I. JOYFUL IMPRESSIONS ON ARRIVING IN THE COUNTRY
   Allegro ma non troppo

   II. SCENE BY THE BROOK
   Andante molto moto

   III. MERRY-MAKING OF THE COUNTRY FOLK
   Allegro

   IV. THUNDER-STORM, TEMPEST
   Allegro

   V. SHEPHERD'S SONG; GLADNESS AFTER THE STORM
   Allegretto

   INTERMISSION

3. **WEBER-WEINGARTNER**   -   Invitation to the Dance
4. **LISZT**   -   -   Symphonic Poem "Les Preludes"

The Steinway Piano is the Official Piano of the Philharmonic Society

New York Philharmonic Concert Program of February 16, 1911. Courtesy of the New York Philharmonic Archives

PARSONS' THEATER

HOME of HIGH CLASS PLAYS

TONIGHT at 8:15.

A GREAT MAN WITH A
GREAT BIG ORCHESTRA

Symphonic Event Of The Season.

FIRST ANNUAL APPEARANCE

PHILHARMONIC

SOCIETY OF NEW YORK.

World's Greatest Symphonic Conductor,
GUSTAV MAHLER.

100 Performers. Superb Novel Program.
Seats on Sale. $2.00, $1.50, $1.00, 75c.
Mr. Mahler will play the Harpsichord
in the Bach Suite.

Hartford advertisement, February 16, 1911. Courtesy of Hartford Courant

Gustav Mahler on board to New York from Bremen, 1910.
Courtesy of the Kaplan Foundation Collection, New York

CHAPTER FIVE

~

Great Lakes Tour of December 1910

After Mahler agreed to renew his contract as director for the 1910–1911 season, the Philharmonic quickly outlined an expanded schedule of concerts. Management planned a tour covering the Great Lakes area, a second tour in New England, and several concerts in Philadelphia and Washington, D.C. For December 1910, the Philharmonic organized an extensive tour reaching Pittsburgh,[1] Cleveland, Buffalo, Rochester, Syracuse, and Utica, New York. Very conveniently, Penn Station in New York City opened on November 27, 1910, which provided easy transportation for personnel and instruments from Manhattan.[2] Unlike the previous tour, however, the management hired no instrumental or vocal soloists to appear with the orchestra.

The Philharmonic visited six cities during December 1910, starting with Pittsburgh on Monday, December 5. The following day the orchestra traveled to Cleveland, Ohio, for a concert on Tuesday, December 6. By Wednesday, December 7, the orchestra reached Buffalo, New York, for an evening concert, and on Thursday, December 8, they performed in Rochester, New York. The next morning they traveled further east and arrived in Syracuse, New York, for a Friday evening performance on December 9. On Saturday, December 10, the Philharmonic played their final concert of the tour in Utica, New York.

For this tour Mahler programmed music featuring three major German composers: Bach, Beethoven, and Wagner. Each concert began with Mahler's arrangement of the Bach Suite and again, the Philharmonic transported a reconfigured Steinway piano. Mahler originally selected Beethoven's

Symphony No. 8 in F Major, op. 93, as the second selection on the program, but approximately one week before commencing the tour he substituted the Symphony No. 6 in F Major, op. 68, *Pastoral*.[3] After intermission, the second half of each program featured works by Richard Wagner starting with the Prelude and Liebestod from *Tristan und Isolde*, continuing with *Siegfried Idyll*, and concluding with the popular Prelude to *Die Meistersinger von Nürnberg*.

In addition, a number of the local managers were women. At the turn of the century, the role of a local impresario became a respectable profession for women and enabled them to be financially independent. Throughout this tour four prominent women coordinated the local concerts, including May Beegle of Pittsburgh, Adella Prentiss Hughes of Cleveland, Mai Davis Smith of Buffalo, and A. Kathleen King of Syracuse. Beegle, Hughes, and Smith also initiated concert series and were instrumental in creating a following for orchestral music, which were the precursors of establishing permanent orchestras.

The Pittsburgh Concert on Monday, December 5, 1910

Pittsburgh offered a convenient stop for traveling musicians and orchestras en route to the Midwest and South from New York. The haven of Andrew Carnegie's fortune, Pittsburgh prospered at the turn of the twentieth century as mills manufactured steel and iron to meet the growing demands of the American economy. As the city's population surged to roughly half a million in 1910,[4] Pittsburgh became known as home of the steelworker. From 1900 to 1913, the production of steel ingots and casting tripled from ten million to thirty-one million tons,[5] and the expansion of river and rail tonnage increased from 65,818,630 in 1900 to 167,733,268 in 1910.[6]

Unfortunately, the formation of musical institutions in Pittsburgh did not parallel its industrial growth. As the *Pittsburgh Bulletin Index* noted, "The hard-headed, stern-hearted Scotch Presbyterians and Germans that settled in Western Pennsylvania were a different breed than those who took root in New England or other Eastern cultural centers. It took them longer to come around to music."[7] After a number of conductors made unsuccessful attempts to sustain a reputable local orchestra, today's Pittsburgh Symphony Orchestra finally formed in 1926.

In 1895, a Pittsburgh Orchestra was created under the umbrella of the Pittsburgh Orchestra Association, and by 1910, the orchestra was classed third in artistic importance in the United States.[8] Unfortunately, the cost to maintain the orchestra far surpassed its revenue. Due to the lack of a strong foundation of guarantors and a successful endowment drive in early 1910, the orchestra dissolved at the end of the season, in May 1910. In the fall Carl Bernthaler managed to organize a new orchestra containing roughly sixty-five remaining musicians from the Pittsburgh Orchestra.[9] With assistance from the Pittsburgh Orchestra Association, this orchestra planned fifteen concerts for the 1910–1911 season.

Even though the association also coordinated concerts featuring visiting orchestras, its primary objectives were "to secure an endowment fund for the local orchestra and to keep musical interest alive with concerts by visiting orchestras."[10] Hence, the committee believed it never acted in violation of the organization's goals when it planned a concert series. On the contrary, the association believed if visiting orchestras impressed local concertgoers, then the public would be inspired to subsidize a local orchestra. Articles in local newspapers commended the association for limiting the number of visiting orchestras during the season and applauded their dedication in generating civic pride.[11] The writer of the *Pittsburg Press* believed the concert series would surpass in "importance and educational value any single orchestra offering ever before presented in Pittsburgh"[12] and help rehabilitate the Pittsburgh Orchestra on a more refined basis comparable to the prestigious traveling orchestras.

For the 1910–1911 season the Pittsburgh Orchestra Association outlined a group of four concerts featuring the New York Philharmonic Orchestra, the Boston Symphony Orchestra, and the Theodore Thomas Orchestra.[13] In June of 1910, arrangements were completed for Gustav Mahler and the Philharmonic Orchestra of New York to open the season at Soldiers and Sailors Memorial Hall in Pittsburgh on Monday, December 5, 1910.[14] For the first time in sixteen years the Boston Symphony Orchestra intended to visit Pittsburgh and offered a concert on January 20, 1911, with Anton Witek as violin soloist.[15] With eighty musicians the Theodore Thomas Orchestra from Chicago also planned to offer the final two concerts, featuring cellist Bruno Steindel on February 21, and violinist Hans Letz on March 27, 1911. The cost to produce the series in Pittsburgh amounted to roughly eleven thousand dollars.[16]

From New York, Loudon Charlton coordinated the Pittsburgh concerts for all the visiting orchestras, and locally the Pittsburgh Orchestra Association appointed May Beegle to represent Charlton at meetings and assist with local arrangements.[17] Beegle's experience with managing musical events started in 1907, when she first worked as secretary for the Pittsburgh Orchestra. She later handled all publicity for the organization. In the years to follow, Beegle was instrumental in developing the musical scene in Pittsburgh and gained recognition as "dean of Pittsburgh's impresarios."[18] Starting in 1913, she managed the Ellis concerts and from 1923 until her death in

1943, she organized her own concert series. Throughout her career Beegle also managed the Art Society Concerts (1927–1937) and coordinated the Summer Pop Concerts.[19]

In early October 1910, advertisements for the concerts began appearing in the *Pittsburgh Post, Pittsburg Dispatch, Pittsburg Press, Pittsburgh Gazette Times, Pittsburgh Sun, Pittsburgh Bulletin, Pittsburgh Index, Pittsburgh Chronicle-Telegraph, Pittsburgh Leader,* and the *Pittsburgh Volksblatt und Freiheits-Freund.*[20] For the four concerts that featured visiting ensembles the Pittsburgh Orchestra Association sold season subscriptions for $7.50, $5.50, $3.50, $2.50, and $1.75.[21] With seating capacity of 2,378 available at Soldiers and Sailors Memorial Hall, this pricing structure appealed to concertgoers. Single tickets were later available for the Philharmonic concert and ranged between $.50 and $2.00.[22]

Advertisements

Similar to the publicity that circulated in New England newspapers for the Philharmonic's tour in February 1910, Loudon Charlton distributed press releases detailing Mahler's career as a conductor and composer. The Philharmonic guaranteed to appear in Pittsburgh with at least eighty-five members.[23] Likewise, the other orchestras visiting Pittsburgh for the season also featured a larger number of musicians; the Boston Symphony Orchestra committed to eighty-five musicians on tour and the Theodore Thomas Orchestra promised eighty players for their concerts.

An article in the *Pittsburgh Gazette Times* anticipated that the performance would "create a sensation among music lovers of Pittsburgh, because nothing like it has ever been presented in this city."[24] The latter part of the program highlighted Wagner's music and required no introduction, as a writer for the *Pittsburg Press* commented "that it needs bu[t] the mere announcement to arouse interest and delight of all concertgoers."[25]

Early ticket sales signaled a successful start to the season. As the *Pittsburg Press* reported, "Teachers and students throughout the city, and parties from towns within a radius of one hundred miles of the city have taken blocks of seats."[26] By October 30, 1910, the Pittsburgh Orchestra Association expected a financially lucrative season, as ticket sales were reported overwhelmingly large "with the cheapest seats exhausted and the better seats rapidly being allotted."[27] The ticket demand continued, and less than a week before the event, the *Pittsburg Press* predicted that any remaining seats would be sold by opening night.[28] Ticket holders ranged from members of high society to music lovers of the working class. Yet, similar to patrons of the former Pittsburgh

Orchestra, these supporters included the "most important Pittsburgh families and the best of Pittsburgh music lovers."[29] To thank local citizens for their support, the Pittsburgh Orchestra Association supplied the names of season subscription holders to the local newspapers. Beyond coverage for the concerts in the music section of newspapers, the society section of several newspapers, such as the *Gazette Times*, printed the full name of each season subscriber, which filled more than three columns of a page.[30]

Articles assured wealthy concertgoers that improvements in the Soldiers and Sailors Memorial Hall would accommodate their every need. Maids would be in attendance in the ladies' cloak room on the main corridor, and attendants would also be provided in the gentlemen's check room. In addition, the management offered areas for sitting, and smoking rooms on the main corridor.[31] Management even enlarged the stage to accommodate the larger orchestra[32] and added additional draperies to improve the acoustics.[33]

Opened in October 1910, the Soldiers and Sailors Memorial Hall was founded by the Grand Army of the Republic and styled after the ancient mausoleum of Halicarnassus, one of the Seven Wonders of the Ancient World. After the Pittsburgh Orchestra's first concert of the season, however, critics and musicians complained about the poor acoustics in the hall. As a result, the local orchestra moved their remaining concerts to Carnegie Music Hall and even changed the day of the upcoming concert from Friday, December 2, 1910, to Thursday, December 1, 1910. As plans for the Symphony Series progressed, the financial condition of the local orchestra moved from fair to dismal. Even though a patron could pay fifty cents to hear the New York Philharmonic or a mere twenty-five cents to hear the New York Symphony in Pittsburgh, the Pittsburgh Orchestra charged a minimum price of one dollar. Thus, while a touring orchestra attracted thousands of people, when the local orchestra performed on December 1, 1910, only four hundred people attended the concert.[34] The local orchestra even discounted tickets on the concert day to appeal to more listeners. Although these purchasers had no seat selection, they could enjoy a prime seat in the orchestra circle for a mere fifty cents, or for twenty-five cents they could sit in the balcony.[35] On Thursday, December 1, 1910, only four days before the New York Philharmonic event, the local orchestra presented a concert, and on Saturday afternoon, December 3, 1910, at 2:15 p.m. they repeated the program. Despite vigorous marketing efforts, the orchestra failed to sustain a large audience at every concert, and without a group of guarantors or season subscribers, their survival remained in jeopardy.

Throughout the first week in December 1910, numerous articles addressed the dire condition of the local orchestra and pleaded with readers to step forward and commit to the future of Pittsburgh through their financial contributions. When the Orchestra Association held an emergency meeting on Wednesday, November 30, 1910, they decided to continue the concerts and again solicit contributions.[36] Several individuals even stepped forward and increased their donations to the orchestra. After exhausting appeals in local newspapers, the association decided to address the public at the beginning of the New York Philharmonic concert.

Reviews of the Pittsburgh Concert

On Sunday evening, December 4, 1910, Gustav Mahler, Loudon Charlton, and eighty-five musicians of the Philharmonic left New York City on the Iron City Special and arrived in Pittsburgh Monday morning, December 5, 1910.[37] Even though the Philharmonic concert engaged music lovers in Pittsburgh, the plight of the local orchestra dominated the newspapers.

As Monday evening drew near, ticket holders filled the hall. Martha Root from the *Pittsburgh Post* reported that twenty-two hundred patrons attended the concert with another five hundred turned away at the doors.[38] Within this crowd appeared all the guarantors of the former seasons and the city's most distinguished men and women. Complete with jewels and jetted ornaments, Pittsburgh's elite arrived in lavish gowns of velvet, satin, marquisette, and chiffon.[39] Theodore Rentz from the *Pittsburgh Gazette Times* observed that patrons occupied nearly every seat in the hall and the "audience was all that could be desired."[40] Besides the usual spectators, Rentz noticed a large delegation from the surrounding towns.[41] In addition to filling Soldiers and Sailors Memorial Hall, the *Pittsburgh Index* documented that the audience was the largest ever assembled in the city for a symphony concert.[42]

When the concert commenced at eight fifteen in the evening, local attorney A. M. Imbrie approached the podium. As a representative of the Pittsburgh Orchestra Association, Imbrie made one last effort to implore support for the local orchestra. He reminded the audience that although the association secured the three most distinguished musical organizations in the country, they hoped listeners would "assist in securing for our city a permanent orchestra worthy of its name."[43] Imbrie attempted to abolish rumors of internal strife among the local musical circles and proclaimed, "There is not the slightest controversy between this association and that of the Pittsburgh Symphony Orchestra."[44] As he concluded the speech, Imbrie reaffirmed the association's desire to establish a permanent orchestra in Pittsburgh.

Bach

The real focus of the evening, however, was Mahler's appearance in Pittsburgh. After Imbrie left the stage, a "thrill of curiosity ran through the large audience as a striking figure, small of stature, but absolutely individual in looks, walked to the front of the stage with quick, nervous strides, and perching himself in a high chair with his back to the audience, directed the orchestra."[45] Mahler began the concert with his Bach Suite, and critics immediately evaluated his use of a modified piano in this work. Rentz noted the altered tone of the instrument as theoretically a very interesting plan but "hardly a success in a large hall" when the instrument competes against the volume of many strings.[46] The critic for the *Pittsburgh Index* expressed a similar opinion as he acknowledged the harpsichord as a reminder of "by-gone customs," and a "doubtful proposition in these days of large orchestras and large halls."[47]

Although the so-called instrument may have sounded inappropriate for this hall, the audience expressed sheer approval as they produced a hearty applause after each movement. The critics praised the arrangement of the Air as the first violins bowed the melody in unison.[48] The *Press* applauded Mahler for his "wonderful musical and somewhat athletic feat of presiding at the harpsichord and conducting the orchestra at the same time."[49] Charles Wakefield Cadman of the *Dispatch* offered the most favorable review as he wrote, "Wisdom and musical acumen run through the sympathetic adaptation in veins of pure gold. The calling into use of the harpsichord is in itself a masterstroke. As handled by Mr. Mahler, it enhances the character of the work twofold."[50] While controversy existed over Mahler's interpretation of Bach's work, his enhancements to the next selection quickly gained approval.

Beethoven

After the Philharmonic performed Beethoven's Sixth Symphony, the audience recalled Mahler four times.[51] Compared with other performances of this symphony in Pittsburgh, the Philharmonic made the piece "newer and even more delightful than ever before."[52] In previous renditions, conductors typically treated each movement as a detached piece, but Mahler connected the successive movements as members of a "complete whole" that led up to a grand climax in the final movement.[53] The *Volksblatt und Freiheits-Freund* review noted the orchestra played with devotion, as if they meant to pay homage to Beethoven.[54] The Philharmonic's rendition convinced listeners they were actually experiencing spring, as the critic noted, "It was as you heard the brook murmuring, the birds singing and the peasants rejoicing and dancing, and on the other hand as if you stood right in the middle of the thunderstorm."[55]

According to Theodore Rentz in the *Gazette Times*, Mahler took a dangerously slow tempo in the "Scene by the Brook" and the flute's poor intonation "marred the beauty of phrases in this and other numbers."[56] As the review continued, Rentz commented on the great freedom Mahler employed in the Scherzo, which began rather slowly and gradually increased in force and tempo. With "extraordinary vividness" Mahler conducted the last movement and produced a close that "was invested with a new meaning."[57]

As in the Bach work, Mahler took great liberties in updating the composition for a larger orchestra and modern hall. Compared to the Bach selection, however, critics unanimously respected and approved the enhancements to Beethoven's work. In the *Dispatch* Charles Cadman expressed admiration for Mahler's changes, and he concluded, "No matter what was done to the symphony it was simply great music, and everybody had to gasp for breath to admire such a virile reading."[58] Writing for the *Post*, Jennie Mix also commended the alterations, as she stated, "It sounded in places almost as though one were listening to something from the pen of a modern and it was fascinating, beautiful and magnetic. There was not a trace for an instant of the over sentimentality so frequently put into this score."[59] Other critics noticed Mahler expanded the instrumental lines and added "piercing high notes of the piccolos in the storm."[60]

During intermission listeners only briefly visited in the foyer. From the animated discussions within the hall it appeared everyone was very interested in the concert and desired the creation of a permanent orchestra for Pittsburgh.[61]

Wagner

In William Siviter's review for the *Chronicle Telegraph* he mentioned the necessity of a large orchestra in successfully bringing out the diverse dynamics and tones in Wagner's music.[62] Siviter believed Mahler created beauty with a proper balance of instruments and concluded, "The hearer feels that he is listening to all the instruments in the orchestra and not merely to a group of the loudest."[63]

Theodore Rentz summarized the works as a fitting close, which "displayed the qualities of conductor and orchestra to the best possible advantage."[64] In his review Rentz also noted that the audience hardly missed the usual soloist that orchestras typically included and found it "hard to imagine how the pleasure of the evening would be enhanced by any solo offerings."[65]

As a conductor, Mahler satisfied concertgoers and displayed qualities that made him famous. Rentz captured Mahler's style of conducting as follows:

> His temperamental qualities and personal magnetism compel immediate attention. His intellectual grasp of the compositions is remarkable and demands immediate response from the players. There were occasions last night when he appeared to prefer broad lines to fine detail, and some of the lights and shadows, as well as the more delicate phrasings gave place to a wider sweep of his general plans.[66]

Overall, the concert received a superior rating from the critics. The reviewer of the *Press* noted, "There comes but few times in a person's life when he is permitted to hear such a program as that of last evening."[67] Prior to the concert the crowd appeared enthusiastic, and as the program progressed, they expressed frequent signs of appreciation with thunderous applause. The audience recalled Mahler and Philharmonic numerous times, and "there was continuous evidence that the program was entirely acceptable."[68]

Rentz was still apprehensive in declaring the New York Philharmonic superior to the local orchestra. He noticed a number of musicians in the Philharmonic served as former members of the Pittsburgh Orchestra.[69] The critic for the *Press* supported Rentz's viewpoint and acknowledged the Philharmonic as a wonderful organization, but "no better than one which Pittsburg could support if it would and which it will have if the public meets the association half way in its work."[70]

The morning of December 6, 1910, greeted Pittsburgh with a heavy fall of snow reaching four to five inches in the city, with temperatures approaching twenty degrees.[71] In addition, snowdrifts of four to five feet covered the railroad tracks in the mountainous surrounding areas. As a result, trains from both the east and the west arrived from a half hour to one hour and forty minutes late.[72] As Mahler and the Philharmonic prepared to leave for Cleveland, their train most likely encountered a delay. After traveling 127 miles west, the Philharmonic reached Cleveland in time to perform that evening.

Failure of the Pittsburgh Orchestra

Despite the success of the Philharmonic program, tensions continued to mount regarding the economic conditions of the local orchestra. The concert did not inspire enough supporters to step forward and finance a local

organization. Quite the contrary, citizens realized they could hear a prestigious orchestra for the same price as a mediocre local orchestra. Therefore,
citizens quickly closed their wallets, and the association decided to cancel all
upcoming Pittsburgh Orchestra concerts. When the local orchestra returned
from their tour of Detroit and Ohio on December 11, 1910, it planned to re-
sume rehearsals on December 12, 1910.[73] Instead of rehearsing, conductor
Carl Bernthaler announced no further practices would be held and advised
musicians to seek their final check at the orchestra's headquarters.[74] Many
musicians refused to accept this news and entered into a spirited protest
against the orchestra's executive committee. Since some musicians declined
opportunities with other ensembles throughout the country at the start of the
musical season, they believed they were entitled to the year's full salary. In
addition, the musicians never received any legal notification that the orchestra had disbanded. Bernthaler voiced his disappointment to the *Chronicle Telegraph*:

> I have made no plans for the future, but I want to leave Pittsburgh. I have
> given the best years of my life to the advancement of music in this city. I have
> worked conscientiously in the Pittsburgh Orchestra for fifteen years under
> Archer, Herbert, and Paur, and now I see all my painstaking work come to
> naught. If I were inclined to complain I might say that Pittsburgh has no grat-
> itude, but I will not say that. I want to remember those friends who have been
> kind and true.[75]

In the following weeks the orchestra fully dissolved, and many musicians left
Pittsburgh to seek employment with other organizations.

The Cleveland Concert on Tuesday, December 6, 1910

Located halfway between Chicago and New York, Cleveland offered a prime
stopping point for traveling musicians and orchestras. Originally part of the
Western Reserve, Cleveland's population soared in the 1830s with the industrial development of Ohio and the opening of the Erie Canal. With the
establishment of the railroads in the mid-nineteenth century its population
surged again, and at the start of the twentieth century Cleveland had the
sixth largest population in the United States.[76] Local tycoons such as John
D. Rockefeller Sr., John Huntington, Jepthe Wade, and John L. Severance
quickly amassed fortunes from the oil and steel industries, yet no permanent
orchestra had managed to survive in Cleveland for more than a few years.
Unfortunately, touring orchestras competed with local ensembles and de-

layed the development of a permanent orchestra until 1918. After the failure of a local Cleveland Symphony Orchestra in 1901,[77] Adella Prentiss Hughes quickly organized a Cleveland Symphony Concert Series featuring out-of-town orchestras, and in November 1901, the series commenced with the Pittsburgh Orchestra. As the years passed, Hughes added more orchestras to the series, including the Boston Symphony Orchestra, Cincinnati Symphony Orchestra, the Minneapolis Symphony Orchestra, the Chicago Symphony Orchestra, and the New York Symphony. For the first five years audiences heard ensembles with roughly fifty players. Beginning with the 1906–1907 season larger orchestras arrived in Cleveland, as the Boston Symphony Orchestra brought seventy-five musicians and other ensembles typically traveled with sixty-five musicians.[78]

Similar to Pittsburgh, a local association of rich and prominent citizens, including John D. Rockefeller Sr., John L. Severance, David Z. Norton, and Samuel Mather, backed the series financially.[79] Hughes convinced these individuals to invest in the series, rather than donate their fortunes to a local orchestra with an uncertain future. As time passed, this same group secured a foundation for the Cleveland Orchestra in the 1920s.

In the spring of 1910, Hughes added the New York Philharmonic to the list of orchestras scheduled to perform in Cleveland during the following 1910–1911 season. Subscribers quickly reserved seats, and in early June 1910 sales quickly surpassed the previous season by over one thousand dollars.[80] In October 1910, the announcement for the tenth season of Symphony Orchestra concerts appeared in the local media, including the *Cleveland Plain Dealer*, *Cleveland Leader*, *Cleveland Town Topics*, *Cleveland News*, *Cleveland Press*, and the *Cleveland Wächter und Anzeiger*.[81] Hughes advertised the season as "Seven Magnificent Concerts" and offered subscriptions for six and nine dollars.[82] The season featured the Theodore Thomas Orchestra with Frederick Stock as conductor and soloist Frances Alda on November 16, 1910. The second concert on February 20, 1911, offered Yolando Mérö as pianist, and on March 29, 1911, soloist Perceval Allen planned to perform with the orchestra. Mahler and the New York Philharmonic scheduled their first concert in Cleveland for Tuesday, December 6, 1910. Slightly more than a month later the New York Symphony with director Walter Damrosch arranged a concert for January 20, 1911, and at the end of the month on January 31, 1911, the Boston Symphony Orchestra with Max Fiedler planned to arrive in Cleveland. The Cincinnati Symphony Orchestra with Leopold Stokowski and violinist Mischa Elman rounded out the season with a concert on March 8, 1911.

Hughes now boasted the addition of the New York Philharmonic to the series, and reporters ranked the quality of concerts on par with those in New York, Boston, and Chicago.[83] Advertisements for the season publicized that in value nothing compared to the Symphony Concert Series, which featured "five of the greatest orchestras, and five of the best soloists who are to be in America this winter."[84] Bradley of the *Cleveland Leader* remarked that the most notable event of the season would be the Philharmonic and its distinguished leader Gustav Mahler.[85] She believed Mahler interpreted Beethoven as "if Beethoven were alive today and acquainted with the scope of the modern orchestra."[86] Writing for the *Cleveland News*, Marcosson notified readers that Hughes added the Philharmonic to the series and remarked, "Its radiance has already penetrated our atmosphere considerably in advance of its bodily presence."[87] Compared with the other concerts in the series, the Philharmonic planned to revive many classics and introduce some of the greatest modern masterpieces.[88]

Well before the fall of 1910, Hughes coordinated orchestras to visit Cleveland for the upcoming season. On August 9, 1910, Hughes entered into a legal agreement with Loudon Charlton for the services of the New York Philharmonic Orchestra. In the document, Charlton promised a minimum of eighty players with Gustav Mahler as the conductor for the evening of Tuesday, December 6, 1910, in exchange for two thousand dollars.[89]

Hughes also signed contracts with the management of other orchestras to guarantee their performances. With the recent failure of the Pittsburgh Orchestra, Hughes refused to include the defunct orchestra in the schedule. Many of the upcoming performances featured a renowned soloist; however, the New York Philharmonic and the Boston Symphony Orchestra programmed no soloists on their concerts.

As the Philharmonic concert approached, articles detailed the history of Mahler and the orchestra. *Town Topics* acknowledged Mahler as one of the giants in music who would not likely remain in the country.[90] The *Leader* announced the season as Mahler's last year with the famous old New York orchestra and assured concertgoers they would have the opportunity to witness Mahler's ability as a director and hear his interpretations.[91] The most positive endorsement reached readers as the *Town Topics* commended Mahler for reshaping the Philharmonic and creating an accomplished orchestra that deserved the name of a virtuoso orchestra.[92]

Little competition stood in the way of a large turnout at Grays Armory for the Philharmonic concert. Even though another local manager offered concerts at the Hippodrome in Cleveland, the Symphony Concert Series appealed to a more refined group of listeners. Nevertheless, entertainment at the Hippodrome still attracted large audiences. Ten days prior to Mahler's appearance, the Sousa Band offered two concerts at the Hippodrome on Sunday afternoon and evening, November 27, 1910.[93] With over fifty members in the organization Sousa conducted two outstanding programs, and the large audiences immensely enjoyed his charm and music.[94]

Reviews of the Cleveland Concert

Town Topics praised the magnificent program, and the critics recognized that while "the Philharmonic was great, Mahler was even greater."[95] In a review for the *Cleveland News* Marcosson concluded Mahler's greatness "is so marked that one came away from the concert easily acknowledging having heard the best concert of the entire ten years' series."[96] Compared to reviews in other cities, the critics in Cleveland focused on Mahler's ability as a conductor. Writers referred to Mahler as "a wizard with a magic wand,"[97] "an extraordinary genius,"[98] "a little giant,"[99] and "one of the greatest directors Cleveland ever had as a guest artist."[100] Several articles captured Mahler's physical description and his distinctive traits. Miriam Russell created a colorful depiction of Mahler in the *Cleveland Plain Dealer* stating,

> Little Mahler with the big brain. Little Mahler with the might force. Little Mahler with the great musical imagination. Little Mahler, whose gigantic power make the other conductors seem like pygmies. It is this Herculean little Mahler who directs the New York Philharmonic Orchestra which furnished the second concert of the symphony series at Grays armory last night. . . And this from little Gustav Mahler, that mere wisp of a man, with the slight form, the long slender hands, the loose shock of black hair standing away in all directions from the delicate, ascetic face. Little Mahler, the giant![101]

Writing for the *Cleveland Leader* Bradley recounted Mahler's personality to readers as she wrote,

> Perhaps the greatest thing about Mahler is his own personality. Quick, nervous, full of vitality in every movement, one has the impression of a man with mind in every muscle. His characteristic eccentricity of attitude was apparent in an amusing way as he turned towards the audience at the end of the intermission, evidently wondering when the conversation would cease. Perhaps he was not accustomed to so informal an assemblage. As he stood waiting with baton in hand he made a perfect picture of a human interrogation point.[102]

As a critic for the *Press*, Smith described the leader as "small in stature, but great in intellectual and emotional grasp of his art. He paints in all colors, from the conservative and harmonious blend of the severer classic to the vivid and glowing glare of the moderns."[103]

Rather than evaluate the Philharmonic on the basis of other orchestras, reviewers compared Mahler's conducting style with that of other directors. The writer for *Town Topics* regarded Mahler as a counterpart to Dr. Carl Muck, former conductor of the Boston Symphony Orchestra.[104] He noted both men as "quiet in their conducting gestures" as they "secured climaxes of wonder in the easiest manner."[105]

Smith thought only one conductor in the world could rival Mahler in perfection of detail and unity of dynamic shading, namely Arthur Nikisch.[106] Yet, Smith explained the differences in their approaches to music. He recognized Mahler "at all times the intellectual and consummate musician,"[107] and viewed Nikisch as a splendid musician who at times suggested the virtuoso and placed effect before the musical thought.[108]

Mahler immediately captured the attention of concertgoers and musicians. The writer for the *Town Topics* noted that Mahler's baton behaved like a magic wand as he created "the most wonderful effects imaginable."[109] Just the mere point of the baton toward the player produced the desired effect. His charisma captured the critic of the *Town Topics*, who found himself so immersed in the music that he lost track of the length of the program. Moreover, this critic noted, if another conductor had attempted this program, many listeners would have left well before the evening concluded.[110]

Although Mahler encountered negative comments in the past regarding his revisions of music, Alice Bradley applauded his ability to intrigue the ordinary listener even if he "made some of the sternly judicious grieve."[111] For the average listener Mahler generated new life into the old text and finally produced the spirit of the music.[112] Unlike other orchestras Mahler's musicians were ready to perform, and there appeared "no getting ready, working up, and no preliminary warming process before the orchestra found itself."[113]

Bach

In the *Plain Dealer* Russell observed that when the concert commenced the orchestra plunged into the suite "like a race horse at a signal."[114] Throughout the evening the orchestra continued to play in this same manner and the program offered "no vacillation, no weakening, no hesitancy, no drag."[115]

Even though the Bach selection delighted a number of critics, several writers expressed extremely negative comments on the use of the modified piano. Wilson Smith noted in the *Press* that while Mahler modernized the scoring of the suite for a modern orchestra, he should have provided listeners with the sound of a modern piano. Mahler's use of the harpsichord reminded Smith of the "reading of some antique to me by candlelight."[116] Smith recommended the instrument should be donated to the "junk pile or museum" and believed the "modern concert stage has forgotten it."[117]

Nevertheless, Alice Bradley was convinced that Mahler captured Bach's spirit and omitted any possible dull moment as he melded the "true feeling of the light-hearted ancient composer into intimate sympathy with modern moods."[118] In the Badinerie and the Gavotte, Bradley noticed how the harpsichord accented each measure and added to the proper interpretation of eighteenth-century music.[119] Marcosson also believed Mahler gave "youthful vigor" to the Gavotte, which made it refreshing and inspiring.[120] The popular Air also pleased listeners and critics as Mahler created "a revelation of beauty in the fusion of tone that flowed from the string body of the Philharmonic."[121] Thus, Mahler transformed the famous Air into "a divine piece of tone-poetry" as the Philharmonic created "its rightful body and color" and the work became "tender and spiritual."[122] Compared with other renditions Mahler managed to spark interest in baroque music, as Marcosson concluded: "He manipulates tradition with a bold hand and imbues with fresh life and vigor the spirit too often dormant in the musty manuscript."[123]

Although Boston critics opposed Mahler's tampering with the original manuscript, Cleveland critics supported Mahler's changes to modernize the music. Thus, Mahler shaped a work where "the dull moments were eliminated."[124] Critics continued with enthusiasm for Mahler as he proceeded to the Beethoven selection.

Beethoven

Although other orchestras had performed Beethoven's Sixth Symphony in Cleveland before this season, these previous interpretations never made the impact Mahler achieved through his critical interpretation of the score.[125] Russell believed Mahler succeeded in updating the symphony and in still preserving Beethoven's "spirit" by creating "not a metamorphosed Beethoven at all, but a sort of glorified Beethoven."[126] After hearing the work, the writer for *Town Topics* ranked the Beethoven selection as the superior piece of the evening and raved that he never heard a better interpretation of the work nor enjoyed the piece as much as when Mahler conducted in Cleveland.[127] He anticipated that listeners would long remember the "marvelously clean presentation" and it would "long linger in the minds of those who attended."[128]

Bradley expressed a more in-depth description of the work, as she wrote in the *Cleveland Leader*: "More beauty of rendition it would be hard to imagine.

The poetic expression of country happiness was all there, and a breadth of interpretation, a clarity of theme in hidden voices, as well as in the more obvious one, quite new and wonderful."[129]

Wagner

With Beethoven and Bach holding the spotlight, the Wagner pieces received limited coverage. The review in *Town Topics* acknowledged them as "excellently done," but it did not compare or equal the Beethoven symphony.[130] In the *Leader*, however, Bradley believed the Wagner pieces could ask for "no more intense, and soulful interpretation" than what Mahler produced.[131]

After the concert, the orchestra remained in Cleveland for the evening, but Mahler and Loudon Charlton immediately left on an overnight train headed 185 miles northeast for Buffalo, New York. Alma Mahler planned to join Gustav in Buffalo on Wednesday morning, so that they could spend the day at Niagara Falls.

The Buffalo Concert on Wednesday, December 7, 1910

Known as the Queen City of the Great Lakes, Buffalo offered a vast network of railroads and featured the western terminus of the largest barge canal system in the country. Although the iron and steel mills represented approximately 61 percent of industry in Pittsburgh at the turn of the twentieth century, in Buffalo it represented only 11 percent.[132] As the decade progressed, other industries and major corporations arrived in Buffalo, including the Ford Motor Company. Compared to previous cities along the tour, Buffalo was renowned for its significant snowfall, and December 1910 marked no exception. Beginning on December 5, 1910, only two days before the Philharmonic concert, the city endured a blizzard.[133]

News of the Philharmonic's success along the tour reached Buffalo well before the orchestra's arrival. On December 6, 1910, the *Buffalo Evening Times* confirmed that Pittsburgh's Soldiers and Sailors Memorial Hall "was packed to the doors" with an audience that demonstrated keen interest in the Bach Suite.[134] The concert presented an admirable rendition of Beethoven's Sixth Symphony, and the Wagnerian excerpts brought the evening to a dramatic close.[135]

For a number of years orchestras had appeared in Buffalo, and in 1906, Louis Whiting Gay and Mai Davis Smith organized the first concert series featuring visiting orchestras. Smith later worked independently, and in 1910 coordinated a concert series in Buffalo, which included Mahler and the New

York Philharmonic. Throughout her life Smith brought the finest soloists and orchestras to Buffalo and helped develop the city's culture. Upon her death in 1924, Marian de Forest assumed her work and soon formed the Buffalo Musical Foundation as a memorial to Mai Smith.[136] This organization created the backbone of support for the current Buffalo Symphony Orchestra, formed in 1935.

Similar to the Cleveland series, Smith offered subscription tickets for the 1910–1911 season. Unlike the Cleveland series, some of the Buffalo concerts featured only soloists. The season welcomed Johanna Gadski of the Metropolitan Opera on October 7, 1910, followed by Marcella Sembrich on November 22, 1910. The New York Philharmonic planned a concert for December 7, 1910, and on January 10, 1911, Francis Alda, soprano, and George Hamlin, tenor, scheduled a joint recital. Max Fiedler and the Boston Symphony Orchestra presented an orchestral concert on February 3, 1911. Smith invited pianist Olga Samaroff to conclude the concert series on March 3, 1911. For the six concerts Smith sold subscription tickets between $3.00 and $7.50. Otherwise, concertgoers purchased individual tickets for as low as $.75 and as high as $2.00.[137]

Concerts for the series were held in Buffalo's Convention Hall, which originally stood as the Seventy-fourth Armory Building on the northeast corner of Virginia and Elmwood Avenues. The hall was originally built in 1886, but when the regiment outgrew the facility in 1900, the city took over the management and renamed the building Convention Hall. In 1901, J. N. Adams purchased the organ for the hall from the Pan-American Exposition of 1901 in Buffalo. After the city installed the organ on a remodeled stage, weekly organ recitals soon followed.[138]

News of the New York Philharmonic's premiere in Buffalo began circulating in local newspapers on September 4, 1910, when the *Buffalo Morning News* announced that "no musical event of the season will arouse more interest" than the New York Philharmonic concert.[139] Two weeks later, advertisements for subscription tickets ran in the *Buffalo Courier*, *Buffalo Enquirer*, *Buffalo Evening News*, *Buffalo Evening Times*, *Buffalo Illustrated Times*, *Buffalo Morning Express*, *Buffalo Illustrated Express*, and the *Täglicher Buffalo Volksfreund*.[140]

Several weeks prior to the concert, newspapers printed feature articles on Mahler and the New York Philharmonic and highlighted the Bach Suite. The *Buffalo Commercial Advertiser and Journal* defined the upcoming event as "doubly noteworthy" since Mahler planned to appear as a performer on the "harpsichord" and simultaneously conduct the orchestra in the Bach Suite.[141] Moreover, the *Express* commended Mahler's understanding of baroque music and believed his "mastery of musical effect of the day" would guarantee a "wonderfully perfect reproduction of the Bach music."[142] As in other promotions, this article referred to the work as a novelty and "an artistic revelation."[143] This writer believed knowledge of the clavichord or harpsichord was still relevant to music students and thought the instrument brought to light the true beauty of the classics.[144] A press release in the *Enquirer* informed readers that after Mahler recently performed the Bach work in New York, it became the chief point of conversation, and in response to the many requests, the organization added the piece to the program in Buffalo.[145]

General seat sales for the series opened on December 1, 1910, at the Denton, Cottier and Daniels Company. Individual tickets for the concert sold for $2.00, $1.50, $1.00, and $.75 and were comparable in price to tickets for other concerts in the series. At a recent Sousa concert in Buffalo, however, ticket prices had ranged significantly lower, from only $.75 to $1.00.[146]

The upcoming event also marked the first orchestral concert of the season, and news soon reached cities well beyond Buffalo. In Lockport, New York, located just north of Buffalo and south of Niagara Falls, the *Lockport Union-Sun* announced the appearance of the New York Philharmonic Orchestra as one of the important concerts of the season.[147] Only two brief articles announced the upcoming concert in the local German newspaper, *Täglicher Buffalo Volksfreund*. On the day of the concert a brief notice in the *Volksfreund* declared: "This evening a large concert by the New York Philharmonic Society, with Gustav Mahler as director and soloist, in the Convention Hall [Heute Abend großes Konzert der New Yorker Philharmonischen Gesellschaft, mit Gustav Mahler als Dirigent und Solist, in der Konventshalle]."[148]

A Short Trip to Niagara Falls

On the morning of the concert, Gustav met Alma in Buffalo. Alma noted in her memoirs that Mahler arrived at the hotel, and "after a short rest we took the train to Niagara and from there in an antediluvian carriage to the Falls."[149] It was no surprise that Alma picked Buffalo to reunite with Mahler since Mahler hoped to view the falls while living in America and ranked it as one of his top tourist attractions.[150] Many years later when Alma recalled the excursion to Niagara Falls, she described the sight as follows:

> It was a day of wintry sunshine. Every twig was coated in ice. When we got right up to the Falls and then beneath them by the lift, the strength of the greenish light hurt our eyes. The thunder of the water beneath the roof of ice,

the trees mantled far and wide in frozen foam, and the distant view over the snow-covered plain all had a dreamlike beauty.[151]

After a day at Niagara Falls, Mahler and Alma returned to Buffalo in the late afternoon. Meanwhile the orchestra had departed from Cleveland and had reached Buffalo in the afternoon.[152] As the evening approached, the *Evening News* reported that many dinner parties commenced prior to the concert and that music lovers anticipated a rare evening of fine music.[153] Another article cautioned readers that latecomers would not be allowed to enter the hall when the orchestra was playing; therefore, "promptness in arrival will be necessary."[154]

Reviews of the Buffalo Concert

As the concert began at Convention Hall, another winter blizzard blew into Buffalo with a forty-six mile southeast wind. For roughly two hours the city was "swept by the swirling snowstorm," and before the concert ended, roughly four inches of snow fell, and the wind formed enormous snow-drifts.[155] As the blizzard raged outside, the writer for the *Evening Times* noted, "Buffalo's most cultured audience witnessed the greatest musical achievement of many years."[156] Critics declared the concert a huge success, and the titles of local reviews proclaimed the event as a "Superb Concert Philharmonic Orchestra,"[157] "Superb Poetry in Philharmonic's Art,"[158] "Brilliant Concert,"[159] "Philharmonic Concert a Musical Triumph,"[160] "Delightful Concert by Philharmonic,"[161] and "Music Hath its Charms."[162]

Bach

While evidence survives to confirm the presence of an organ in Convention Hall for the opening Bach Suite, none of the reviews or the program mentioned an organist for this work. Overall, the audience and critics enjoyed Mahler's modifications of the Bach composition, and the *Courier* remarked, "To many this was the favorite of the evening."[163] The critic for the *Evening News* praised Mahler for emulating Bach's spirit as he performed the music with "a vitality that pulsated with life and energy."[164] Mahler captured the excitement of the composer as the "elastic rhythm and nuance of each phrase made Bach seem the human being he was in his music and not the automaton that pedantry often makes him appear."[165]

Critics approved of Mahler's enhancements, and some even endorsed the reconfigured piano as an appropriate replacement for the harpsichord. The critic for the *Enquirer* described the instrument to readers as a pianoforte with modified action that produced a tone similar to an old harpsichord, but somewhat louder.[166] Although the writer for the *Express* enjoyed listening to the Bach work, he disapproved of the modified piano and rated it as an unsatisfactory replacement for the instrument of Bach's time since it "lacked the gentle, thin sweetness of the harpsichord and both in the Overture and Gavotte it was disagreeably strident."[167] Yet, the same critic admitted the instrument lent itself better in the Rondeau and created a delightful performance that transported listeners to the days of Bach.[168] In an article for the *Evening Times* the reviewer believed the reconfigured piano created the only blemish on the evening's enjoyment as it "lacked the richness of tone of an original instrument of Bach's time."[169]

Beethoven

Mahler conducted an inspiring rendition of Beethoven's Sixth Symphony for the second selection. A storm of applause followed as the audience displayed their appreciation and forced Mahler to return to the stage to acknowledge their praise.[170] Beginning with the first movement, Mahler took a quicker than usual tempo and proceeded to the second movement with a slower than accustomed tempo.[171] The critic for the *Express* noticed the music in the second movement, "A Scene by the Brook," displayed a richness of coloring,[172] and the third movement, "Merry Gathering of Country Folk," was especially pleasing with the "rhythmic incisiveness" that marked Mahler as a leader.[173] During the climactic fourth movement, the critic for the *Evening News* recorded the "Thunderstorm" as truly colossal with the "kettle drums out doing nature in her most riotous and volcanic moments."[174] Moreover, the critic for the *Express* recounted the success of Mahler's interpretation as he wrote, "A more tremendously realistic portrayal of the thunderstorm has certainly never been given, and the conductor himself seemed like the very genius of the storm, driving his forces on to fiercer and yet fiercer outbursts."[175] After hearing the final fifth movement, the writer further commended the orchestra on its constant rhythmic surety and on Mahler's ability to bring "to the foreground certain inner voices which listeners seemed never to have heard before."[176]

Critics detected Mahler's attention to detail and phrasing throughout the Beethoven selection. A reviewer in the *Evening News* observed that Mahler grasped the "smallest details of structural design and musical concert," while he never lost sight of "the large outline of the work as a whole and fine ensemble."[177] The writer also noticed Mahler commanded the symphony and controlled the music rather than having the music control him.[178] In the *Enquirer* the critic praised Mahler's attention to detail and exacting ideals, which created a performance of exquisite refinement with "a perfect balance in every phrase and every nuance in that phrase."[179]

The journalist for the *Commercial Advertiser and Journal*, comparing other selections on the program, noticed the orchestra played the movements of this symphony with the "innermost spirit of the creator."[180] The critic for the *Evening Times* congratulated Mahler for capturing Beethoven's passion for nature and believed "the interpretation showed the audience the wonderful skill of the orchestra and Mr. Mahler's baton as perhaps did no other number on the program."[181]

Wagner

Unlike critics in other cities, those in Buffalo extensively critiqued the final selections on the program. The *Commercial Advertiser and Journal* concluded the works "were magnificently played,"[182] and the writer for the *Evening News* corroborated that they were presented with splendid effect.[183] He observed the most compelling parts of this section occurred when the dramatic element entered as in the changing aspect of the love theme of Tristan, the memories of Siegfried, and at the opening of the Prelude from *Die Meistersinger von Nürnberg*.[184] Unlike the prior works, Wagner's music offered the orchestra the first chance to demonstrate their full power. Upon hearing the Prelude and Liebestod from *Tristan und Isolde* the reviewer for the *Enquirer* rated the orchestra as magnificent, the "body of strings and woodwind instruments produced a tone which under the wand of the great conductor took on a plastic joyous beauty."[185] The critic for the *Evening News* observed that even though Mahler's constant subtle changes appeared almost unnoticed, they "heightened the fascination immeasurably and the performance made a strong impression."[186]

As the final selection on the program, the Prelude to *Die Meistersinger von Nürnberg* delighted listeners with Mahler's addition of emotion and radiant color that "almost overpowered the audience and ignited thunderous applause which rang through the hall."[187]

Mahler as a Conductor

Mahler impressed critics and listeners in Buffalo as a "great director,"[188] "great musician,"[189] and a "giant of the musical world"[190] who showed the "power of a strong man and the gentleness of a child."[191] Throughout the evening Mahler kept a keen eye on every section of the orchestra as he conducted with only his right hand as his left hand rested on his hip.[192] The writer for the *Enquirer* viewed Mahler's attractive personality as magnetic, yet unaffected by interruptions.[193] In the *Courier*, the journalist saw a personality not to be denied, and in Mahler's rendition "there was nothing stilted and while keeping close to the musical text he invested each number with new beauty of interpretation."[194]

The reporter for the *Commercial Advertiser and Journal* also commended Mahler as a fabulous and inspiring conductor who possessed "rare intellect and a great deal of magnetism."[195] Without significant effort Mahler appeared to produce astonishing effects. The same critic regarded Mahler's presence in Buffalo as a noteworthy moment in the orchestral field:

> In flight of fancy, in poetry of conception, Mahler is among the foremost of orchestra conductors. His subtle magnetism appeals alike to orchestra and audience, and his fine artistic reading and intellectual treatments of the different work afforded the deepest pleasure to all who were present last evening.[196]

The critic for the *Express* voiced a different opinion, as Mahler appeared to him a "thin, small man, with a serious, determined face, crowned with a mass of shaggy hair and with a manner absolutely devoid of self-consciousness."[197] Rather than a conductor who attracted the public, this reporter viewed Mahler as "indifferent as to the effect upon the listeners of his readings" and "wholly absorbed in giving out the musical message as he feels it."[198] The same critic found Mahler more engrossed in the "effect of colossal grandeur," and his sincerity demonstrated no mannerisms or affectations.[199]

The Orchestra

A number of writers in Buffalo studied the relationship between Mahler and the ensemble throughout the performance. Although Mahler appeared a quiet individual, he governed the orchestra, and the musicians instantaneously responded to his every gesture.[200] The review in the *Advertiser and Journal* acknowledged the readiness of the musicians, as Mahler played "the orchestra as a master organist plays on his instrument" and demonstrated his absolute command of the musicians.[201] The critic for the *Express* noticed that Mahler stood quietly as "he dominated the men in unusual degree."[202]

Several critics discussed the quality and unique sound of the New York Philharmonic. The writer for the *Commercial Advertiser and Journal* believed the musicians played with firmness and delicacy and remarked that their most distinguishable feature was "the accuracy in pitch and the clearness of the attacks."[203] Without much visible strain, the musicians created an immense tonal volume that seemed effortless, simple, and natural.[204] Rather than evaluate the orchestra's sound, the writer for the *Express* compared the Philharmonic's sound with other unnamed orchestras, presumably the Boston Symphony Orchestra or the Theodore Thomas Orchestra. The critic initially noticed the Philharmonic lacked the "mellowness and beauty of tonal quality which marks the work of some other orchestra bodies in the land."[205] At the same time, however, the writer complimented the sound as "compact and well-blended" and for the most part marked "by unity, generally good balance and splendid attack."[206]

Afterthoughts

Following the concert, Mahler returned to the hotel where Alma and a simple supper awaited him. Alma recorded that Gustav arrived at the room in an exalted mood and declared, "I have today realized that articulate art is greater than inarticulate nature."[207] He was most likely referring to the evening's performance of Beethoven's Sixth Symphony. Alma concluded in her memoirs that after conducting the piece, Gustav found it "more tremendous than all the Niagara Falls."[208]

The Rochester Concert on Thursday, December 8, 1910

Located sixty miles northeast of Buffalo, Rochester boasts an extensive history of music and business. Still known today as the Flower City, Rochester's slogan at the turn of the twentieth century encouraged citizens to "Do it for Rochester."[209] In the business world Rochester represented the home of the Eastman-Kodak Company. As advancements in photography soon became part of the American lifestyle, George Eastman quickly accrued a vast fortune that helped to establish several centers of culture, including the Eastman School of Music, in the early 1920s.[210] Yet, even prior to this institution, citizens enjoyed local and imported entertainment. With the assistance of several impresarios, traveling orchestras and musicians also added to Rochester's culture. When the local media announced that the world-famous Gustav Mahler might conduct a concert at Convention Hall, readers were encouraged to "Do it for Musical Rochester."[211]

Recognized today as the GeVa Theater, Rochester's Convention Hall offered the perfect space for the New York Philharmonic's first visit on Thursday, December 8, 1910. Although the building originated as home for the

Fifty-fourth Regiment of the New York National Guard in 1871, the city took over the space in 1909 and renamed it Convention Hall.[212] For many years the hall featured entertainment, political debates, rallies, dances, and music. Although the "Chronological History of Convention Hall" documented prominent moments such as tenor Enrico Caruso's appearance in 1908,[213] Theodore Roosevelt's visit in 1910,[214] and pianist Ignacy Jan Paderewski's concert in 1916,[215] Mahler's performance failed to make the list.

The record of the New York Philharmonic's concert appeared limited to Stewart B. Sabin's *Music in Rochester: From 1909 to 1924.*[216] According to this source the Philharmonic performed twice in Rochester between 1909 and 1912, but Sabin provided no date for the first appearance and failed to mention that Gustav Mahler was the director. As a well-respected authority on local history, Blake McKelvey provided substantial material on local culture in *Rochester: The Quest for Quality 1890–1925*, but he focused on other ensembles such as Walter Damrosch and the New York Symphony.[217] With the organization of John F. Furlong's concert series in 1912, several sources acknowledged the Philharmonic's first significant appearance in Rochester as 1913, when Josef Stransky conducted and violinist Mischa Elman appeared as the featured soloist.[218] Unfortunately, even more recent articles such as Vincent Lenti's "A History of the Eastman Theater"[219] relied on these earlier sources for authenticity and never examined materials from local newspapers. Therefore, Mahler's performance with the New York Philharmonic in Rochester remained absent from the list of historical events until now.

As in other cities along this tour, a local impresario organized a concert series. In the spring of 1910, Walter Bentley Ball planned seven evenings of superb popular music for the 1910–1911 season. In a postcard sent to potential subscribers, Ball promised a series of fabulous orchestras and soloists if he received a sufficient number of orders by July 15, 1910. In the card Ball featured pictures of each conductor and several soloists. Readers responded positively to Ball's request, and on August 21, 1910, news of the upcoming season appeared in local newspapers, including the *Rochester Democrat and Chronicle*, the *Rochester Herald*, the *Rochester Post Express*, and the *Rochester Union and Advertiser.*[220]

Marketed as a "Popular Concert Series," the season opened with American basso Herbert Witherspoon on October 24, 1910. Several weeks later, violinist Francis Macmillan presented a concert on November 11, 1910, followed by Mahler and the New York Philharmonic on December 8, 1910.[221] The first month of 1911 offered two concerts with tenor Alessandro Bonci on January 2, and Walter Damrosch and the New York Symphony on January 17. Soprano Johanna Gadski stepped into the spotlight the following month with a concert on February 10, 1911. The series concluded with a joint recital featuring the great French pianist Adolphe Borchard and cellist Boris Hambourg on March 6, 1911.

In early November 1910, an article in the *Rochester Union and Advertiser* declared Rochester as the only city in the United States where the world's greatest musical artists could be heard at a reasonable price.[222] Ball anticipated moderate prices would attract attention in local musical circles and the surrounding areas. Local musicians even advised potential concertgoers that the standing room sign would likely appear for many concerts.[223] Ball hoped this recommendation would invigorate season ticket sales and persuade interested parties not to postpone their ticket purchases.

In the weeks preceding the concert, several inaccurate statements appeared in the local newspapers. Although Mahler and the Philharmonic traveled to New England cities the previous season, several reports still declared the upcoming concert as part of the Philharmonic's first tour in their sixty-nine years of existence.[224] In addition, these notices declared Rochester only the fourth city outside of New York to hear the Philharmonic, hence not citing any cities from the prior season.[225]

For individuals unable to attend the entire series, Ball sold individual tickets for the Philharmonic concert ranging from $.75 to $2.50.[226] Surprisingly, of the three thousand seats in Convention Hall, five hundred seats were still available on Tuesday, December 6, 1910.[227] According to *Post Express*, Ball needed to collect at least two thousand five hundred dollars to break even for the Philharmonic concert.[228]

Walter Ball also arranged for George Barlow Penny to offer a free preconcert lecture at the Hotel Seneca on Wednesday, December 7, at four o'clock in the afternoon. Local concertgoers recognized George Penny as a local music teacher and head of the Rochester Oratorio Society. As part of the lecture, Penny planned to provide background on Beethoven and Wagner and outline the structure of Beethoven's Sixth Symphony as "plain as possible with reproductions of the principal themes."[229] Penny promised to be entertaining as well as instructive with his lecture, which incorporated lantern slides and examples performed on the piano.[230]

For readers unfamiliar with Mahler's accomplishments, several articles detailed his numerous successes. Readers learned of Mahler's recognition as "one of the most notable masters of orchestral force" who enjoyed an international reputation and achieved great progress with the Metropolitan Opera House in New York. With his recent direction over the Philharmonic, the ensemble "scored some of the most emphatic successes of its career."[231] The *Herald* reported that even the music critics in New York united in tributes to Mahler's programs and renditions.[232] As a composer, Mahler brought excitement, enthusiasm, and controversy to the stage, and his compositions excited as much interest and controversy "as a Bruckner symphony used to provoke in the old days when the Brahmsites raged together and the Wagnerians imagined vain things."[233] Several days before the performance, another article in the *Post Express* captured Mahler's position in the current musical environment as follows:

> Gustav Mahler is one of the most striking figures in contemporary music. He is the devout champion of Mozart; his readings of Wagner are revelatory in their reverent originality; and he is the composer of a series of symphonies which reach to colossal proportions. The remarkable thing about the man's intellectual make up is his combination of the old and the new.[234]

Reviews of the Rochester Concert

The week the Philharmonic toured Upstate New York, temperatures reached the lowest mark of the season. The *Union and Advertiser* recorded that at the northern portions of New York the temperature dipped to sixteen degrees below zero.[235] Even with this extremely frigid weather, Walter Bentley Ball convinced three thousand people to leave their comfortable homes and arrive at Convention Hall before eight fifteen in the evening for the New York Philharmonic Concert.[236] Once concertgoers filled the hall they "listened to the noble music in a fervor of enthusiasm," and the *Post Express* declared the concert to be "one of the best given in Rochester."[237] Other critics commended the musicians, and the reviewer for the *Herald* rated the evening as a treasured memory of the musical season.[238] The *Democrat and Chronicle* also concluded the concert would "long linger in the memories of musical enthusiasts."[239]

Bach

Compared to other works on the program, the *Union and Advertiser* acknowledged the opening Bach Suite as the primary attraction.[240] As verified in several accounts, Mahler again directed from his seat at the piano[241] and appeared as "some old cembalist from the eighteenth century who improvised a part from the continuous bass line of Bach and led with only look and gesture."[242] The critic for the *Post Express* described the instrument as a "grand piano" constructed to produce the sound of a magnified harpsichord.[243] The reviewer for the *Herald* complimented Mahler for his arrangement and ability to reconstruct and adapt Bach's music for modern audiences. According to this critic, Mahler achieved an offering "not Bach sacrosanct" but "Bach in his proper setting for modern hearers and for modern means."[244] Compared with other performances of Bach's music in Rochester, this selection appeared "full of reverence and veneration for Bach,"[245] which "satisfied the soul,"[246] and demonstrated the music of Bach as "a living, a pulsating, and emotional language."[247] In the fourth movement, the Air from Bach's Suite No. 3, Mahler captured the interest of listeners as he "produced a devout song of nature, which soon satisfied critics and listeners."[248] Moreover, no reporter criticized Mahler's attempt to modernize Bach's music with a larger ensemble or reconfigured piano.

During this performance the critic for the *Herald* admired the "brilliancy, incisiveness, and virtuosity" of the string section as the peer of any orchestra heard in Rochester in many years.[249] The reviewer emphasized he meant nothing derogatory about the woodwinds or brass, but believed the strings created a convincing effect that demanded recognition.[250]

Beethoven

In the next selection Mahler brought Beethoven's Sixth Symphony alive with an inspired performance well beyond the traditional reading.[251] Many critics noted the enhancements produced a symphony where Beethoven's symphony was no longer "archeology, but music in which the spirit of the master lives and rejoices."[252] The *Herald* acknowledged Mahler not only as a scholar and artist, but also as an "exemplar of the modern mechanism" who materialized such a storm as the "orthodox Beethovenite never realized."[253] Furthermore, the writer for the *Democrat and Chronicle* observed, "Mr. Mahler conducted it with reflective and calculated effect, and gave it an eminently revealing, glowing, and tender performance."[254]

Based on this performance, a number of local critics, including the reviewer for the *Post Express*, hailed Mahler as a genius. This critic watched as the great conductor shaped the music and took pleasure in conducting the piece. Hence, the writer concluded that "Mahler achieved the secret of good conducting, which was also the secret of playing and good singing."[255] Mahler approached the composition as program music and made "a vivid piece of tonal music suggestive of material things."[256] The writer for the *Democrat and Chronicle* noticed that during the thunderstorm in the fourth movement there was a "crashing of brilliant tonality that was terrifying in its realism of the storm."[257]

Wagner

Most critics focused on one or two of the final Wagner selections. One reviewer even voiced that the *Siegfried Idyll* could have easily been removed from the program since the audience was, at that moment, a "little beyond the saturation point."[258] As an interpreter of Wagner's music, Mahler approached this music in a subdued manner and "reserved the usual booming and crashing for select moments."[259] When needed, however, Mahler created tremendous climaxes "where the crescendos seemed to go on amplifying to infinity."[260]

The critic for the *Democrat and Chronicle* commended Mahler's conducting and praised his interpretation: "They were all played with illuminating, overwhelming power and emotional effect that aroused persistent and tumultuous applause."[261] Moreover, some critics heralded Mahler for the Wagner selections, which presented contrast and superb effect.[262]

After the Prelude and Liebestod from *Tristan und Isolde*, the critic for the *Democrat and Chronicle* concluded the work "was magnificently read and played with tremendous fire and appreciation of its musical substance."[263] A brief review of the rendition in the *Herald* concluded Mahler's insight lost no episode in the dramatic orchestration or the passionate mood.[264]

During the final selection of Prelude to *Die Meistersinger von Nürnberg*, the brass section gained attention, as the critic for the *Rochester Post Express* opined, "Mahler sees to it that his brass is not unsexed; it is masculine, virile; the blare sends cold shivers down your spine."[265] Other reviewers described the interpretation as "gorgeous in color"[266] and performed "with electrifying brilliancy"[267] as the pace and tonal splendor created a grand effect.

Hence, with the successful performance and a packed concert hall, Rochester experienced a musical awakening. With great anticipation the writer for the *Democrat and Chronicle* hoped the New York Philharmonic would again visit the following season.[268] Under Ball's management Rochester leaped over the hurdle of unstable financial support and ended the period of "tentative efforts and nervous experimentation" and moved Rochester into a period of "actual realization."[269] In the following years Rochester continued to thrive not only in commercial activity, but also in its support and appreciation of the arts.

The Syracuse Concert on Friday, December 9, 1910

As Mahler conducted the concert in Rochester, snow began falling in Syracuse. Located eighty-nine miles east of Rochester in the Finger Lakes region,

Syracuse averages 140 inches of snow per year, and December 1910 marked no exception. From dusk on Thursday, December 8, 1910, until dawn on Friday, December 9, 1910, nearly four inches of snow accumulated on the ground. To combat the weather, Commissioner Westcott ordered out the largest force of snow removal with twenty-five plows and 225 men with shovels.[270]

Although snow still falls on many winter days in Syracuse, the majority of the buildings and landmarks from the turn of the twentieth century exist only as mere glimpses of the past. From the late eighteenth century to the end of the nineteenth century, however, Syracuse stood as the national provider of salt in the United States and acquired the nickname "Salt City."[271] The natural salt springs near Onondaga Lake offered a wealth of salt, and by the late nineteenth century over three hundred salt suppliers stretched from Liverpool to Syracuse. In 1825, the Erie Canal extended to Syracuse and opened a main stopping point for barges. When the New York Central Railway expanded, Syracuse once again became a major station and welcomed traveling entertainers, musicians, and orchestras. Syracuse never boasted the same population or percentage of upper-class households as other cities along the tour such as Cleveland or Rochester. Nevertheless, citizens eagerly awaited the arrival of Mahler and the Philharmonic on Friday, December 9, 1910.

Long before the snow arrived in Syracuse, Loudon Charlton had arranged with local manager A. Kathleen King for the Philharmonic to offer a concert on Friday evening, December 9, 1910. Similar to her counterparts in other cities, such as Cleveland and Pittsburgh, King came from an upper-class family, traveled through Europe, received a formal education, and even took several courses under Theodor Leschetizky.[272]

On the list of "Representative Women of Syracuse" the Onondaga Historical Association ranked King as one of Syracuse's most talented pianists and an authority upon the works of Chopin.[273] She also possessed expert knowledge of Hungarian music, corresponded with scholars in Europe, and even presented a series of lectures on Hungarian music in New York City. According to her obituary in the *Syracuse Journal*, King acquired local recognition for bringing the Boston Symphony Orchestra to Syracuse, and participated in the Morning Musical Series and Salon Musicales.[274] For a number of years the Boston Symphony Orchestra traveled through upstate New York, and in 1909 King engaged Walter Damrosch and the New York Symphony to visit Syracuse. King organized three major concerts for the 1910–1911 season at the New Wieting Opera House, starting with the New York Philharmonic's concert on Friday, December 9, 1910, and on January 17, 1911, Walter

Damrosch and the New York Symphony arrived. Under the auspices of the Morning Musicale of Syracuse, Max Fiedler and the Boston Symphony Orchestra offered the third concert on February 4, 1911.[275]

The New Wieting Opera House

King arranged many performances for the 3,000-seat New Wieting Opera House. Although the hall has not survived, historians documented many of the concerts, operas, plays, and state conventions that occurred in the building. Located directly across from the train station, the hall offered convenient access for unloading equipment, sets, instruments, and even fragile grand pianos. The Philharmonic presented its first concert not in the original hall, but in the fourth and last Wieting Opera House constructed in 1897.

Advertisements in Syracuse

Announced as an "Engagement Extraordinary,"[276] news of the Philharmonic concert appeared by late November in the *Syracuse Herald, Syracuse Journal*, and the *Syracuse Post-Standard*.[277] Several promotional stories featured Mahler's positive qualities and allowed readers to draw their own conclusions about the mysterious conductor. One of the most popular articles throughout the tour captured Mahler's physical appearance as:

> . . . a small man, delicate looking and extremely nervous, a long, clean-shaven face, the head high in the center and surmounted with very black hair, an extraordinary forehead. Behind large round spectacles gleam brilliantly sharp, dark eyes, which give the impression of inflexible will, and this is strengthened by a large, prominent nose. The mouth (fine almost to effeminacy) frequently breaks into a smile of childlike frankness and great kindness, forming a striking contrast to the austerity of the upper portion, which is continually agitated by involuntary movement.[278]

An article in the *Herald* encouraged readers to witness Mahler in action and indicated that Mahler planned to devote time to composition at the end of the season.[279] Unfortunately, this statement failed to specify whether the time specifically referred to only the summer.

Several articles drew a parallel between Mahler and the great master Beethoven and acknowledged Mahler as the "one musician since the death of Beethoven who has dared to follow in the pathway hewn by the Ninth Symphony to liberty of form and expression in its noblest and most elevating influence."[280] The *Journal* commented that "his [Mahler's] readings of even hackneyed scores are always refreshing, for he inspires his men with his own personality to such a degree that it is as if he were interpreting the music on a single instrument. He is intense and forceful, but at all time dignified and quiet."[281] Beyond hearing the typical orchestral works, Mahler's performance with a Steinway harpsichord promised to be not only the "most interesting," but also the most fascinating.[282]

Mahler's demand for perfection made the concert an event not to be missed, as the *Journal* stated, "Mr. Mahler seems to throw himself heart and soul into the spirit of the music, striving by voice and gesture to convey to his players his conception of the composition. He keeps up a running fire of comment and instruction, addressing the men in German."[283]

A number of reports emphasized the players' potential to produce a flawless performance. Compared with other ensembles these musicians were "unequaled in individual qualifications as well as in discipline and training" and thus offered an attraction that "may rightly be considered one far out of the ordinary."[284]

Developing civic pride and culture in a growing city offered another reason to observe Mahler in Syracuse. As populations throughout cities increased at the turn of century, writers often rated the level of culture on the number of tickets sold for an event. In Syracuse, as in other locations, concertgoers seemed less concerned about understanding the music and more concerned about making an appearance at the event and meeting other socialites. A report in the *Herald* on December 4, 1910, noted, "Local music lovers are keenly alive to the importance of the forthcoming engagement, and Mr. Mahler is certain to be welcomed by a crowded house. No orchestral organization in the country enjoys a greater reputation. But few cities will be included in the present tour."[285] During the following days subsequent articles reinforced the idea of Syracuse's rising position in culture and observed that "Syracuse is forging ahead among cities of its class as a patron of musical art in its grandest form of instrumental interpretation—the orchestra."[286] In a final attempt to persuade readers to purchase tickets, the *Herald* wrote, "For the sake of music culture in Syracuse, we trust that the patronage of each of these noble concerts will justify and requite the enterprise of local promoters. In no other way can the city maintain the standard now happily set."[287]

Referring to the concert as "the talk of the town" since the first announcement, promoters hoped a large audience would fill the Wieting Opera House.[288] Tickets were made available at the beginning of the week and ranged in price from $.75 to $2.50,[289] which was significantly higher than the most expensive ticket of $2.00 set for the upcoming Boston Symphony Orchestra concert.[290] During the same week of the Philharmonic event a modernized rendition of *The Bohemian Girl*[291] played at the Wieting on all the other remaining evenings with matinees on Wednesday, Friday, and Saturday and a final performance on Saturday, December 10, 1910. Matinee tickets for *The Bohemian Girl* ranged from only $.25 to $1.00 and tickets for evening performances started at $.25 and reached $2.00.[292] Earlier in the week the Syracuse Arts Club sponsored soprano Jeanne Jomelli in a recital at the Hotel Onondaga on Tuesday, December 6, 1910. This occasion marked her first appearance as a soloist in Syracuse.[293]

Reviews of the Syracuse Concert

Unfortunately, on the night of the concert many seats in the New Wieting Opera House remained vacant. The *Herald* reported: "From the musical point of view the orchestral concert of the New York Philharmonic Society at the Wieting last night will rank among the great successes of its kind in the musical history of Syracuse. As a business enterprise, be it said with regret, a similar claim cannot be made for it."[294] The critic also noted the size of the audience as only moderate, similar in size to the crowd at a popular play on a third night.[295] Although music lovers filled the hall for two symphony concerts in the prior year, critics denounced managers for setting ticket prices too high, which "at once excited resentment and repelled patronage."[296] In a review from the *Post-Standard*, a second writer blamed the New York management for poor attendance rather than the "Syracuse music loving public."[297] In addition, the critic of the *Herald* believed if management set two dollars as a maximum for admission, the hall's capacity would "probably have been exhausted."[298]

For individuals who attended the concert, the result "was one of pure delight to the appreciative and discerning" audience.[299] Similar to concerts in Pittsburgh and Cleveland, a social aspect influenced concert attendance. The reviewer for the *Journal* concluded, "The so-called music lovers of Syracuse—the crowd that 'attends' only social affairs so as to be numbered 'among the present,' was not there. Only the earnest ones who love music for music's sake were there."[300] Unfortunately, the writers who compiled newspaper clippings in *Famous Visitors to Syracuse: 1825 to April 1990*[301] also overlooked this significant concert. While other musicians such as John Philip Sousa acquired a full page of coverage in this source,[302] Mahler's visit received no attention. Even on the day following the concert, reviews in Syracuse newspapers appeared more brief and general than those in larger cities along the tour such as Pittsburgh, Cleveland, and Buffalo. After listening to the works from various periods, the critic for the *Herald* viewed the program as an educational study of orchestral compositions in three stages of development.[303]

Bach

Only one of the three major newspapers in Syracuse, namely the *Post-Standard*, offered specific comments and details relevant to the Bach work. In this review, unlike others from previous performances, the writer reported that several men placed the keyboard instrument on pedestals. Mahler then sat down, faced the audience, and conducted the orchestra as he played.[304] This review marked the first time along the tour Mahler actually faced the audience, either partially or completely, rather than perform with his back turned to the audience.

Mahler's interpretation of Bach obviously pleased the audience and critics. Hence, not one reviewer disapproved of the reconfigured Steinway piano or Mahler's tampering with the score. On the contrary, the critic for the *Post-Standard* concluded,

> The effect, probably as near an approach as has been made since Bach's own time, two centuries ago, to the effects which Bach himself used to create, was indescribably picturesque and telling. The somewhat nasal voice of the harpsichord sounded through the bright fabric of the composition like some oriental pattern appearing and reappearing amid the broad color of the orchestral score in contrast and yet in exquisite harmony with the rest.[305]

The program emphasized Mahler performed only on a Steinway piano throughout the tour. In addition to printing the piano manufacturer underneath the selection in the program, a full-page advertisement encouraged readers to purchase a Steinway.[306]

Beethoven

Compared with other works on the program, Mahler's interpretation of Beethoven's Sixth Symphony created the "supreme delight of the evening" and, on the whole, reviewers believed this work would linger the longest in the memory of listeners.[307] Mahler's commitment to perfection and attention to detail paid off as the *Herald* noted that "with all its wealth of imagery and beauty of melody, [the work] was never before made articulate in Syracuse with such fervor and accuracy of execution as the Philharmonic devoted to it last night."[308] The critic praised the string section of the orchestra as a "magnificent aggregation of trained performers" whose labor presented the best example of musical expression ever presented in Syracuse.[309] Moreover, the same reviewer believed the Philharmonic surpassed other orchestras "in the superior number of instruments and a finer precision of sheer technique."[310]

Wagner

The final portion of the concert offered solely Wagner selections, and Mahler demonstrated his ability as a conductor of opera. The extensive review in the *Herald* applauded Mahler for his interpretation and pointed out that the orchestra was at its best during these selections. These compositions provided "a brilliant exhibition of artistic skill and enthusiasm and an eloquent tribute to the breadth and profundity of Herr Mahler's directive power."[311] In regard to programming, the critics commended Mahler for illustrating the three phases of Wagner's musical art, from tragedy to romance and finally to refined comedy.[312]

The Last Telegram

Shortly after Mahler arrived in Syracuse on Friday, December 9, 1910, he sent a brief telegram to Alma at the Hotel Savoy at 1:08 P.M. Although Alma reunited with Gustav in Buffalo, she returned the following day to New York City. In a telegram Mahler wrote, "My journey with almiosha even more splendid, wonderful snowy weather today, woo Gustav."[313] Even though the note was brief, it marked the last piece of correspondence Gustav sent to Alma.

The Utica Concert on Saturday, December 10, 1910

On the following morning, Saturday, December 10, the orchestra departed Syracuse for the final leg of the tour in Utica, New York, located only fifty miles east of Syracuse in Oneida County and twenty miles east of the geographical center of the state.[314] The Philharmonic arrived in Utica before noon and had ample time to relax before the evening concert. Although the other stops in the Great Lakes tour remained major cities throughout the twentieth century, Utica's economy and status declined, and in more recent years, the population has substantially decreased. Hence, scarce evidence related to the Philharmonic's visit in 1910 and only fragmented details of

Utica's history surfaced from the sources available in the Utica Public Library and Oneida County Historical Association. Unfortunately, an original program from the concert has not survived in the Oneida County vicinity or at the New York Philharmonic.

When the Philharmonic arrived in Utica in 1910, the city flourished with businesses and culture. During the early eighteenth century capitalists built large textile mills in the region, and Utica quickly attracted Welsh, Polish, Irish, and Italian immigrants. At its peak in 1910, the textile industry employed roughly 18,000 workers in the Oneida-Herkimer region, thus accounting for roughly 44 percent of the area's total manufacturing employment.[315] Over the following decades the textile industry migrated to the South, and by 1958, only 1,700 workers remained in Utica's textile industry.[316] In 1942, General Electric opened its first plant in Utica and temporarily rejuvenated the economy, but less than a half a century later General Electric closed the facilities in the area. Once again the city experienced further economic struggles.

At the turn of the twentieth century, however, business and entertainment thrived in Utica. Numerous musicians, composers, orchestras, and traveling entertainers made frequent visits to Utica, including Walter Damrosch and the New York Symphony. Beginning in 1908, with subsequent visits in 1910 and 1911,[317] Damrosch made successful visits to the region and played a vital role in Utica's Midwinter Music Festival in 1912 and 1914.[318] Unlike Mahler's visit, however, Damrosch included local choral groups and amateurs in his programs. Many traveling musicians frequently arrived at the New York Central train station, performed at the magnificent Majestic Theater, and spent the night at Utica's Majestic Hotel. Unfortunately, these sites survive only on historical maps of the city.

In addition to visiting musicians, the area featured the Utica Conservatory of Music[319] and a local philharmonic orchestra.[320] The influx of Polish immigrants to Utica led to the formation of several choral groups including the Chopin Choir of Holy Trinity Church and the Kolka Filaretow, often referred to as the Filarets.[321]

During this period readers chose from several local newspapers, including the *Utica Herald Dispatch*, *Utica Observer*, *Utica Daily Press*, and *Utica Sunday Tribune*.[322] Compared with newspapers in other cities along the tour, however, publications in Utica featured no standard music section, column, or critic. Although several critics reviewed the concert, the Philharmonic's management created standard press releases, and thus, many of the promotional articles in Utica appeared in other newspapers in Pittsburgh, Cleveland, Buffalo, Rochester, and Syracuse.

Working with Loudon Charlton, Hugh T. Owen of Utica managed the local preparations for the Philharmonic concert. Owen had recently provided Uticans with the famous coloratura soprano Marcella Sembrich in concert and he eagerly coordinated the Philharmonic's visit. He arranged for the orchestra to perform at the Majestic Theater, which was "the handsomest, best equipped, and most luxurious theatre between New York and Buffalo."[323] This hall easily accommodated traveling ensembles and provided adequate space for a large orchestra. The theater hosted many performances, including the first recital of the great Wagnerian singer Kirsten Flagstad and the initial performance of the hit tune "Tea for Two" from the operetta *No, No, Nanette*.[324]

Although Keith's Vaudeville Show at the Shubert Theater offered the only major competing event on the same evening as the Philharmonic concert, more publicity appeared in local media for the Philharmonic concert than for the vaudeville show. From the first announcement, Owen informed the public that ticket prices were divided into various ranges to suit everyone and to guarantee seats for all interested parties.[325] Only two days before the concert on Thursday, December 8, 1910, at nine o'clock in the morning, subscription ticket sales opened at Buckingham and Moak's. A number of standard press releases filled the newspapers during December 1910. These articles promoted the concert as "one of the great musical evenings of the year, if not many years"[326] and "the talk of the town since announcement of the engagement."[327] A featured story in the *Utica Sunday Times* noted, "No greater concert attraction will be heard here this season than the Philharmonic Orchestra, which comes to the Majestic on Saturday evening for one concert only under the distinguished leadership of Gustav Mahler."[328]

Unlike the standard articles replicated in newspapers along the tour, these articles aimed to invigorate sales, document the success of tour, and introduce the music. A report from the *Observer* from Thursday, December 8, 1910, declared that the Philharmonic achieved tremendous success in other cities and cited the unique character of the Bach Suite, which Mahler played and conducted; is rendition of the Beethoven's *Pastoral* Symphony; and several Wagnerian numbers.[329] On Friday, December 9, 1910, another article confirmed the tour's triumph, as the reporter observed a large audience present in Buffalo on Wednesday evening, followed in Rochester with a wonderful reception on Thursday evening, and with a sold-out engagement planned in Syracuse for Friday evening.[330] Even on the morning of the concert details from the previous evening's performance in Syracuse hit local media as the *Observer* reported a "very enthusiastic" audience filled Syracuse's Wieting Opera House and enjoyed the great Bach Suite as Mahler played and conducted at the same time.[331]

Reviews of the Utica Concert

Frigid temperatures continued to cover upstate New York during the second week of December 1910, and the day of the concert marked no exception. An article in the *Observer* pointed out that for more than a week the mercury remained below freezing, and most of the time the temperature averaged twelve degrees.[332] Only for three or four days in the past two weeks had considerable warmth allowed some ice to thaw. Surprisingly, subzero conditions were more commonplace during January and February, and the report considered these present circumstances extremely abnormal for December.[333]

When the performance commenced at eight fifteen in the evening, an unconfirmed number of listeners appeared in Utica's Majestic Theater. Reviews printed in local newspapers on the following day reported drastically different stories. Although freezing temperatures may have deterred some individuals from attending, the *Observer* proudly reported that Utica offered one of the largest audiences along the tour since the orchestra's first concert in Pittsburgh. Moreover, the same writer cited the size of the audience as proof to any doubters of "Uticans' ability to appreciate the classical."[334] Writers from other local newspapers contradicted this statement, such as the critic for the *Daily Press*, who indicated the number of concertgoers less than adequate and believed the program deserved a larger audience.[335] A reporter from the *Sunday Tribune* further stated that "only a small audience enjoyed the delights of the occasion."[336] Although many of Utica's music lovers supported the event, this critic admitted the showing was not creditable for a city that boasted a large class of appreciative people. The writer also detected as many musicians in the orchestra itself as people on the main floor of the theater.[337] Nevertheless, those who attended overwhelmingly approved of Mahler and the Philharmonic and offered nothing but flattering expressions, which were heard throughout the evening and at the completion of the program.[338]

Bach

Local critics voiced no derogatory remarks regarding Mahler's alterations to the score or playing on a reconfigured Steinway piano. Of the movements in the suite, the Air quickly became a favorite among listeners and critics as the writer for the *Sunday Tribune* remarked, "This was the most beautiful and called forth hearty applause."[339] The reporter for the *Daily Press* noticed the audience enjoyed the third movement and the Gavotte of the fourth movement.[340] Throughout this work Mahler displayed his thoroughness in the manner of conducting,[341] demonstrated another instance of his ability as a musician,[342] and took the audience back two centuries to the days of Bach.[343]

Beethoven

As the second selection on the program, Mahler's rendition of Beethoven's Sixth Symphony soon became the most popular number of the evening. The critic for the *Observer* regarded the entire program as masterful, yet the "orchestral tunes appealed stronger to the audience" in this composition than in other offerings on the program.[344] As in previous stops along the tour, the thunderstorm of the fourth movement quickly captivated listeners. During this short movement the "brass instruments were played with power" as they offered the greatest impression, and thus, "it was thrilling."[345] In addition, the reviewer for the *Sunday Tribune* noted the "truly colossal" playing of the tympani during the storm.[346] Compared with other selections, the Beethoven symphony delivered the full dynamic range of the Philharmonic from the softest piano to the greatest forte.[347] Even though the following Wagnerian pieces were brilliant and credited as the finest technical portion of the program, the writer for the *Observer* believed the rendition of the Beethoven work would linger in the memory of the audience long after the Philharmonic departed Utica.[348]

Mahler as Conductor

The writer for the *Sunday Tribune* noted the orchestra presented the Wagner pieces with "splendid effect" and that the "elation of the appreciative audience was present at all times."[349] Although the Beethoven work may have received the greatest response, the writer of the *Observer* noted the audience showered Mahler with applause after every work.[350] A few closing remarks compared the Philharmonic with other visiting orchestras, such as the New York Symphony. The writer for the *Observer* confirmed that the organization differed from others "by a marked preponderance of the strings over the wind instruments in a finer precision of technique."[351] In conclusion, the critic for the *Daily Press* painted Mahler as a genius and described him as follows:

> Add to an ability to interpret with feeling the work of master musicians, an influence which can bring three score and more artists to act as one and a personality which has its influence upon his audience instantly, and you have a picture of Gustav Mahler."[352]

The critic for the *Sunday Tribune* indicated the expectations for the event were met as "one of the greatest orchestras with the greatest of conductors" created a superb performance and showed "admirably the perfection of the organization's work."[353] As readers purchased newspapers the following morning, they absorbed the critics' opinions, and although the writer for the *Daily Press* expressed disappointment in the small attendance, he knew those who heard Mahler and the Philharmonic would be recounting the event to the many others who missed a historical moment in music.[354]

The Philharmonic Returns to New York City

Though the musicians sought to rest after the concert, this tour marked only the onset of a very busy schedule for the New York Philharmonic season, which began on November 1, 1910. An article in the *Daily Press* indicated that the orchestra left immediately after the concert on a train headed for New York City and that they rehearsed the following day.[355] The ledger records for Carnegie Hall revealed, however, that the Philharmonic received a day off on Sunday, December 11, and resumed rehearsals on Monday, December 12, 1910.[356]

During the Philharmonic's absence in New York City, music lovers experienced no decrease in musical events, as the Boston Symphony Orchestra arrived and offered a concert at Carnegie Hall on Thursday evening, December 8, which they repeated on Saturday evening, December 10, 1910. Compared with other reviews of the period, critics were less impressed with these Boston Symphony Orchestra performances than with prior ones. In their rendition of Tchaikovsky's Symphony No. 5 in E Minor, op. 64, Henry T. Finck of the *New York Evening Post* remarked, the music was "not so well played, from either a technical or an emotional point of view, as it has been repeatedly in the same hall by our Philharmonic Orchestra, under Safonoff and Mahler—yes, Mahler."[357] Although the crowd cheered, neither the orchestra nor conductor performed "at their best" and Mahler's recent rendition of the work produced an "inspired and memorable performance."[358]

In Mahler's absence some critics began to notice and even appreciate his progress with the Philharmonic. On Wednesday, December 13, 1910, Mahler and the Philharmonic commemorated the one hundred and fortieth anniversary of Beethoven's birth with an all-Beethoven concert at Carnegie Hall.[359]

Notes

1. Throughout this period "Pittsburgh" and "Pittsburg" appeared as accepted spellings. Therefore, some newspapers such as the *Pittsburg Press* and *Pittsburg Dispatch* adapted the spelling "Pittsburg," while others used "Pittsburgh." As the century progressed, "Pittsburgh" became the official spelling, but for historical purposes and in direct quotations both spellings will be used.

2. "Open Pennsylvania Station Tonight," *New York Times*, 26 November 1910, 5. The station opened on November 27, 1910, and offered sixty-one through westbound and fifty-five through eastbound daily trains.

3. "Musical Devotees are Preparing for Treat," *Pittsburg Press*, 27 November 1910, Theatrical sec., 8.

4. Gerald W. Johnson, "The Muckraking Era," in *Pittsburgh: The Story of an American City*, ed. Stefan Lorant (Garden City, NY: Doubleday and Company, 1964), 272. Pittsburgh's population was 553,905 in 1910.

5. Johnson, 275.

6. Johnson, 275.

7. "Season's Series," *Pittsburgh Bulletin Index*, 11 October 1934, 4.

8. Edward G. Baynham, "Pittsburgh," *The New Grove Dictionary of Music and Musicians*, ed. Stanley Sadie (London: Macmillan, 1980), 14:793.

9. "In the Music World," *Pittsburgh Gazette Times*, 30 October 1910, sec. 2, 8.

10. "In the Music World," 30 October 1910, sec. 2, 8.

11. "In the Musical World," *Pittsburgh Gazette Times*, 25 September 1910, sec. 6, 4.

12. "Music of the Week," *Pittsburg Press*, 9 October 1910, theatrical sec., 5.

13. The committee in charge of the concerts included: Dr. P. J. Eaton, Mr. and Mrs. Frank Moore, William Flinn, Dr. Arthur Hammerschlag, A. M. Imbrie, H. H. McClintic, Mr. and Mrs. Enoch Rauh, H. C. Terrance, Mrs. Lawrence Litchfield, Mrs. Josiah Cohen, Mrs. Charles L. Taylor, Mrs. John C. Slack, and William H. Donner. For more information refer to Edward G. Baynham, "A History of Pittsburgh Music 1758–1958," vol. 2 (Pittsburgh: Carnegie Library, Music and Art Department, photocopied), 265.

14. Baynham, 265.

15. "Music and Musicians," *Pittsburgh Bulletin*, 18 November 1910, 23.

16. "Music of the Week," *Pittsburg Press*, 9 October 1910, theatrical sec., 5.

17. "In the Music World," *Pittsburgh Gazette Times*, 9 October 1910, sec. 2, 6.

18. "Season's Series," *Pittsburgh Bulletin Index*, 11 October 1934, 4.

19. Baynham, 357. Upon May Beegle's death on December 8, 1943, her brother Thomas Beegle took over the series. When he passed away in 1946, his sons Thomas P. Jr. and William H. Beegle managed the business.

20. The *N. W. Ayer and Son's Newspaper Annual and Directory of 1910* (Philadelphia: N. W. Ayer and Son, 1910) printed the daily/weekly circulation of each paper as follows on pages 794–796: *Pittsburgh Post*, 52,642, Sunday edition 71,925; *Pittsburg*

Dispatch, 65,554, Sunday edition 76,941; *Pittsburgh Gazette Times*, 75,501, Sunday edition 65,000; *Pittsburgh Leader*, 81,233, Sunday edition 61,871; *Pittsburg Press*, 85,000, Sunday edition 72,000; *Pittsburgh Sun*, 66,820; *Pittsburgh Bulletin*, 4,500; *Pittsburgh Index*, 12,000; Pittsburgh *Chronicle-Telegraph*, 75,609; *Pittsburgh Volksblatt und Freiheits-Freund*, 12,500.

21. *Pittsburg Press*, 2 October 1910, theatrical sec., 3. As indicated in the advertisement, mail order subscriptions were available at the Pittsburgh Orchestra Association located at 1517 Farmers Bank Building or via telephone at 526 Grant.

22. "Concert Ticket Sale Opened at Nixon Today," *Pittsburg Press*, 28 November 1910, 3.

23. "Music and Musicians," *Pittsburgh Bulletin*, 3 December 1910, 14.

24. "In the Music World," *Pittsburgh Gazette Times*, 23 October 1910, society and women's club sec., 1.

25. "Musical Devotees are Preparing for Treat," *Pittsburg Press*, 27 November 1910, theatrical sec., 8.

26. "Music of the Week," *Pittsburg Press*, 20 November 1910, sec. 6, 5.

27. "In the Music World," *Pittsburgh Gazette Times*, 30 October 1910, sec. 2, 8.

28. "Demand Continues for Concert Tickets," *Pittsburg Press*, 29 November 1910, 10.

29. "In the Music World," *Pittsburgh Gazette Times*, 30 October 1910, sec. 2, 8.

30. "Society," *Pittsburgh Gazette Times*, 4 December1910, Society sec., 3.

31. "Orchestra Plays Monday," *Pittsburgh Gazette Times*, 3 December 1910, 11.

32. "Big Orchestra Arrives: Will Play Tonight," *Pittsburg Press*, 5 December 1910, 8.

33. "New York Orchestra to Start Here To-day," *Pittsburg Post*, 3 December 1910, 7.

34. "Good Music and Money," *Pittsburgh Gazette Times*, 2 December 1910, 4.

35. "To Continue Fight for Symphony Orchestra," *Pittsburgh Post*, 1 December 1910, 8.

36. "Music News of the Week: Symphony Orchestra Plans," *Pittsburgh Press*, 3 December 1910, Sports sec., 3.

37. "New York Orchestra to Start Here To-day," *Pittsburgh Post*, 3 December 1910, 7.

38. Martha L. Root, "Concert a Brilliant Society Event," *Pittsburgh Post*, 6 December 1910, 2.

39. "Society," *The Pittsburg Dispatch*, 6 December 1910, 15.

40. Theodore Rentz, "Orchestra Given Grand Reception," *Pittsburgh Gazette Times*, 7 December 1910, 4.

41. Rentz, 4.

42. "Music," *Pittsburgh Index*, 10 December 1910, 13.

43. "N.Y. Orchestra Makes Its Debut in Pittsburg," *Pittsburg Press*, 6 December 1910, 14.

44. "N.Y. Orchestra Makes Its Debut in Pittsburg," 14.

45. Charles Wakefield Cadman, "Brilliant Welcome to Mahler," *Pittsburg Dispatch*, 6 December 1910, 7.

46. Rentz, 4.

47. "Music," *Pittsburgh Index*, 10 December 1910, 13.

48. Rentz, 4.

49. "N.Y. Orchestra Makes Its Debut in Pittsburg," 4.

50. Cadman, 7.

51. Rentz, 4.

52. "N. Y. Orchestra Makes Its Debut in Pittsburg," 4.

53. Rentz, 4.

54. "Der Töne Zauber," *Pittsburgh Volksblatt und Freiheits-Freund*, 6 December 1910, sec. 3, 3. Das Orchester spielte mit einer Hingabe, als ob es galt den Manen Beethovens zu huldigen.

55. "Der Töne Zauber," sec. 3, 3. Es war, als ob man die Bächlein rauschen, die Vögel jubiliren und die Bauern jauchzen und tanzen hörte, und wiederum, als ob man mitten im Gewitter stände.

56. Rentz, 4.

57. Rentz, 4.

58. Cadman, 7.

59. Jennie Irene Mix, "Brilliant Gathering at Concert," *Pittsburgh Post*, 6 December 1910, 1.

60. Cadman, 7.

61. "Society," *Pittsburg Dispatch*, 6 December 1910, 15.

62. William H. Siviter, "First Concert Great Success," *Pittsburgh Chronicle Telegraph*, 6 December 1910, 6.

63. Siviter, 6.

64. Rentz, 4.

65. Rentz, 4.

66. Rentz, 4.

67. "N. Y. Orchestra Makes Its Debut in Pittsburg," 14.

68. Rentz, 4.

69. Rentz, 4.

70. "N. Y. Orchestra Makes Its Debut in Pittsburg," 14.

71. "Snow Ties Up Trains and Trolley Lines," *Pittsburg Press*, 6 December 1910, 1.

72. "Snow Ties Up Trains and Trolley Lines," 1.

73. The Pittsburgh Orchestra tour also included Oberlin, Ada, Piqua, Lima, and Alliance, Ohio.

74. "Orchestra Players Refuse to Quit Without Full Pay," *Pittsburgh Chronicle Telegraph*, 12 December 1910, 1.

75. "Orchestra Players Refuse to Quit Without Full Pay," 1.

76. William Ganson Rose, *Cleveland: The Making of a City* (Cleveland: World Publishing Company, 1950), 374.

77. Johann Beck conducted the Cleveland Symphony Orchestra from 1900 to 1901. For more information refer to Mary Wagner, "Early Orchestras in Cleveland" (Master's thesis, Kent State University, 1998).

78. Donald Rosenberg, *The Cleveland Orchestra Story: Second to None* (Cleveland: Gray and Company, 2000), 38.

79. Rosenberg, 40. Severance was an industrialist. Norton accrued his fortune as a partner in the iron ore and shipping firm Oglebay Norton Company. Mather achieved wealth as an iron ore and steel magnate.

80. "Music and Musicians," *Cleveland Leader*, 18 September 1910, sec. 6,7.

81. The *N. W. Ayer and Son's Newspaper Annual and Directory of 1910* printed the daily/weekly circulation of each paper as follows on pages 682–684: *Cleveland Plain Dealer*, 79,601, Sunday edition 102,725; *Cleveland Leader*, 30,000, Sunday edition 45,000; *Cleveland Town Topics*, 4,500; *Cleveland News*, 65,000; *Cleveland Press*, 159,275; and *Cleveland Wächter und Anzeiger*, 29,000, Sunday edition 19,000.

82. *Cleveland Leader*, 23 October 1910, sec. 6, 2.

83. Sol Marcosson, "Brilliant is Outlook for Cleveland's Musical Season Soon to be Opened," *Cleveland News*, 1 October 1910, 12.

84. Alice Bradley, "Music," *Cleveland Leader*, 23 October 1910, sec. 5, 5.

85. Bradley, "Music," 23 October 1910, sec. 5, 5.

86. Bradley, "Music," 23 October 1910, sec. 5, 5.

87. Sol Marcosson, "Many Notable Artists and Musical Bodies will Appear in Concert Season," *Cleveland News*, 8 October 1910, 2.

88. Marcosson, "Many Notable Artists and Musical Bodies," 2.

89. Agreement from the Office of Loudon Charlton, in MAA Board of Trustees Contracts Series, Symphony Orchestra Series 1909–1910, Cleveland Orchestra Association, Cleveland.

90. "In Musical Circles," *Cleveland Town Topics*, 26 November 1910, 10.

91. Alice Bradley, "Music," *Cleveland Leader*, 4 December 1910, sec. 6, 2.

92. "In Musical Circles," *Cleveland Town Topics*, 3 December 1910, 10.

93. Sol Marcosson, "Sousa's Band Here Sunday; Famous Artists to be Heard in Winter's Concerts," *Cleveland News*, 26 November 1910, 2.

94. "In Musical Circles," *Cleveland Town Topics*, 3 December 1910, 8.

95. "In Musical Circles," *Cleveland Town Topics*, 10 December 1910, 8.

96. Sol Marcosson, "Mahler Calls Back Spirits of Masters," *Cleveland News*, 7 December 1910, 4.

97. Marcosson, "Mahler Calls Back Spirits of Masters," 4.

98. Alice Bradley, "Concert Delight to Big Audience," *Cleveland Leader*, 8 December 1910, 9.

99. Miriam Russell, "Mahler, Leading, Shows his Power," *Cleveland Plain Dealer*, 7 December 1910, 2.

100. Wilson G. Smith, "Little Mahler Looms Giantlike in Concert," *Cleveland Press*, 7 December 1910, 6.

101. Russell, 2.

102. Bradley, "Concert Delight to Big Audience," 9.

103. Smith, 6.

104. Muck was director of the Boston Symphony Orchestra from 1906 to 1908, and from 1912 to 1917. In March 1918 he was arrested and interned for the duration of the war.

105. "In Musical Circles," 10 December 1910, 8.

106. Smith, 6.

107. Smith, 6.

108. Smith, 6.

109. "In Musical Circles," 10 December 1910, 8.

110. "In Musical Circles," 10 December 1910, 8.

111. Bradley, "Concert Delight to Big Audience," 9.

112. Bradley, "Concert Delight to Big Audience," 9.

113. Russell, 2.

114. Russell, 2.

115. Russell, 2.

116. Smith, 6.

117. Smith, 6.

118. Bradley, "Concert Delight to Big Audience," 9.

119. Bradley, "Concert Delight to Big Audience," 9.

120. Marcosson, "Mahler Calls Back Spirits of Masters," 4.

121. Marcosson, "Mahler Calls Back Spirits of Masters," 4.

122. Bradley, "Concert Delight to Big Audience," 9.

123. Marcosson, "Mahler Calls Back Spirits of Masters," 4.

124. Bradley, "Concert Delight to Big Audience," 9.

125. Bradley, "Concert Delight to Big Audience," 9.

126. Russell, 2.

127. "In Musical Circles," 10 December 1910, 8.

128. "In Musical Circles," 10 December 1910, 8.

129. Bradley, "Concert Delight to Big Audience," 9.

130. "In Musical Circles," 10 December 1910, 8.

131. Bradley, "Concert Delight to Big Audience," 9.

132. "Buffalo in 1910," *Buffalo Enquirer*, 23 November 1910, 1.

133. "Storm Reported, Headed This Way," *Buffalo Commercial Advertiser and Journal*, 5 December 1910, 1.

134. "Philharmonic Orchestra," *Buffalo Evening Times*, 6 December 1910, 9.

135. "Philharmonic Orchestra," 6 December 1910, 9.

136. Ossip Gabrilowitsch, a long-time friend of Mai Davis Smith, offered a memorial concert for Smith when the Detroit Symphony Orchestra toured to Buffalo in the fall of 1924.

137. "Sunday News Music Page: Concert Series of Eminent Artists Planned for Season," *Buffalo Sunday Morning News*, 18 September 1910, 8. Season tickets were

divided into four groups based on the design of Convention Hall: first sixteen rows, $7.50; regular price per concert $2. Next fifteen rows, $6.00; regular price per concert $1.50. Next fifteen rows, $4.50; regular price per concert, $1. Best of the lower floor and the balcony, $3; regular price per concert, 75 cents. The hall offered 2,658 seats.

138. Mildred E. Wolf, *History of Music in Buffalo: 1820–1945* (Buffalo: Kleinhans Musical Hall Management, 1945), 18. In October 1912, Convention Hall officially became the Elmwood Music Hall.

139. "Sunday News Music Page," *Buffalo Morning News*, 4 September 1910, 8.

140. The *N. W. Ayer and Son's Newspaper Annual and Directory of 1910* printed the daily/weekly circulation of each paper as follows on pages 577–578: *Buffalo Courier*, 43,136, Sunday edition 83,009; *Buffalo Enquirer*, 25,000; *Buffalo Evening News*, 94,660, Sunday edition (*Buffalo Sunday News*) 25,000; *Buffalo Evening Times*, 40,000, Sunday edition (*Buffalo Illustrated Times*) 35,000; *Buffalo Morning Express*, 35,143, Sunday edition (*Buffalo Illustrated Express*) 55,000; *Täglicher Buffalo Volksfreund*, 8,077.

141. "Musical News," *Buffalo Commercial Advertiser and Journal*, 3 December 1910, 5.

142. M. M. H., "Music Hath its Charms," *Buffalo Express*, 8 December 1910, 5.

143. M. M. H., "Music Hath its Charms," 5.

144. M. M. H., "Music Hath its Charms," 5.

145. "Music," *Buffalo Enquirer*, 3 December 1910, 7.

146. "The Musical World," *Buffalo Illustrated Sunday Times*, 20 November 1910, 53. A matinee earlier that day offered tickets to adults for $.50 and to children for $.25.

147. "Brilliant Score for Grand Concert," *Lockport Union-Sun*, 6 December 1910, 4.

148. "Notizen," *Täglicher Buffalo Volksfreund*, 7 December 1910, 8.

149. Alma Mahler, *Gustav Mahler: Memories and Letters*, 3rd ed., ed. Donald Mitchell, trans. Basil Creighton (Seattle: University of Washington Press, 1975), 183.

150. "Philharmonic Players to Arrive Wednesday," *Buffalo Evening Times*, 5 December 1910, 9.

151. Alma Mahler, *Gustav Mahler: Memories and Letters*, 211.

152. "Mahler Tonight," *Buffalo Express*, 7 December 1910, 6.

153. "Superb Concert Philharmonic Orchestra," *Buffalo Evening News*, 8 December 1910, 18.

154. "Great Concert Tonight," *Buffalo Commercial Advertiser and Journal*, 7 December 1910, 5.

155. "Lively Blizzard Hits the Town," *Buffalo Enquirer*, 8 December 1910, 3.

156. "Philharmonic Concert a Musical Triumph," *Buffalo Evening Times*, 8 December 1910, 5.

157. "Superb Concert Philharmonic Orchestra," 18.

158. "Superb Poetry in Philharmonic's Art," *Buffalo Courier*, 8 December 1910, 8.

159. "Brilliant Concert," *Buffalo Commercial Advertiser and Journal*, 8 December 1910, 5.

160. "Philharmonic Concert a Musical Triumph," 5.

161. "Delightful Concert by Philharmonic," *Buffalo Enquirer*, 8 December 1910, 12.

162. M. M. H., "Music Hath its Charms," 5.

163. "Superb Poetry in Philharmonic's Art," 8.

164. "Superb Concert Philharmonic Orchestra," 18.

165. "Superb Concert Philharmonic Orchestra," 18.

166. "Delightful Concert by Philharmonic," 12.

167. M. M. H., "Music Hath its Charms," 5.

168. M. M. H., "Music Hath its Charms," 5.

169. "Philharmonic Concert a Musical Triumph," 5.

170. "Delightful Concert by Philharmonic," 12.

171. "Superb Concert Philharmonic Orchestra," 18.

172. M. M. H., "Music Hath its Charms," 5.

173. M. M. H., "Music Hath its Charms," 5.

174. "Superb Concert Philharmonic Orchestra," 18.

175. M. M. H., "Music Hath its Charms," 5.

176. M. M. H., "Music Hath its Charms," 5.

177. "Superb Concert Philharmonic Orchestra," 18.

178. "Superb Concert Philharmonic Orchestra," 18.

179. "Delightful Concert by Philharmonic," 12.

180. "Brilliant Concert," 9.

181. "Philharmonic Concert a Musical Triumph," 5.

182. "Brilliant Concert," 9.

183. "Superb Concert Philharmonic Orchestra," 18.

184. "Superb Concert Philharmonic Orchestra," 18.

185. "Delightful Concert by Philharmonic," 12.

186. "Superb Concert Philharmonic Orchestra," 18.

187. "Superb Poetry in Philharmonic's Art," 8.

188. "Delightful Concert by Philharmonic," 12.

189. "Superb Poetry in Philharmonic's Art," 8.

190. "Brilliant Concert," 9.

191. "Brilliant Concert," 9.

192. M. M. H., "Music Hath its Charms," 5.

193. "Delightful Concert by Philharmonic," 12.

194. "Superb Poetry in Philharmonic's Art," 8.

195. "Brilliant Concert," 9.

196. "Brilliant Concert," 9.

197. M. M. H., "Music Hath its Charms," 5.

198. M. M. H., "Music Hath its Charms," 5.

199. M. M. H., "Music Hath its Charms," 5.

200. "Delightful Concert by Philharmonic," 12.

201. "Brilliant Concert," 9.

202. M. M. H., "Music Hath its Charms," 5.

203. "Brilliant Concert," 9.

204. "Brilliant Concert," 9.

205. M. M. H., "Music Hath its Charms," 5.

206. M. M. H., "Music Hath its Charms," 5.

207. Alma Mahler, *Gustav Mahler: Memories and Letters*, 184.

208. Alma Mahler, *Gustav Mahler: Memories and Letters*, 184.

209. Blake McKelvey, *Rochester: The Quest for Quality 1890–1925* (Cambridge, MA: Harvard University Press, 1956), 106.

210. McKelvey, 381.

211. Walter Bentley Ball, "Postcard: The Popular Concert Series," Local History Programs File 1910, Special Collections, Sibley Music Library, Eastman School of Music, University of Rochester, Rochester, New York.

212. "Reminiscing Rochester," *Rochester Democrat and Chronicle*, 20 November 1999, sec. 2, 5.

213. "Chronological History of Convention Hall," typewritten, Vertical File, Local History Division, Rochester Public Library, Rochester. The file noted May 13, 1908, as the date of Caruso's concert.

214. "Chronological History of Convention Hall." Roosevelt gave a speech at Convention Hall on October 29, 1910.

215. "Chronological History of Convention Hall." Paderewski performed in Rochester in 1916. He also performed at the Eastman Theater on March 29, 1928, February 5, 1932, and May 21, 1939.

216. Stewart B. Sabin, *Music in Rochester: From 1909 to 1924*, The Rochester Historical Society Fund Series, ed. Edward R. Foreman, vol. 3 (Rochester: Rochester Historical Society, 1924).

217. McKelvey, 201.

218. Sabin, 15.

219. Vincent Lenti, "A History of the Eastman Theater," ed. Ruth Rosenberg-Naparsteck, *Rochester History* 49, no. 1 (January 1987), 10.

220. The *N. W. Ayer and Son's Newspaper Annual and Directory of 1910* printed the daily/weekly circulation of each paper as follows on pages 629–630: *Rochester Democrat and Chronicle*, 55,667, Sunday edition 40,649; Rochester Herald, 22,899; Rochester Post Express, 20,127; Rochester Union and Advertiser, 26,986.

221. "Play and Players: Popular Concert Series," *Rochester Herald*, 21 August 1910, 20.

222. "There is only one City in the United States Today," *Rochester Union and Advertiser*, 5 November 1910, 14.

223. "Play and Players: Popular Concert Series," 20.

224. "In Local Playhouses: Philharmonic Orchestra," *Rochester Union and Advertiser*, 19 November 1910, 13.

225. "In Local Playhouses: Philharmonic Orchestra," 13.

226. "Advertisements," *Rochester Herald*, 4 December 1910, 22. Tickets were available for $.75, $1.00, $1.50, $2.00, and $2.50 and could be purchased at Gibbons and Stone's or at 105 Beckley Building.

227. "Advertisements," *Rochester Democrat and Chronicle*, 6 December 1910, 18.

228. "Music and Drama: Theater Notes," *Rochester Post Express*, 1 December 1910, 5.

229. "Music and the Drama: Theater Notes," *Rochester Post Express*, 7 December 1910, 5.

230. "Philharmonic Orchestra," *Rochester Union and Advertiser*, 3 December 1910, 11.

231. "Notable Concert," *Rochester Herald*, 4 December 1910, 24.

232. "Notable Concert," 24.

233. "In Musical Circles," *Rochester Post Express*, 19 November 1910, 5.

234. In Musical Circles," *Rochester Post Express*, 3 December 1910, 5.

235. "Coldest Day in Season," *Rochester Union and Advertiser*, 10 December 1910, 8.

236 "Music and the Drama: Convention Hall," *Rochester Post Express*, 9 December 1910, 11.

237. "Music and the Drama: Convention Hall," 11.

238. "Mahler and the Philharmonic," *Rochester Herald*, 9 December 1910, 11.

239. "Amusements: Convention Hall," *Rochester Democrat and Chronicle*, 9 December 1910, 20.

240. "In Local Playhouses: Convention Hall," *Rochester Union and Advertiser*, 9 December 1910, 16.

241. "In Local Playhouses: Convention Hall," 16.

242. "Music and the Drama: Convention Hall," 11.

243. "Music and the Drama: Convention Hall," 11.

244. "Mahler and the Philharmonic," *Rochester Herald*, 11.

245. "In Local Playhouses: Convention Hall," 16.

246. "Mahler and the Philharmonic," *Rochester Herald*, 11.

247. "Music and the Drama: Convention Hall," 11.

248. "Music and the Drama: Convention Hall," 11.

249. "Mahler and the Philharmonic," *Rochester Herald*, 11.

250. "Mahler and the Philharmonic," *Rochester Herald*, 11.

251. "Music and the Drama: Convention Hall," 11.

252. "Music and the Drama: Convention Hall," 11.

253. "Mahler and the Philharmonic," *Rochester Herald*, 11.

254. "Amusements: Convention Hall," 20.

255. "Music and the Drama: Convention Hall," 11.

256. "Mahler and the Philharmonic," *Rochester Herald*, 11.

257. "Amusements: Convention Hall," 20.

258. "Music and the Drama: Convention Hall," 11.

259. "Music and the Drama: Convention Hall," 11.

260. "Music and the Drama: Convention Hall," 11.

261. "Amusements: Convention Hall," 20.

262. "Mahler and the Philharmonic," *Rochester Herald*, 11.

263. "Amusements: Convention Hall," 20.

264. "Mahler and the Philharmonic," *Rochester Herald*, 11.

265. "Music and the Drama: Convention Hall," 11.

266. "Mahler and the Philharmonic," *Rochester Herald*, 11.

267. "Amusements: Convention Hall," 20.

268. "Amusements: Convention Hall," 20.

269. "Music and the Drama: Convention Hall," 11.

270. "Storm Wraps Syracuse in a Blanket of Snow," *Syracuse Post-Standard*, 10 December 1910, 6.

271. Reid A. Hoey, "Syracuse," in *Encyclopedia Americana* (Danbury, CT: Grolier, 1988), 187.

272. "Miss A. K. King, Musician, Dies at Age of 74," *Syracuse Journal*, January 14, 1935, 4. Leschetizky lived from 1830 to 1915. King most likely studied piano with him in Vienna where he retired from performing and developed his own school of piano.

273. "Kathleen King," Vertical File, Onondaga Historical Association, Syracuse, New York.

274. "Miss A. K. King, Musician, Dies at Age of 74," sec. 4, 4.

275. "Three Great Concerts," *Syracuse Herald*, 5 December 1910, 8.

276. "Amusements," *Syracuse Herald*, 4 December 1910, sec. 4, 6.

277. The *N. W. Ayer and Son's Newspaper Annual and Directory of 1910* printed the daily/weekly circulation of each paper as follows on pages 635–636: *Syracuse Herald*, 32,918, Sunday edition 41,952; *Syracuse Journal*, 28,474; *Syracuse Post-Standard*, 39,517.

278. "Next Week in the Theaters: Gustav Mahler," *Syracuse Post-Standard*, 3 December 1910, 11.

279. "The Theaters," *Syracuse Herald*, 8 December 1910, 14.

280. "Next Week in the Theaters," *The Syracuse Journal*, 3 December 1910, 11.

281. "Coming to Theaters," *The Syracuse Journal*, 5 December 1910, 8.

282. "Opera Made to Look Like Three-Ring Circus: Remarkable in Music," *Syracuse Journal*, 8 December 1910, 8.

283. "Mahler is a Wonder," *Syracuse Journal*, 7 December 1910, 8.

284. "The Theaters," 14.

285. "Wieting-The New York Philharmonic Orchestra," *The Syracuse Herald*, 4 December 1910, sec. 4, 6.

286. "Three Great Concerts," 8.

287. "Wieting-The New York Philharmonic Orchestra," sec. 4, 6.

288. "Coming to the Theaters," *The Syracuse Journal*, 2 December 1910, 8.

289. "Amusements," *Syracuse Herald*, 4 December 1910, sec. 4, 6. Tickets were available for $.75, $1.00, $1.50, $2.00, and $2.50.

290. *Wieting Programs 1910–1911*, Onondaga Historical Association, Syracuse, New York. Tickets were available for $.50, $.75, $1.00, $1.50, and $2.00.

291. Created as an opera in three acts by Michael William Balfe, this work was adapted after a ballet named *The Gipsy*. Alfred Bunn wrote the text.

292. "Amusements," *Syracuse Herald*, 4 December 1910, sec. 4, 6.

293. "Music," *Syracuse Journal*, 5 December 1910, 8.

294. "Grand Concert of the New York Philharmonics," *Syracuse Herald*, 10 December 1910, 7.

295. "Grand Concert of the New York Philharmonics," 7.

296. "Grand Concert of the New York Philharmonics," 7.

297. "When the Curtain Rises," *Syracuse Post-Standard*, 10 December 1910, 9.

298. "Grand Concert of the New York Philharmonics," 7.

299. "Grand Concert of the New York Philharmonics," 7.

300. "Music," *Syracuse Journal*, 10 December 1910, 8.

301. *Famous Visitors to Syracuse: 1825 to April 1990*, 3 vols. Local History/Special Collections, Onondaga County Public Library, Syracuse, New York, 1991.

302. *Famous Visitors to Syracuse: 1825 to April 1990*, vol. 3, 385.

303. "Grand Concert of the New York Philharmonics," 7.

304. "When the Curtain Rises," 9.

305. "When the Curtain Rises," 9.

306. *Wieting Programs 1910–1911*.

307. "Grand Concert of the New York Philharmonics," 7.

308. "Grand Concert of the New York Philharmonics," 7.

309. "Grand Concert of the New York Philharmonics," 7.

310. "Grand Concert of the New York Philharmonics," 7.

311. "Grand Concert of the New York Philharmonics," 7.

312. "Grand Concert of the New York Philharmonics," 7.

313. Gustav Mahler, *Letters to his Wife*, ed. Henry-Louis de La Grange and Günther Weiss, in collaboration with Knud Martner, trans. Antony Beaumont, 2d ed. (Ithaca, NY: Cornell University Press, 2004), 393.

314. "The Stage: Philharmonic Orchestra Here," *Utica Observer*, 10 December 1910, 12.

315. David M. Ellis, James A Frost, Harold C. Syrett, and Harry J. Carman, *A History of New York State* (Ithaca, NY: Cornell University Press, 1967), 529.

316. Ellis et al., 529.

317. Damrosch appeared in Utica on Easter Monday, 1908; January 15, 1910; and January 16, 1911. For further information refer to the *Local Area Scrapbooks*, Oneida County Historical Association, Utica, New York.

318. The Midwinter Music Festival took place February 12 and 13, 1912, and January 5 and 6, 1914. For further information refer to the *Local Area Scrapbooks*, Oneida County Historical Association, Utica, New York.

319. The conservatory formed in 1889.

320. Louis Lombard first led this orchestra. Several years later the group dissolved and was not connected with the current Utica Symphony Orchestra that formed in 1933.

321. John J. Walsh, *Vignettes of Old Utica* (Utica: Utica Public Library, 1982), 254.

322. The *N. W. Ayer and Son's Newspaper Annual and Directory of 1910* printed the daily/weekly circulation of each paper as follows on page 638: *Utica Herald Dispatch*, 19,691; *Utica Observer*, 17,855, weekly edition 8,000; Utica Daily Press, 15,117, Tuesday and Friday edition 6,309; *Utica Sunday Tribune*, 9,073.

323. *1907 Utica City Directory* (Utica: Utica Directory Publishing), 64.

324. H. E. Whittemore, "Many a Start First Thrilled to Applause on Stages Here," *Utica Observer-Dispatch*, 25 May 1958, sec. 3, 12.

325. "Tips on Things Theatrical," *Utica Daily Press*, 3 December 1910, 15.

326. "The Stage: Is a Great Orchestra," *Utica Observer*, 8 December 1910, 6.

327. "New York Philharmonic Orchestra," *Utica Daily Press*, 8 December 1910, 6.

328. "The Philharmonic Orchestra," *Utica Sunday Times*, 4 December 1910, 13.

329. "The Stage: Is a Great Orchestra," 6.

330. "The Stage: Mahler, The Great Conductor," *Utica Observer*, 9 December 1910, 6.

331. "The Stage: Philharmonic Orchestra Here," *Utica Observer*, 10 December 1910, 12.

332. "Everybody Says That It's Cold," *Utica Observer*, 12 December 1910, sec. 2, 7.

333. "Everybody Says That It's Cold," sec. 2, 7.

334. "The Stage: Philharmonic Orchestra Here," 12.

335. "A Delight to Music Lovers," *Utica Daily Press*, 12 December 1910, 15.

336. "Mahler and the Philharmonic," *Utica Sunday Tribune*, 11 December 1910, 2.

337. "Mahler and the Philharmonic." According to Walsh's *Vignettes of Old Utica*, 363, the main floor offered 420 seats, the balcony featured 425 seats, and the gallery provided 75 seats and standing room for as many more.

338. "Mahler and the Philharmonic," *Utica Sunday Tribune*, 2.

339. "Mahler and the Philharmonic," *Utica Sunday Tribune*, 2.

340. "A Delight to Music Lovers," 15.

341. "A Delight to Music Lovers," 15.

342. "Mahler and the Philharmonic," *Utica Sunday Tribune*, 2.

343. "The Stage: The Philharmonic Orchestra," *Utica Observer*, 12 December 1910, 7.

344. "The Stage: The Philharmonic Orchestra," 7.

345. "A Delight to Music Lovers," 15.

346. "Mahler and the Philharmonic," *Utica Sunday Tribune*, 2.

347. "Mahler and the Philharmonic," *Utica Sunday Tribune*, 2.

348. "The Stage: The Philharmonic Orchestra," 7.

349. "Mahler and the Philharmonic," *Utica Sunday Tribune*, 2.

350. "The Stage: The Philharmonic Orchestra," 7.

351. "The Stage: The Philharmonic Orchestra," 7.

352. "A Delight to Music Lovers," 15.

353. "Mahler and the Philharmonic," *Utica Sunday Tribune*, 2.

354. "A Delight to Music Lovers," 15.

355. "A Delight to Music Lovers," 15.

356. *Carnegie Hall: Collection of Ledgers and Cash Book Covering the Period 1891–1925*, vol. 6, 175, Fine Arts Division of the New York Public Library.

357. [Henry T. Finck], "Music and Drama," *New York Post*, 9 December 1910, 9.

358. [Henry T. Finck], "Music and Drama," 9.

359. [Henry T. Finck], "Music and Drama," *New York Post*, 14 December 1910, 9. This program included the *King Stephen* Overture, the *Coriolan* Overture, op. 62, Overture No. 3 to *Leonore*, op. 72, Symphony No. 6, op. 68, and the Piano Concerto No. 5, op. 73, with Franz Xaver Scharwenka as the soloist.

~

CHAPTER SIX

Tours to Philadelphia and Washington, D.C., 1910–1911

In addition to the New England and the Great Lakes tour, the New York Philharmonic made a number of visits to Philadelphia and Washington, D.C. Mahler conducted three concerts in Philadelphia at the Academy of Music between 1910 and 1911, beginning on Monday, January 17, 1910. This event marked the Philharmonic's first concert outside Greater New York in its sixty-eight years of existence. Two months later the orchestra returned to Philadelphia, and on Monday, March 14, 1910, presented a second concert which featured violinist Fritz Kreisler.[1]

For the following 1910–1911 season the Philharmonic organized three brief tours south of New York beginning with an afternoon concert in Philadelphia on January 23, 1911, followed by a concert at the New National Theatre in Washington, D.C., on January 24, 1911. One month later the Philharmonic planned to perform at Alexander's Hall in Princeton, New Jersey, on February 27, and in Washington, D.C., on February 28. The orchestra offered a final set of concerts on March 27 in Princeton and on March 28, in Washington, D.C. Of these three planned journeys Mahler appeared only on the first tour in January 1911. Johanna Gadski joined the Philharmonic for the January concert in Philadelphia, and afterward, she accompanied the ensemble to Washington, D.C., for the performance on the following afternoon. When Mahler fell deathly ill on February 22, 1911, newspaper articles in Princeton and Washington, D.C., continued to promote him as director of the Philharmonic, and concertgoers expected he would conduct the remaining concerts. Unfortunately, he never conducted again.

The Philadelphia Concert on Monday, January 17, 1910

Mahler first visited Philadelphia as conductor of the New York Metropolitan Opera on February 18, 1908, when he conducted Mozart's *Don Giovanni*. The next day a critic from the *Philadelphia Inquirer* noted the performance "had its good points and was excellent and enjoyable in some important respects," but still left "a good deal to be desired."[2] In the years to follow, however, critics and citizens of Philadelphia overwhelmingly respected and praised Mahler as a conductor and composer. After his death, and under the direction of Leopold Stokowski, the Philadelphia Orchestra gave the American premiere of Mahler's Symphony No. 8 in E-Flat on March 2, 1916.[3] During this period Mahler was still viewed as a "fairly exotic figure,"[4] and this significant concert marked an event in the music history of Philadelphia to which no previous event was comparable.[5] The enthusiasm sparked nine performances of the symphony in Philadelphia during the season, and then the ensemble traveled to New York and presented the work at the Metropolitan Opera House on Sunday, April 9, 1916.

Musical resources such as Herbert Kupferberg's *Those Fabulous Philadelphians* thoroughly recounted this event and other significant musical occasions in Philadelphia. Although Kupferberg noted the dates that Richard Strauss, Edward MacDowell, and Arthur Rubinstein performed in Philadelphia, he failed to document any of Mahler's visits.[6] Fortunately, newspapers preserved the details of these concerts in the advertisements, promotions, and reviews of the *Philadelphia Evening Bulletin*, *Philadelphia Evening Item*, *Philadelphia Inquirer*, *Philadelphia Public Ledger*, *Philadelphia Press*, and the *Philadelphia Record*.[7]

Musical Activities

At the turn of the twentieth century Philadelphia offered a wealth of musical activities during the winter, including annual concerts featuring the Boston Symphony Orchestra and the New York Symphony Orchestra. Throughout the 1909–1910 season the Boston Symphony Orchestra offered five concerts in Philadelphia,[8] and one week before the New York Philharmonic's debut the Boston orchestra presented an outstanding concert on Monday evening, January 10, 1910.[9] In its tenth season, the Philadelphia Orchestra under the direction of Carl Pohlig usually offered concerts on Friday and Saturday evenings at the Academy of Music. Individual tickets for the Philadelphia Orchestra concerts ranged between $.25 and $.75.

The week of the Philharmonic concert offered several cultural events, including a Philadelphia Orchestra concert on Friday afternoon, January 14, and on Saturday evening, January 15. On the following day at the Academy, Toscanini conducted Wagner's *Tristan und Isolde* with the Metropolitan Opera Company with world-renowned soprano Johanna Gadski in the role of Isolde. Another musical event filled Wednesday evening, January 19, as the Philadelphia Orchestra offered its "seventh popular concert" with local soloist soprano Marie Zeckwer.[10]

Many of these events took place at Philadelphia's Academy of Music. Still in use today as a music facility, the Academy, built in 1857, was originally designed to be an opera house. Although the hall easily accommodates almost three thousand listeners, it still provides an intimate and warm interior. Throughout the past century the facility experienced numerous improvements, and joined the list of National Historical Landmarks.[11]

Advertisements for the Philharmonic's first concert began appearing in local newspapers on Sunday, January 2, 1910, and announced that the program would include Beethoven's Symphony No. 5 in C Minor, Op. 67, Smetana's Overture to *The Bartered Bride*, Richard Strauss' *Till Eulenspiegels lustige Streiche*, and Wagner's Prelude to *Die Meistersinger von Nürnberg*.[12] Tickets for the Philharmonic concert were made available on January 16, 1910, at Heppe's Piano Room and ranged in priced from fifty cents to two dollars.[13]

Even though subsequent Philharmonic concerts in Philadelphia included a soloist, Mahler decided not to program one for its debut. As reported in four newspapers, the Philharmonic also selected familiar works in order "to permit the playing ability of the Philharmonic to be judged purely on its merits."[14] Critics prepared to evaluate the Philharmonic on two main points: first, Mahler's interpretation of the music and second, the orchestra's sound, including tone quality, technical ability, and finish.[15]

The Philharmonic hoped the Philadelphia concert would spark additional trips, because the ninety-mile journey could easily be completed in one day. On January 17, 1910, the Philharmonic arrived in the late morning on a "special train" from New York, and at the conclusion of the concert they immediately returned home.[16] Even before their first performance in Philadelphia, local newspaper writers anticipated future concerts, as the *Philadelphia Press* stated: "It is not unlikely that occasional pilgrimages from Manhattan to Philadelphia will grow out of this first visit which has been delayed for the larger part of the sixty-eight years of the Philharmonic's existence."[17]

Reviews of the First Concert in Philadelphia

Even though local newspapers promoted the event and local critics anticipated the concert would sell out, a number of seats remained vacant in the

Academy of Music.[18] Critics cited three major reasons for the poor attendance. First of all, the reviewer for the *Philadelphia Record* predicted a larger audience would have patronized the concert if a distinguished soloist had appeared with the orchestra.[19] Secondly, the writer for the *Philadelphia Inquirer* noted that the "paucity of the attendance was not surprising" based on the number of other cultural events throughout the week.[20] Finally, several critics blamed the "inclement weather" for less than a full house at the Academy.[21]

Nevertheless, the Philharmonic created a "favorable impression" and Philadelphians "found an orchestral conductor of the first rank."[22] The *Record* credited Mahler for reorganizing the orchestra and "bringing to perfection one of the best-equipped organizations in the world."[23] In addition, the writer for the *Inquirer* commended Mahler and the Philharmonic and noted the "occasion was one of the most noteworthy and enjoyable in a season which has been full of musical interest."[24]

While critics admired Mahler's achievements with the Philharmonic, they hesitated to declare the orchestra superior to their own. The writer for the *Inquirer* noticed the competency of musicians with superior training, but in essential areas such as "beauty of tone and high finish of execution," he believed the Philharmonic did not compare with "some other" unnamed orchestras.[25] Nevertheless, the *Record* reported that the audience broke into cheers for the conductor at the conclusion of the concert, whereupon Mahler returned to the stage to acknowledge the ovation.[26] In addition, the musicians were encouraged to accept a portion of the applause for a wonderful performance.

Beethoven

Mahler's rendition of Beethoven's Fifth Symphony immediately generated several critical reviews. The critic for the *Record* remarked how unusual it was for an orchestra to start with a symphony, but the "novelty of the arrangement proved attractive."[27] In a review from the *Evening Item* the writer commended Mahler for beginning the program with the Beethoven work and for giving an interpretation that "truly justified the reputation of the world-famed conductor."[28] In addition, the selection rewarded the listeners for "braving the elements" of the weather to attend the concert.[29]

Unfortunately, Mahler did not so easily impress the reporter for the *Evening Bulletin*. Overall, the critic believed Mahler's interpretation "was a bit disconcerting" to the aficionados of Beethoven and "lacked the usual graceful dignity that characterizes its rendition by the Boston and Philadelphia orchestras."[30] After disapproving of Mahler's rendition of the andante movement, the same critic complimented the trio section as "most beautifully sung," and noticed the orchestra "rose to the highest flights of musical interpretation" in the closing allegro.[31]

Mahler's rendition, however, proved to be very distinct from previous performances of Beethoven's Fifth Symphony in Philadelphia and stimulated substantial reviews. The writer for the *Inquirer* expressed both positive and negative comments regarding the performance. He admitted the work attracted the closest attention throughout the evening and was "the most striking, the most admirable and the most significant."[32] Compared with other performances, Mahler sparked new energy into the work as the same critic observed:

> What it showed was that the performance of a classic masterpiece does not need to be dull and dry and wholly impersonal for it to remain faithful to the spirit of the score. He gave one of the most highly colored and strongly accentuated renderings of this familiar music that can be recalled, and yet it contained nothing that could give legitimate offense to the most sensitive stickler for the maintenance of the classical traditions.[33]

In spite of offering a number of positive points, this same critic disapproved of the unusually fast tempo Mahler took in the first movement. Although Beethoven marked this movement allegro "con brio," the faster tempo distracted from the finale and even created a "sense of anticlimax" at the end of the symphony.[34]

Nevertheless, Mahler's rendition impressed the writer more than that of other popular conductors, and the critic remarked that Mahler "did not seek to modernize the spirit of the composition and to animate it with an emotion essentially foreign to its character."[35] Even on more recent occasions some other conductors played the piece "with a sentiment appropriate to the ballads of a Claribel or a Tosti."[36] Mahler's rendition contained none of these qualities as the critic concluded:

> Strength, sanity, virility, dignity and lucidity, a total absence of self-consciousness, and absolute freedom, from any suggestion of insincerity or affectation, such were the salient elements of as fine a performance of the C minor in all the features of truly interpretative greatness as has been heard here since Theodore Thomas laid the baton down.[37]

Upon hearing the performance, the reporter for the *Public Ledger* commended "the vigorous earnestness of the cellos, the mellow utterance of the oboes, and the spirited performance of the first violins."[38] At the conclusion of the symphony the audience expressed "enthusiastic approval" and "shouts of stentorian acclaim" rose from the galleries.[39] After Mahler and the orchestra received an ovation, the program continued with Smetana's Overture to *The Bartered Bride*.

Smetana

Critics paid much less attention to the remaining works on the program. The writer of the *Evening Bulletin* credited Mahler for introducing Smetana's Overture to America during the previous year.[40] After hearing the work, the critic of the *Inquirer* remarked on the "peculiar and pleasing accelerando" and the "joyful spirit" of this nationalist work.[41] Since Mahler was a "Bohemian" himself, the reporter of the *Evening Item* credited him for understanding the music and knowing how to bring out "the national spirit of the odd and pretty melodies."[42] Overall, listeners and critics seemed unfamiliar with the selection and even appeared unsure of where the work ended. Hence, the audience expressed only brief applause as Mahler took only a short break before leading directly into the next selection.

Strauss

Mahler unanimously impressed the critics with *Till Eulenspiegels lustige Streiche*. Writing for the *Evening Bulletin*, the critic regarded the program music as the "merriest" number heard in the Academy in a long period of time.[43] Mahler and the Philharmonic quickly won the approval of the critic for the *Evening Item*, who thought that to properly understand the composition, one must actually hear the work in a performance. He commended Mahler's conducting skills and noted, "It is possible that few conductors could as perfectly interpret the music and bring out its meaning."[44]

This selection allowed several sections of the orchestra to display their virtuosity, and they "reveled in the plangent tone coloring" that Strauss offered.[45] In particular, the writer for the *Public Ledger* applauded the inspirational playing of the percussion section as they handled the work with "dexterity and precision."[46] The same reporter noted Mahler's delight in the kettledrum line as the musicians "fell upon the bombardment of the polyphony like a freight locomotive charging furiously up a heavy grade."[47]

Wagner

The evening concluded with Wagner's Prelude to *Die Meistersinger von Nürnberg*. Writing for the *Record*, the reviewer regarded Mahler's conducting on a par with that in Bayreuth and Munich and encouraged listeners to embrace Wagner operas.[48] Rather than the usual noisy orchestration, the music appeared to change under Mahler's baton and "the orchestra was made subservient to the drama."[49] In contrast, the review in the *Evening Bulletin* regarded the performance of the Strauss work as rather tame.[50] After completing the piece, Mahler put down the baton, the crowd vigorously recalled him several times, and he bowed "his thanks for the appreciation shown."[51]

Mahler's Conducting

Not all critics ranked Mahler superior to conductors such as Max Fiedler of the Boston Symphony Orchestra or Karl Pohlig of the Philadelphia Orchestra, but they did acknowledge him as a unique conductor, and even the *Evening Item* declared Mahler "a prince among conductors."[52] Rather than the "ridiculous gymnastic devices" some conductors used, Mahler conducted primarily with his head and arms.[53]

Throughout the evening Mahler created a variety of effects through the use of acceleration and diminuendo of tempo and the "exquisite phrasing of the different notes."[54] Mahler's concern for balance with the orchestra also characterized his conducting style. The writer for the *Record* recorded that "the balance and tone of the orchestra approached perfection" and when the "full power is employed the effect is stupendous, overwhelming."[55] Moreover, the critic for the *Inquirer* realized Mahler's remarkable powers as a conductor created an exceptional occasion and made the orchestra play in a "convincing and impressive nature."[56]

Some reporters elaborated on Mahler's physical appearance and drew attention to his "intellectual face" and "quick nervous manner."[57] The writer of the *Public Ledger* created a very detailed analysis of Mahler as a conductor and summarized:

> Mahler revealed himself an extraordinarily skillful musical field general. He rejoices in paradoxes and does not hesitate to be utterly unconventional. He does not passively superintend the players; he adjures and pleads with all the fervor of the old-time camp-meeting exhorter, and is as urgent as a first-rate jockey on the homestretch. He is all fire and temperament, and his enthusiasm

is communicative and contagious. Every player last night seemed on his mettle to give the best that was in him.[58]

Beyond praising Mahler's leadership, the reviewer for the *Evening Telegraph* offered only praise for the musicians and the sound of the ensemble as he concluded:

> The playing of the orchestra was distinguished by remarkable precision and finesse. The fullness and breadth of tone in the fortissimo passages without any suggestion of coarseness; the mellowness of the brass and freedom from blatancy; the balance of the instruments; the clearness and sonority of the strings; the purity of tone and the smoothness of the wood-wind all contributed to make a favorable impression of the orchestra's excellence.[59]

Even though no critic believed Mahler and the New York Philharmonic surpassed the quality of the Boston Symphony Orchestra, they accepted, allowed, and even encouraged the orchestra to give another concert in Philadelphia. In closing remarks, the reviewer for the *Public Ledger* observed that the audience gave a "prolonged demonstration" of appreciation to the orchestra and believed the Philharmonic demonstrated "its right in the future to a cordial welcome in this city."[60] Hence, the management of the Philharmonic soon confirmed Mahler and the Philharmonic would return on Monday, March 14, 1910, for a second concert.

The Philadelphia Concert on Monday, March 14, 1910

Perhaps the management of the Philharmonic took a local critic's advice when they added the distinguished violinist Fritz Kreisler to their second concert on Monday, March 14, 1910.[61] The program for this occasion consisted of Berlioz's *Symphonie Fantastique*, Beethoven's Violin Concerto in D Major, Op. 61, with Kreisler as the soloist, and Wagner's Overture to *Tannhäuser*. The evening marked the Philharmonic's second and last concert in Philadelphia for the season and also Kreisler's final appearance in Philadelphia for the season.[62]

To draw more attention to this visit, promotions highlighted the recent success of the Berlioz work in New York and New England cities. In both the *Record* and the *Inquirer*, press releases reported that in New York the *Symphonie Fantastique* "aroused the audience to a high pitch of enthusiasm" and in a recent tour of New England, the same conditions prevailed.[63] An article in the *Press* informed readers that upon the conclusion of the Berlioz work at Carnegie Hall, patrons who were ordinarily unmoved "sprang to their feet and shouted" and gave the "greatest demonstration ever witnessed during the many hundred concerts given by the Philharmonic in the last sixty-seven years."[64]

Less than two months had passed since the Philharmonic first performed in Philadelphia, and publicity described the orchestra as rejuvenated and improved. Even Mahler believed the musicians now played much better than when they first appeared at the Academy of Music, and he expected concertgoers would long remember this upcoming concert.[65] In an attempt to elevate the Philharmonic's status in Philadelphia, another article in the *Press* noted that a number of music critics from the cities where the Philharmonic recently toured unanimously ranked the Philharmonic "as one of the first half dozen symphony orchestras of the world."[66] Advertisers used this commanding statement to increase ticket sales, but it may have also persuaded readers and critics to reconsider their opinion of Mahler and the New York Philharmonic.

On the same day as the Philharmonic's second concert, the popular Kneisel Quartet gave their third recital in a series to a large audience in Witherspoon Hall at quarter of three o'clock in the afternoon.[67] Several days earlier on Friday evening, March 11, and Saturday evening, March 12, the Philadelphia Orchestra offered the closing concert of its tenth season. Since October, the local orchestra offered eighty concerts and ended the year with a "high level of interpretative ability" as the critics praised its accomplishments.[68] Exactly one week after the Philharmonic concert the Boston Symphony Orchestra gave its final concert of the season at the Academy of Music on March 21, 1910.[69]

Reviews of the Philadelphia Concert on Monday, March 14, 1910

The Philharmonic once again performed on a Monday, and in spite of adding a world-renowned violinist to the program, attendance remained "discouragingly small."[70] The critic for the *Record* even seemed surprised the Philharmonic returned in the same season based on the attendance at the first concert.[71] Although no one documented an exact number of concertgoers, the reviewer for the *Evening Bulletin* observed only one quarter of the seats occupied in the Academy.[72] The writer for the *Inquirer* also indicated the audience "was not all it should have been in view of the music consequence of the occasion," but its size increased considerably from the previous concert.[73] Furthermore, a reporter for the *Evening Telegraph* deplored the small audience, "whose numbers disgraced Philadelphia's reputation as a center of music taste and appreciation."[74] Only one writer from the *Public Ledger* offered insight into the dismal situation when he concluded that the small audience resulted from the concert being held toward the last part of an "unusually arduous music season."[75]

Although a number of seats remained vacant, the upper tiers of the hall contained "row upon row" of eager listeners who warmly greeted the musicians.[76] Hence, even though a small audience turned out, they appeared more receptive and supportive of the orchestra than in previous months. Some critics observed this reaction, including the writer for the *Inquirer*, who noted the crowd "was intelligently appreciative and there was a great deal of well deserved applause."[77] Additional reports in the *Evening Bulletin* and *Record* stated that concertgoers expressed "sincere and intelligent enthusiasm,"[78] and likewise the praise after each selection indicated those present "represented a musical element of the city."[79]

Critics soon verified improvement in the orchestra's sound. A writer for the *Evening Item* noticed the orchestra represented not only the largest symphony orchestra in America, but also one of the greatest, due to the "persistent efforts and untiring zeal of the talented director."[80] Rather than focus on Mahler's ability as a conductor, critics described the orchestra as a group of fine musicians whom Mahler led to produce a "great beauty of tone with a sweeping breadth of conception and with illuminating precision."[81] In addition to being "beautifully balanced,"[82] the musicians also created the sense of "one grand musical instrument of unity."[83] Some critics testified to this account, including the writer for the *Evening Telegraph*, who believed the ensemble displayed "additional access of finish," more so than in the preceding January concert.[84]

Berlioz

The second concert opened with the *Symphonie Fantastique*, and Mahler anticipated that Philadelphians would be delighted with his interpretation. Karl Pohlig and the Philadelphia Orchestra had performed the piece earlier in the season, giving listeners a rendition for comparison. The Philharmonic's performance received mixed reviews, but the critic for the *Evening Bulletin* commended Mahler's performance and remarked, "It is doubtful if Berlioz's great work has ever been given a more appreciative and significant interpretation in this city."[85] The writer for the *Evening Item* observed a realistic rendering which "so impressed the listeners that a short silence ensued before the applause burst forth."[86] Other reporters praised Mahler's rendition and noticed the audience paid tribute to the conductor and offered him "the greatest enthusiasm."[87] Furthermore, his original reading of the work proved "illuminating and dramatic" and demonstrated an "absolute knowledge of the resources of an orchestra."[88] Unfortunately, the reviewer for the *Inquirer* was not convinced that the Philharmonic gave a superb performance and believed one hearing per season of the work was enough.[89] Although Mahler selected the piece to exhibit how differently the Philharmonic could play, this critic believed the "demonstration was hardly worth while" and furthermore "did not prove to be so tremendously important."[90]

Contradictory views appeared, as the critic for the *Evening Bulletin* thought Mahler interpreted the second movement with "fine insight into the poetic significance of the music."[91] The writer for the *Record*, however, considered Mahler's rendition "not half so ravishing in rhythm and expression"[92] as when Karl Pohlig conducted the piece. Favorable and detailed statements continued in the *Evening Bulletin* and described the following movements as follows:

> The waltz was given with dash and sensuousness. The pastoral episode, where the plaintive piping of a shepherd is interrupted by the approach of a thunderstorm, was a marvelous exhibition of tone painting and showed Mahler's sure instinct for delicate shading and effective orchestral contrasts. The weird march to the scaffold was read with an impressiveness that was almost terrible, and the Witches Sabbath, with its unearthly and riotous sequences of musical ingenuities, formed a climax of tremendous beauty."[93]

In the *Inquirer* the journalist reminded readers how conductors frequently applied more freedom when leading this work and how the piece even invited "all sorts of startling accentuations."[94] Mahler also produced a number of effects, which "were quite original and singularly moving."[95] The reviewer in the *Evening Bulletin* offered a very different perspective as he heard a performance "rich in imaginative warmth" and "marked by musicianly restraint."[96] Although some conductors may be tempted to indulge in "noisy clamors," Mahler avoided an "abundance of obnoxious sound" to produce a beautiful tone.[97]

Beethoven

The second selection featured violinist Fritz Kreisler in Beethoven's Violin Concerto and created "a revelation of supreme art and beauty of tone."[98] In the prior week Kreisler performed the Brahms's Violin Concerto with the Philharmonic at Carnegie Hall on March 10 and March 11, and the reviewer for the *New York Sun* remarked, "It was one of the truly eloquent readings of this concerto which this town has heard."[99]

Kreisler's performance in Philadelphia triggered glowing comments in the local newspapers. Starting with the *Evening Item*, the writer praised Kreisler's rendition as he created "intricate stirring passages" and "aroused the greatest enthusiasm."[100] Kreisler quickly won over listeners, as the *Inquirer* described the interpretation as "nobly eloquent,"[101] and the writer for the *Evening Bulletin* heard the purity and delicate warmth in his tones.[102] Kreisler executed the two cadenzas with extreme grace, and the technical difficulty "seemed almost nonexistent."[103] He created cadenzas in the first and last movement of the concerto and demonstrated his ability "in writing episodes that so perfectly dovetailed into the music mosaic."[104] Upon its completion the audience "vociferously applauded," and Kreisler returned to the stage a number of times to greet his admirers.[105]

In addition, at least one reporter acknowledged the orchestra's role in the concerto and concluded, "It would be difficult to say which was more enjoyable, Kreisler's virtuosity, or the extraordinary accompaniment given by Mahler."[106] Throughout the playing Mahler balanced Kreisler and the orchestra, creating a piece "wonderfully artistic, and a revelation of what scientific accompanying may be."[107]

Wagner

Surprisingly, this concert consisted of only three selections. As the last piece on the program, Wagner's Overture to *Tannhäuser* impressed concertgoers. However, the writer for the *Record* believed the interpretation created a "stupendous performance."[108] Despite a recent performance of the work in Philadelphia, the critic believed those who heard Mahler's rendition experienced "something they never heard before."[109] In contrast with the other performances, Mahler positioned the brass in the center of the string section and placed the bass viols forward and divided into two sections.[110]

In retrospect, the writer for the *Record* probably formed the best analysis of Mahler as an interpreter of music. He acknowledged Philadelphia's own Karl Pohlig as an energetic conductor full of "temperament and fire," which concertgoers grew to accept as normal.[111] Even though Mahler's actions were less physical than Pohlig's, they might have appeared cold to some concertgoers; yet even using a more reserved style, Mahler still produced an outstanding performance.

The Philadelphia Concert on Monday, January 23, 1911

The following season the Philharmonic again planned to appear in Philadelphia. Rather than schedule single concerts in Philadelphia for the

1910–1911 season, management grouped concerts in Philadelphia with those in Washington, D.C. Although the orchestra would appear at the Academy of Music on Mondays, they scheduled the performances for three o'clock in the afternoon rather than later in the evening. After each concert in Philadelphia, the orchestra traveled south and gave the same program in Washington, D.C., on the following afternoon at four thirty in the afternoon in the New National Theatre.

The Philharmonic planned their first concert of this season in Philadelphia for Monday, January 23, 1911. This week of January offered many cultural events, and several hours after the Philharmonic concert, the Philadelphia-Chicago Opera Company presented Puccini's *The Girl of the Golden West*. On Wednesday afternoon violinist Mischa Elman offered a recital, and Bizet's *Carmen* appeared in the evening at Philadelphia's Metropolitan Opera House. A busy week continued as the Philadelphia Operatic Society performed Gounod's *Faust* on Thursday night, and the Philadelphia Orchestra presented a concert on Friday afternoon. The weekend began with Puccini's *La Bohème* on Friday evening, followed on Saturday night with Verdi's *Il Trovatore* and another opportunity to hear the Philadelphia Orchestra.

With Loudon Charlton as the new manager for the Philharmonic, a new approach appeared in the publicity for this season. Rather than sell tickets for one concert at a time, the Philharmonic promoted the upcoming three concerts in Philadelphia, as a series and offered a soloist with each program. In addition, local articles highlighted the accomplishments of Johanna Gadski, who planned to perform as a soloist with the orchestra. Advertisements emphasized the importance of Gadski's appearance and her name appeared as large as the Philharmonic's in the announcements. This upcoming concert featured strictly Wagnerian music and included the Overture to *Rienzi*, the Overture to *Der Fliegende Holländer*, the Prelude to *Lohengrin*, and the Overture to *Tannhäuser*. The works highlighted Gadski in Elizabeth's arias from *Tannhäuser* and Elsa's Dream from *Lohengrin*. Mahler continued the program with *Siegfried Idyll*, the Prelude and Liebestod from *Tristan und Isolde*, and finished with the Prelude to *Die Meistersinger von Nürnberg*. Approximately one week before the concert, on January 16, 1911, Heppe's Piano Rooms sold tickets to the public ranging from $.50 to $2.00.[112]

Rather than focus on Mahler in the promotions, most articles discussed Gadski's accomplishments and even proclaimed her the "supreme artist in Wagnerian roles."[113] In a recent New York recital the audience enthusiastically applauded the prima donna, and in response she repeated the "Cry of the Valkyries" four times.[114] Moreover, before the concert concluded, critics and concertgoers gave her unstinting approval.

A subsequent article portrayed Gadski and Mahler as two foremost experts of Wagnerian music in America.[115] In addition to being a composer, Mahler was regarded as a "daring innovator," and his approach to Wagner's music even "raised violent dispute."[116] Furthermore, Mahler presented a number of patriotic characteristics in his music and, the article concluded, "He has represented his country in all her aspects, Austria gay, Austria oppressed, Austria the tyrant, and again the sentimental nervous slave."[117]

Reviews of the Philadelphia Concert
on Monday, January 23, 1911

Even with Gadski as a featured soloist on Monday afternoon, January 23, 1911, management still struggled to sell tickets, and even with the upper parts full, the audience on the first floor remained small.[118] The reporter for the *Public Ledger*, however, observed a moderately sized audience that was "a great deal larger" than the audience from the previous season.[119] With no evidence of bad weather, some potential concertgoers may have foregone the event and decided to attend Puccini's *The Girl of the Golden West* later in the evening. On the morning of January 24, 1911, reviews of the opera extended significantly longer than those for the Philharmonic concert. In addition, the Philharmonic did not have the same history and following in Philadelphia as the Boston Symphony Orchestra, and two weeks before when the Boston ensemble gave its fourth concert of the season at Philadelphia's Academy of Music on January 9, 1911, they managed to pack the hall from "pit to dome."[120]

Most of the articles critiquing the Philharmonic's performance provided a general review of the orchestra and focused on Gadski's performance. Hearing selections by only one composer, the writer for the *Inquirer* concluded there was perhaps too much Wagner for one afternoon.[121] Nevertheless, the audience seemed to disagree with this critic, as they heartily applauded after each number from the beginning to the end of the concert.[122] Writing for the *Evening Bulletin*, the reviewer observed only a "fair size audience" at the Academy and believed an all-Wagnerian concert was of "unusual interest."[123] The headline in the *Press* proclaimed, "Great Wagner Concert Given," and the writer noted concertgoers fully appreciated this exceptional event and the opportunity to hear the masterpieces of Wagner.[124] Furthermore, the reviewer for the *Evening Item* predicted this rare event offered perhaps the last time for an American audience to witness Mahler before he returned to Europe to lead a German orchestra.[125]

As in previous Philharmonic concerts in Philadelphia, critics continued to offer mixed reviews. In the *Inquirer* the writer observed that "the orchestra itself is nothing extraordinary" and "not so good in some important respects as our own."[126] The reporter, however, acknowledged Mahler as an "exceptionally magnetic and masterful conductor" who offered a supreme interpretation of Wagner's music and concurred that Mahler's reading of the music was "exceedingly luminous."[127] The critic for the *Public Ledger* applauded the orchestra and noticed a measurable improvement in their playing as the musicians produced "a sweet, pure tone, free from rasping and stridence," which displayed "a refined distilment of last year's product."[128]

Based on Mahler's interpretation of the music, the reporter for the *Evening Bulletin* believed hardly anyone would argue he earned the distinction as a superior conductor of Wagner's music. In addition, Mahler directed the musicians in a manner that made the music new and gave it meaning "without over-emphasis on any part, but never slighting or missing a desired effect."[129] Mahler's traits as a great maestro also appeared in the *Evening Item* when the critic praised Mahler's rare gift as "a model for all aspirants to the baton to study from[sic]."[130]

Regarding the musicians, the writer for the *Press* commended the brass section for their fabulous playing in *Tannhäuser* and during the Prelude to *Die Meistersinger von Nürnberg*. The string section excelled during the *Lohengrin* portions, and the woodwinds were superb during the *Siegfried Idyll*. Moreover, the double basses demonstrated their excellence with their "harmonious effects" throughout the afternoon.[131]

Johanna Gadski

Johanna Gadski entered the stage with a "brilliant gown of cerise chiffon, trimmed with a band of white lace, edges in sable and a very striking turban with handsome cerise plumes."[132] Her singing quickly captivated the audience, and the critic for the *Public Ledger* reported, "Madame Gadski does not know how to be anything but a great artist, and she was at her very best yesterday afternoon."[133]

As she began singing, the writer for the *Inquirer* noted her voice sounded somewhat "clouded," but as she continued, it quickly cleared up, and the sound soon became warm and "musically beautiful."[134] Gadski demonstrated her vocal range and versatility as she sang Elsa's Dream and the Liebestod. The reviewer for the *Press* regarded Gadski as an "uncrowned empress of the Wagnerian music-drama" as she quickly gained the audience's attention, and they fell immediately silent.[135] Throughout her portion of the concert,

Gadski received many recalls and at the end was presented with a bouquet of white orchids and calla lilies.[136]

Her interpretation of the Liebestod offered the climax of her portion of the program. In a review in the *Evening Item* the diva "infused all the tender agony of bereaved love, as only so finished an artist could, and aroused the audience to unbounded enthusiasm."[137] After this section, Gadski received six recalls and became the highlight of the Philharmonic's third concert in Philadelphia.

The Washington, D.C., Concert on Tuesday, January 24, 1911

After completing the performance in Philadelphia, the orchestra repeated the concert in Washington, D.C., at the New National Theatre on Tuesday afternoon, January 24, 1911. As early as December 4, 1910, an article in the *Washington Post* announced the Philharmonic series and advertised the concerts as "Three Tuesday Afternoons" on January 24, February 28, and March 28, at half past four o'clock.[138] Tickets for the series could be purchased at T. Arthur Smith's and ranged in price from two dollars to six dollars.[139] The week before the concert individual tickets were made available to the general public and ranged from $.75 to $2.50.[140] Throughout the month of January additional news of the upcoming performance appeared in the *Washington Evening Star*, *Washington Herald*, *Washington Post*, *Washington Sunday Star*, *Washington Times*, and the *Washington World*.[141]

Located only three blocks from the White House on Pennsylvania Avenue, the National Theatre quickly gained the nickname "The Theatre of Presidents," since from its beginning every president has attended performances in the hall. Although it first opened in 1835, fire had damaged and even destroyed the building several times during the nineteenth century. Hence, when the theater reopened in 1885, many writers referred to the hall as the New National Theatre. At the turn of the twentieth century, several touring ensembles made annual appearances at the theater, and during January 1911, three major orchestras performed there. On Tuesday, January 10, 1911, the Boston Symphony Orchestra filled the National Theatre to its capacity and offered its third concert of the season.[142] Only a few days after the New York Philharmonic concert Walter Damrosch and the New York Symphony Orchestra gave an evening concert at the National Theatre on Sunday, January 29, 1911. In comparison, tickets to attend the Philharmonic concert were not any more expensive than those for the New York Symphony Orchestra, which ranged from one dollar to two dollars.[143]

In addition to these events, the local Washington Symphony Orchestra presented its third afternoon concert of the season on January 17, 1910.[144] Finally, on January 23, 1911, one day before the Philharmonic concert, the famous German contralto Ernestine Schumann-Heink gave her only Washington recital of the season at the Columbia Theater.

Similar to the concert in Philadelphia, publicity in Washington newspapers highlighted Gadski as the primary attraction. Throughout the advertisements Gadski's name appeared in print as large as the Philharmonic's name, and in subsequent ads Mahler's name showed up in fine print. Some newspapers even printed Gadski's name first and announced a Wagner recital with the New York Philharmonic Society accompanying her.[145]

As in Philadelphia, several articles described Mahler and Gadski as "two of the greatest living interpreters of Wagner" and alerted readers that the event marked the first appearance of the New York Philharmonic in Washington, D.C.[146] Publicity in the *Washington Post* regarded the approaching concert as "one of the most important musical events of the season,"[147] and a subsequent article noted the performance as another musical treat available to music lovers in Washington.[148]

Although Mahler had never conducted in Washington, readers immediately recognized Gadski's name as one of the leading singers of Wagner's music. Two years prior to this concert Gadski had performed in Washington and concertgoers praised her talent.

Reviews of the Washington, D.C., Concert on Tuesday, January 24, 1911

In Washington's National Theatre at four thirty in the afternoon Mahler and the New York Philharmonic repeated the same program they gave in Philadelphia. The concert coincidentally fell on the same day as the second state reception of the winter where the justices of the Supreme Court were the guests of honor in the evening at the White House.[149] Compared with the audience in Philadelphia, concertgoers in Washington, D.C., represented a more diverse group and filled the hall to capacity. In addition to the many young women that represented the schools of Washington, a number of distinguished international delegates occupied many seats. First Lady Helen Taft appeared in the audience and occupied a box that also included her daughter Helen and several acquaintances.[150] The Washington audience also featured a number of international officials including the Minister of the German Ambassador Count Johann-Heinric von Bernstorff,[151] the Netherlands

Minister Jonkheer John Loudon,[152] and the Secretary of the Interior Richard A. Ballinger.[153] Society writers quickly recorded the list of dignitaries at the concert, and a journalist for the *Washington World* even identified the following:

> Other boxes were occupied by the German Ambassador and Countess von Bernstorff and the latter's sister: Countess Luise-Alexandra von Bernstorff and Count Pourtales; the Turkish Ambassador Zia Youssouf Pacha, and his son and daughter-in-law, the First Secretary Mme. Zia, and the latter's sister, Miss Cary, and the Ambassador's daughter; Mrs. James McMillan, who had with her daughter, Lady Harrington, and her granddaughter Mrs. Preston Gibson; Mrs. C. A. Williams, whose guests were the Secretary of the Interior and Mrs. Ballinger, Mrs. R. R. Hitt, and Mrs. E. H. G. Slater; Mrs. Calderon Carlisle, who had the Countess de Buisseret, wife of the Belgian Minister, Mrs. Mandeville Carlisle, and Miss Mary Carlisle with her and Mr. and Mrs. Hugh Legare, with Mr. and Mrs. Alexander Legare. Others in the audience were Mrs. Clarence Moore and Miss Frances Moore, Mrs. Audenried, Mrs. Foraker, Mrs. Stilson Hutchins, Mrs. William Barret Ridgely, the Netherlands Minister and Mme. Loudon, and Miss Lee.[154]

A writer for the *Post* declared "Mrs. Taft Heads Throng of Society at Concert" as the title for his article. In addition to this list of socialites, the record in the *Post* concentrated on American concertgoers.[155]

The writer for the *Washington Times* quickly declared the concert an "unqualified success" and commended the conductor for a splendid performance.[156] When the critics wrote their reviews, however, some specifically focused on Gadski's performance in the headline as they wrote "Mme. Gadski Wins Honors at Concert"[157] and "Gadski Recital."[158] Only one reviewer specifically named the Philharmonic in the headline "Debut of Philharmonic."[159] Other writers designed more generic titles such as "Music and Musicians"[160] and "In the Social World,"[161] but not one article included Mahler's name in the title.

Even though some critics may have considered the program too narrow in scope, the writer for the *Post* noted the audience found pleasure in Gadski's selections.[162] Mahler and Gadski met the expectations of the audience, and the concert created a moment that lingered in the memory of concertgoers.

Most reviews addressed Mahler's capacity as a conductor and Gadski's technique as a singer, while only a few reviews mentioned specific works. The critic for the *Evening Star* remarked on the "marvelous orchestration" of the Overture to *Der Fliegende Holländer* and the "wealth of expressive shading and beauty" in the Prelude to *Lohengrin*.[163] As the program continued a great volume of "power broke forth" in the Overture to *Tannhäuser*, and "the orchestra fairly covered itself with Wagnerian glory."[164] In the subsequent works of *Siegfried Idyll*, *Tristan und Isolde*, and the Prelude to *Die Meistersinger von Nürnberg*, the orchestra "won its way into the favor of lovers of the great German composer's music."[165] Throughout these selections the ensemble demonstrated "marvelous clarity" that added to the "high honors" the orchestra won in its first appearance in Washington.[166]

Compared with other touring orchestras, the Philharmonic received mixed reviews. The critic of the *Post* preferred the homogeneity of the Boston Symphony Orchestra and the Philadelphia Orchestra to the New York Philharmonic and observed that "greater precision in attack" would have added to the beauty of *Der Fliegende Holländer* and *Lohengrin* selections.[167] Writing for the *Times*, J. R. Hildebrand noted that in the *Lohengrin* selection, Mahler "assembled a string choir of marked proficiency" similar in skill to the Boston Symphony Orchestra.

Mahler's Conducting

Overall, Mahler received more admiration from critics in Washington, D.C., than from those in Philadelphia. In the *Times*, Hildebrand commended Mahler for not creating a new interpretation of Wagner's music and for preserving his works with dignity, force, and appreciation.[168] Mahler's conducting style was marked with a "combination of imagination and keen intelligence for orchestral effects."[169] The critic for the *Post* also noted the "distinction and charm" of Mahler's beat, which he made prominent in the *Tannhäuser* and *Siegfried Idyll* selections.[170]

Gadski's Singing

Critics marveled at Gadski's voice and offered only positive remarks. As the highlight of the afternoon, her voice was "crystal clear, effortless, unembellished, and powerful" throughout the performance.[171] A number of listeners judged Gadski's composure and the resonance of her upper register as far better and more resilient than another great soprano recently heard in Washington.[172] Gadski's rendition of the Liebestod from *Tristan und Isolde* most impressed listeners. In this selection her "marvelous combination of power and sweetness" and strong voice quality "was marked when she vied with the crashing tonal effect of brass and drums behind her."[173] After each piece, the thunderous applause drew Gadski back to the stage where she acknowledged the audience.[174]

Based on a very successful concert, music enthusiasts awaited the second performance of the Philharmonic on Tuesday, February 28, at the National Theatre. Even on the day after the first concert a review announced that Mahler would perform his popular arrangement of the Bach Suite when he returned.[175]

Subsequent Concerts Planned for Princeton and Washington, D.C.

When Mahler fell ill in February 1911, he refrained from conducting any more concerts after February 21, but the newspapers in Princeton, New Jersey, and Washington, D.C., failed to report on his condition. Several days prior to the concerts planned for Monday, February 27, in Princeton, and Tuesday, February 28, in Washington, D.C., promotional articles still anticipated Mahler's arrival and the opportunity to hear the "musical sensation of the New York season," namely Mahler's arrangement of the Bach Suite.[176] Moreover, after Mahler failed to conduct the concert in Princeton, media in Washington, D.C., never reported the incident, and still encouraged readers to purchase tickets.[177]

Although Loudon Charlton and the Philharmonic's management were well aware of Mahler's critical condition, they still publicized that Mahler would lead these concerts. Management might have implemented this tactic to convince readers to attend the concerts and to ensure that concertgoers who purchased series tickets would not be disappointed. Furthermore, management probably already paid for the publicity in local media to run in a specific section of each newspaper for the week preceding the concert. Any further advertisement changes also may have incurred additional cost. Finally, on the day of the concert in Washington, D.C., a brief article in the *Times* alerted readers that due to Mahler's illness Theodore Spiering would conduct the concert.[178]

Many concertgoers became aware of Mahler's absence after they arrived at the theater and opened their program, which contained a slip of paper announcing his sudden illness. The original program presented the same works that Mahler and the Philharmonic recently performed on their tour to Springfield, Massachusetts, and Hartford, Connecticut, on February 15 and 16. Thus, in both Princeton and Washington, D.C., the orchestra still performed Beethoven's Symphony No. 6 in F Major, op. 68, Weingartner's arrangement of *Invitation to the Dance* by Weber, and *Les Préludes* by Liszt, but rather than keeping Mahler's arrangement of the Bach Suite, pianist Ernest Hutcheson played MacDowell's Concerto in D Minor.[179] During this period

Hutcheson served as head of the piano department at the Peabody Conservatory of Music in Baltimore.[180]

Audiences showed evidence of deep disappointment in Mahler's absence, but Spiering's leadership pleased critics and even caused "music lovers to forget the fact that Mr. Mahler's illness not only prevented his direction of the orchestra, but also caused a change in the program."[181] Spiering satisfied concertgoers as he conducted with "quiet dignity" and conveyed "an impression of fine sincerity."[182] In addition, Hutcheson's splendid performance and extraordinary technical ability "elicited a highly enthusiastic reception."[183]

March Concerts for Princeton and Washington, D.C.

When Mahler's health continued to deteriorate throughout March, newspapers reported a different story. Even in New York concertgoers read that Mahler would conduct the last concerts of the season at Carnegie Hall.[184] Only after patrons arrived at Carnegie Hall did the posters in the lobby confirm that Mahler continued to be indisposed and would be unable to conduct.[185] Similar conditions prevailed in Princeton and Washington as an article from the *Washington Post* dated March 1, 1911, reported that Mahler had resumed his place with the orchestra and that in the next concert planned for Tuesday afternoon, March 28, 1911, Mahler would perform at the harpsichord. During the weeks and days preceding the March concerts, advertisements indicated Mahler would conduct the orchestra.[186]

Only two days prior to the concert was there any evidence that something different might occur, when the *Washington Times* announced that the English dramatic contralto Louise Kirkby-Lunn planned to join the program.[187] Kirkby-Lunn had studied at the Royal College of Music in London, and after she became a favorite at the Royal Opera at Covent Garden, she arrived in New York and sang in numerous productions with the Metropolitan Opera beginning in 1902.[188] An article in the *Washington Post* indicated the Philharmonic altered the program to include Kirkby-Lunn singing "Printemps qui commence" and "Mon coeur s'ouvre à ta voix" from Saint-Saëns' *Samson and Delilah*. The rest of the program remained the same and included the Overture No. 3 to *Leonore*, op. 72, by Beethoven, Tchaikovsky's Symphony No. 6, the *Pathétique*, "Siegfried's Journey to the Rhine" from Wagner's *Die Götterdämmerung*, and Chabrier's rhapsody for orchestra, *España*.[189] Thus, Mahler's Bach Suite marked the only work missing from the original program. No articles, however, clearly stated or even suggested Mahler would not be present at the concert, and even in a revised advertisement that included Kirkby-Lunn's name, Mahler still appeared as the conductor.[190]

Once again, concertgoers in Princeton and Washington, D.C., learned that Mahler would not conduct the program after they arrived at the theater. This time, however, the management did not even include a notice in the programs, and the audience expressed much more disappointment. Although a large audience turned out for the concert in Washington, D.C., the writer for the *Times* observed that they expected to see Mahler conduct and "to hear him at the harpsichord when the Bach suite was rendered."[191] The Philharmonic's effort to establish a foundation of supporters in Princeton and Washington failed with this third concert. Although the concerts went on as scheduled, Spiering failed to impress audiences as he had in February. This time the critic for the *Post* noted that Spiering's conducting demonstrated a number of mannerisms not present on the previous occasion, and "at times he seemed to have borrowed the gestures of a prominent American band master instead of wielding the scholarly baton of an interpreter of symphonies."[192]

Notes

1. Fritz Kreisler (1875–1962) studied at the Vienna Conservatory and made several tours to the United States. In 1943, he finally became an American citizen. For more information, refer to Boris Schwarz, "Kreisler, Fritz," *The New Grove Dictionary of Music and Musicians*, ed. Stanley Sadie, 2d ed. (London: Macmillan, 2001), 13: 889–891.

2. *Philadelphia Inquirer*, February 19, 1908, 2; quoted in Zoltan Roman, *Gustav Mahler's American Years: 1907–1911* (New York: Pendragon Press, 1989), 87.

3. Herbert Kupferberg, *Those Fabulous Philadelphians* (New York: Charles Scribner's Sons, 1969), 41. The performance included a chorus of 958 singers and an orchestra of 110 musicians.

4. Kupferberg, 40.

5. "Mahler's Work and Stokowski Score Triumph," *Philadelphia Public Ledger*, 3 March 1916, 1; quoted in Kupferberg, 45. For more details refer to Robert A. Gerson, *Music in Philadelphia* (Philadelphia: Theodore Presser, 1940). Gerson's daughter, Katharine, is married to David DeBolt, professor of bassoon at Kent State University. Katharine also serves as violist in the Kent Camerata.

6. Kupferberg, 22–23.

7. The *N. W. Ayer and Son's Newspaper Annual and Directory of 1910* (Philadelphia: N. W. Ayer and Son, 1910) printed the daily circulation of newspapers on pages 785–792: *Philadelphia Evening Bulletin*, 251,986; *Philadelphia Evening Telegraph*, 175,366; *Philadelphia Inquirer*, 167,187, Sunday edition 205,647; *Philadelphia Public Ledger*, 60,000, Sunday edition 50,000; *Philadelphia Press*, 76,743, Sunday edition 139,809; and the *Philadelphia Record*, 165,744, Sunday edition 140,131. The 1911 edition recorded a circulation of 200,000 for the *Philadelphia Evening Item*.

8. The Boston Symphony Orchestra gave five concerts in Philadelphia during the 1909–1910 season, on November 8, 1909; December 6, 1909; January 10, 1910; February 23, 1910; and March 21, 1910. This was the orchestra's twenty-fifth season touring to Philadelphia. For more information refer to Richard P. Stebbins, "Boston Symphony Orchestra Tours and Special Performances Notebook" (Boston: Boston Symphony Orchestra Archives, typewritten), 17–18.

9. "Boston Symphony," *Philadelphia Bulletin*, 11 January 1910, 9.

10. "In Music," *Philadelphia Press*, January 15, 1910, 9. The article noted, "Miss Zeckwer has a high soprano voice of that rare bell that comes from natural tone and production. Her method is correct, her enunciation faultless and her intonation true." Marie Zeckwer was the daughter of local pianist and teacher Richard Zeckwer (1850–1922). Starting in 1870, Richard Zeckwer taught piano at the Academy of Music and in 1876 he became the director.

11. Kupferberg, 153.

12. "In Music's Realm," *Philadelphia Record*, 2 January 1910, sec. 4, 5.

13. "Amusements," *Philadelphia Record*, 15 January 1911, sec. 4, 7.

14. "The Music World," *Philadelphia Record*, 17 January 1910, sec. 4, 5. This same article also appeared in "The Music World," *Philadelphia Record*, 16 January 1910, sec. 4, 5; "Music and Drama: Music Notes," *Philadelphia Evening Bulletin*, 15 January 1910, 8; and in "Musical Notes," *Philadelphia Public Ledger*, 16 January 1910, sec. 2, 8.

15. "The Music World," *Philadelphia Record*, 17 January 1910, sec. 4, 5.

16. "Musical Notes," *Philadelphia Public Ledger*, 16 January 1910, sec. 2, 8.

17. "Music," *Philadelphia Press*, 2 January 1910, 9. This remark also appeared in "News of the Musical Season," *Philadelphia Inquirer*, 2 January 1910, sec. 2, 11.

18. "New York Philharmonic," *Philadelphia Public Ledger*, 18 January 1910, 8.

19. "Under Mahler Baton," *Philadelphia Record*, 18 January 1910, 6.

20. "Music at the Academy," *Philadelphia Inquirer*, 18 January 1910, 4.

21. "Philharmonic's Fine Concert," *Philadelphia Evening Item*, 18 January 1910, 6.

22. "Under Mahler Baton," 6.

23. "Under Mahler Baton," 6.

24. "Music at the Academy," 4.

25. "Music at the Academy," 4.

26. "Under Mahler Baton," 6.

27. "Under Mahler Baton," 6.

28. "Philharmonic's Fine Concert," 6.

29. "Philharmonic's Fine Concert," 6.

30. "At the Theaters: Philharmonic at Academy," *Philadelphia Evening Bulletin*, 18 January 1910, 11.

31. "At the Theaters: Philharmonic at Academy," 11.

32. "Music at the Academy," 4.

33. "Music at the Academy," 4.

34. "Music at the Academy," 4.

35. "Music at the Academy," 4.

36. "Music at the Academy," 4.

37. "Music at the Academy," 4.

38. "New York Philharmonic," *Philadelphia Public Ledger*, January 18, 1910, 8.

39. "New York Philharmonic," 8.

40. Mahler produced the work for the first time in America at the Metropolitan Opera House on February 19, 1909.

41. "Music at the Academy," 4.

42. "Philharmonic's Fine Concert," 6.

43. "At the Theaters: Philharmonic at Academy," 11.

44. "Philharmonic's Fine Concert," 6.

45. "New York Philharmonic," 8.

46. "New York Philharmonic," 8.

47. "New York Philharmonic," 8.

48. "Under Mahler Baton," 6.

49. "Under Mahler Baton," 6.

50. "At the Theaters: Philharmonic at Academy," 11.

51. "Philharmonic's Fine Concert," 6.

52. "Philharmonic's Fine Concert," 6.

53. "Philharmonic's Fine Concert," 6.

54. "Under Mahler Baton," 6.

55. "Under Mahler Baton," 6.

56. "Music at the Academy," 4.

57. "Philharmonic's Fine Concert," 6.

58. "New York Philharmonic," 8.

59. "The Philharmonic Society Gives First Concert Here," *Philadelphia Daily Evening Telegraph*, 18 January 1910, 8.

60. "New York Philharmonic," 8.

61. "Under Mahler Baton," 6.

62. "News of the Musical Season: New York Philharmonic Orchestra," *Philadelphia Inquirer*, 13 March 1910, 8.

63. "In Music's Realm," *Philadelphia Record*, 13 March 1910, sec. 4, 5. This review also appeared in "News of the Musical Season: New York Philharmonic Orchestra," 8.

64. "The World of Music," *Philadelphia Press*, 13 March 1910, sec. 2, 7.

65. "News of the Musical Season: New York Philharmonic Orchestra," 8.

66. "The World of Music," *Philadelphia Press*, 13 March 1910, sec 2, 7.

67. "Kneisel Quartet," *Philadelphia Record*, 15 March 1910, 10.

68. "Kneisel Quartet," 10.

69. During the 1910–1911 season the Boston Symphony Orchestra presented five concerts in Philadelphia on November 7, 1910; December 5, 1910; January 9, 1911; February 20, 1911; and March 20, 1911. Refer to Stebbins, 17–18.

70. "Philharmonic Concert," *Philadelphia Record*, 15 March 1910, 10.

71. "Philharmonic Concert," 10.

72. "At the Theaters: The Philharmonic," *Philadelphia Evening Bulletin*, 15 March 1910, 8.

73. "The Musical Season: New York Philharmonic Orchestra," *Philadelphia Inquirer*, 15 March 1910, 8.

74. "The Philharmonic Again," *Philadelphia Daily Evening Telegraph*, 15 March 1910, 8.

75. "Philharmonic Orchestra," *Philadelphia Public Ledger*, 15 March 1910, 10.

76. "Philharmonic's Second Concert," *Philadelphia Evening Item*, 15 March 1910, 2.

77. "The Musical Season: New York Philharmonic Orchestra," 8.

78. "At the Theaters: The Philharmonic," 8.

79. "Philharmonic Concert," 10.

80. "Philharmonic's Second Concert," 2.

81. "At the Theaters: The Philharmonic," 8.

82. "Philharmonic Concert," 10.

83. "Philharmonic's Second Concert," 2.

84. "The Philharmonic Again," 8.

85. "At the Theaters: The Philharmonic," 8.

86. "Philharmonic's Second Concert," 2.

87. "Philharmonic Orchestra," *Philadelphia Public Ledger*, 10.

88. "The Philharmonic Again," 8.

89. "The Musical Season: New York Philharmonic Orchestra," 8.

90. "The Musical Season: New York Philharmonic Orchestra," 8.

91. "At the Theaters: The Philharmonic," 8.

92. "Philharmonic Concert," 10.

93. "At the Theaters: The Philharmonic," 8.

94. "The Musical Season: New York Philharmonic Orchestra," 8.

95. "The Musical Season: New York Philharmonic Orchestra," 8.

96. "At the Theaters: The Philharmonic," 8.

97. "At the Theaters: The Philharmonic," 8.

98. "The Philharmonic Again," 8.

99. *New York Sun*, 11 March 1910, 9; quoted in Roman, 355.

100. "Philharmonic's Second Concert," 2.

101. "The Musical Season: New York Philharmonic Orchestra," 8.

102. "At the Theaters: The Philharmonic," 8.

103. "At the Theaters: The Philharmonic," 8.

104. "Philharmonic Orchestra," *Philadelphia Public Ledger*, 10.

105. "Philharmonic Orchestra," *Philadelphia Public Ledger*, 10.

106. "Philharmonic Concert," 10.

107. "Philharmonic Concert," 10.

108. "Philharmonic Concert," 10.

109. "Philharmonic Concert," 10.

110. "Philharmonic Concert," 10.

111. "Philharmonic Concert," 10.

112. "Amusements," *Philadelphia Press*, 15 January 1911, sec. 2, 13.

113. "Great Wagner Concert Given," *Philadelphia Press*, 24 January 1911, 3.

114. "Music: Philharmonic Orchestra," *Philadelphia Press*, 18 December 1910, sec. 4, 14.

115. "The World of Music," *Philadelphia Press*, 22 January 1911, 10.

116. "The Music World," *Philadelphia Record*, 22 January 1911, sec. 4, 8.

117. "The Music World," sec. 4, 8.

118. "A Wagner Concert," *Philadelphia Inquirer*, 24 January 1911, 8.

119. "Philharmonic Society," *Philadelphia Public Ledger*, 24 January 1911, 10.

120. "Boston Symphony," *Philadelphia Evening Bulletin*, 10 January 1911, 11.

121. "A Wagner Concert," 8.

122. "A Wagner Concert," 8.

123. "Philharmonic Orchestra," *Philadelphia Evening Bulletin*, 24 January 1911, 11.

124. "Great Wagner Concert Given," 3.

125. "The Philharmonic Concert Last Night," *Philadelphia Evening Item*, 24 January 1911, 3.

126. "A Wagner Concert," 8.

127. "A Wagner Concert," 8.

128. "Philharmonic Society," 10.

129. "Philharmonic Orchestra," *Philadelphia Evening Bulletin*, 11.

130. "The Philharmonic Concert Last Night," 3.

131. "Great Wagner Concert Given," 3.

132. "Great Wagner Concert Given," 3.

133. "Philharmonic Society," 10.

134. "A Wagner Concert," 8.

135. "Great Wagner Concert Given," 3.

136. "The Philharmonic Concert Last Night," 3.

137. "The Philharmonic Concert Last Night," 3.

138. "Amusements," *Washington Post*, 4 December 1910, sec. 5, 3.

139. *Washington Herald*, 1 January 1914, sec. 2, 7. T. Arthur Smith's was located on 1411 Front Street. Ticket prices for the series were offered at $2.00, $2.50, $4.00, $5.00, and $6.00.

140. "Amusements," *Washington Post*, 22 January 1911, 3.

141. The *N. W. Ayer and Son's Newspaper Annual and Directory of 1910* (Philadelphia: N. W. Ayer and Son, 1910) printed the daily/weekly circulation of each paper as follows on pages 110–112: *Washington Evening Star*, 36,605 Sunday edition, 42,157; *Washington Herald*, 30,000; *Washington Post*, 20,000, Sunday edition, 25,000; *Washington Evening Star*, 36,605, Sunday edition, 42,157; and *Washington Times*, 45,758, Sunday edition, 34,260.

142. "Miss Boardman Hostess to Red Cross Delegates," *Washington Post*, 17 January 1910, 7. The Boston Symphony Orchestra gave five concerts in Washington, D.C., during the season on Tuesday afternoons, November 8, 1910; December 6,

1910; January 10, 1911; February 21, 1911; and March 21, 1911. Refer to Stebbins, 17–18.

143. "Amusements," *Washington Post*, 24 January 1911, 4.

144. "The Theaters," *Washington Sunday Star*, 8 January 1911, sec. 2, 2. The Washington Symphony Orchestra gave three concerts during the season.

145. "Amusements," *Washington Post*, 22 January 1911, 3.

146. "Philharmonic Orchestra," *Washington Herald*, 8 January 1911, sec. 2, 7.

147. "Musical Attractions," *Washington Post*, 8 January 1911, sec. 5, 3.

148. "News of the Theaters," *Washington Post*, 22 January 1911, 4.

149 "Taft Honors Bench," *Washington Post*, 25 January 1911, 1.

150. "Mrs. Taft Heads Throng of Society at Concert," *Washington Post*, 25 January 1911, 7. The box also included Mrs. Franklin Ellis, Miss Anderson, Mrs. Rae, and Miss Dorothy Baldwin of Savannah.

151. *New York Times Index*, vol. 14, *1911* (New York: New York Times, 1912), 28.

152. *Who Was Who in America: With World Notables* vol. 4, *1961–1968* (Chicago: Marquis—Who's Who), 586.

153. *2002 World Almanac* (New York: World Almanac Book, 2002), 81.

154. "In the Social World," *Washington World*, 25 January 1911, 5.

155. "Mrs. Taft Heads Throng of Society at Concert," 7. These concertgoers included: Mrs. Clarence Moore, Mrs. George Howard, Miss Margaret Perin, Mrs. Francis Crowninshield, Mr. and Mrs. William Stirling, Mrs. Slater, Mrs. Preston Gibson, Mrs. Kean, Miss Kean, the Misses Harlan, Mrs. Richard Ballinger, Mrs. Hinckley, Miss Hinckley, Mrs. Hugh Legare, Mr. and Mrs. Gordon Cumming, Mrs. Murray Cobb, Dr. and Mrs. Buckner Randolph, Mrs. Huntington Wilson, Mrs. Thomas H. Carter, Mr. and Mrs. A. J. Parsons, the second secretary of the British embassy and Mrs. Kennard, Mrs. Clarence Wilson, Mrs. William Barret Ridgely, and Mrs. Edward A. Mitchell.

156. J. R. Hildebrand, "Mme. Gadski Wins Honors at Concert," *Washington Times*, 25 January 1911, 7.

157. Hildebrand, 7.

158. "Amusements: Gadski Recital," *Washington Evening Star*, 25 January 1911, 9.

159. R. G., "Debut of Philharmonic," *Washington Post*, 25 January 1911, 9.

160. "Music and Musicians," *Washington Post*, 29 January 1911, sec. 4, 10.

161. "In the Social World," 5.

162. R. G., "Debut of Philharmonic," 9.

163. "Amusements: Gadski Recital," 9.

164. "Amusements: Gadski Recital," 9.

165. "Amusements: Gadski Recital," 9.

166. "Amusements: Gadski Recital," 9.

167. R. G., "Debut of Philharmonic," 9.

168. Hildebrand, 7.

169. Hildebrand, 7.

170. R. G., "Debut of Philharmonic," 9.

171. "Amusements: Gadski Recital," 9.

172. R. G., "Debut of Philharmonic," 9.

173. Hildebrand, 7.

174. "Amusements: Gadski Recital," 9.

175. R. G., "Debut of Philharmonic," 9.

176. "Coming to the Theaters," *Washington Post*, 19 February 1911, 6.

177. "Amusements," *Washington Post*, 28 February 1911, 4.

178. "Spiering to Conduct Symphony Concert," *Washington Times*, 28 February 1911, 5.

179. "Philharmonic at National," *Washington Post*, 1 March 1911, 3.

180. Nicolas Slonimsky, *Baker's Biographical Dictionary of Music and Musicians*, 5th ed. (New York: G. Schirmer, 1958), 752. Ernest Hutcheson served on Peabody's faculty (1900–1912), and later joined the faculty of the Juilliard School as dean (1924) and later as president (1937). The Juilliard School was founded in 1905, and known as the Institute of Musical Art until 1926. Born on July 20, 1871, in Melbourne, Australia, Hutcheson attended the Leipzig Conservatory and studied with Carl Reinecke. In 1900, he arrived in the United States where he continued to perform and teach, and later published a number of symphonic works and compositions until his death on February 9, 1951.

181. "Philharmonic at National," 3.

182. "Philharmonic at National," 3.

183. "Symphony Heard in Long Program," *Washington Times*, 1 March 1911, 2.

184. "The Philharmonic Society," *New York Times*, 12 March 1911, sec. 7, 10.

185. "The Philharmonic Concert," *New York Times*, 13 March 1911, 9.

186. "Amusements," *Washington Post*, 26 March 1911, 3.

187. "Mme. Kirkby-Lunn to Sing in Capital," *Washington Times*, 26 March 1911, 6.

188. Slonimsky, 830. Louise Kirkby-Lunn (1873–1930) was born in Manchester, England, and after her studies toured with the Sir Augustus Harris' Company and the Carl Rosa Opera Company. After arriving in New York she impressed listeners in her Wagnerian roles with the Metropolitan Opera Company and later continued touring in England and Australia.

189. "Musical Attractions," *Washington Post*, 26 March 1911, Magazine sec., 3.

190. "Amusements," *Washington Times*, 26 March 1911, 7.

191. "Mahler's Illness Disappoints Many," *Washington Times*, 29 March 1911, 6.

192. "Last Symphony Concert," *Washington Post*, 29 March 1911, 9.

CHAPTER SEVEN

~

The Final Tour of 1911

Mahler's final tour with the Philharmonic took place less than a week before his last appearance at Carnegie Hall on February 21, 1911. A week earlier on Tuesday evening, February 14, 1911, the orchestra performed a Carnegie Hall concert that featured American and English music. Less than twenty-four hours later, Mahler and the Philharmonic headed north to offer a concert in Springfield, Massachusetts, at the Court Square Theater on Wednesday, February 15. On Thursday evening, February 16, Mahler conducted his last concert outside New York City in Hartford, Connecticut, at the Parsons' Theater. The following day, February 17, the musicians traveled back to New York and in the evening repeated the concert presented on Tuesday, February 14. Without a day of rest the Philharmonic resumed rehearsals at Carnegie Hall on Saturday, February 18,[1] and prepared for a Sunday afternoon concert on February 19.[2]

On Monday, February 20, 1911, Alma Mahler noted in her memoirs that Gustav was "suffering once more from inflammation of the throat and fever."[3] Even though his physician Dr. Fränkel warned Mahler to refrain from conducting a concert on Tuesday, February 21, Mahler insisted on continuing. At the time reporters and the musicians did not realize the severity of Mahler's condition when he conducted the concert. Even years later, in a 1964 radio interview when William Malloch asked several musicians from the Philharmonic to recall Mahler's last concert, they were unable to supply any details of the concert.[4]

While articles and books written after Mahler's death detail his health during his final weeks in New York, none of the reviews from either Hartford or Springfield alluded to any life-threatening illness visible in either his physical appearance or manner of conducting. Quite to the contrary, the reviews portrayed an energetic conductor who "contained the fire of a Napoleon."[5] Years later in the *Musical Memories of Hartford*, however, Frances Hall Johnson recalled Mahler's medical condition during the concert in Hartford, noting, "Even with his health failing at the time, he conducted with much verve and energy" and "one felt his mentality and music fiber in the interpretation of every composition."[6]

In contrast to the gossip that circulated in New York newspapers regarding Mahler's appointment for the 1911–1912 season, several articles from Springfield and Hartford newspapers implied that Mahler might remain at the helm of the Philharmonic if the executive committee offered an acceptable salary. Speculation about Mahler's remaining in America appeared in the *Hartford Evening Post*. The writer noted, "Now come pressing calls for Mahler to return to Vienna, and the question is, will the New York Philharmonic Society be able to keep their great leader?"[7] Even in a letter Mahler wrote to Director Hertzka of Vienna in February 1911, he anticipated spending the next season in New York and adamantly stated it would definitely be the last time.[8]

Unlike the first tour of New England, which featured soloists, this tour depended solely on members of the Philharmonic and featured identical programs in Springfield and Hartford. Each concert opened with Mahler's arrangement of the Bach Suite followed by Beethoven's Symphony No. 6 in F Major, op. 68. The third selection featured cellist Leo Schulz as the soloist in Weingartner's arrangement of *Invitation to the Dance* by Weber.[9] The symphonic poem *Les Préludes* by Liszt closed each concert. By not modifying the program for Hartford, the orchestra did not have to rehearse any new music and mostly likely reduced the need for a prolonged rehearsal. With only twenty-six miles between Hartford and Springfield, the musicians encountered minimal travel time and probably enjoyed more leisure time.

The Springfield Concert on Wednesday, February 15, 1911

For the second year in a row William F. A. Engel handled local arrangements for the approaching Philharmonic concert in Springfield at the Court Square Theater. Since local management failed to meet the expenses in the previous year, Engel implemented several new strategies to entice the public. First of all, Engel decided to start publicizing the concert several weeks beforehand. Numerous press releases and advertisements filled the entertainment sections in the *Springfield Daily Republican*, *Springfield Union*, *Springfield Daily News*, *Springfield Weekly Republican*, and the *Springfield Homestead*.[10] Several promotions reminded readers they missed in the prior season one of the best musical events and one of the most distinguished conductors in the world. A writer for the *Daily Republican* recalled that some members of the audience from last year rated the occasion as the "greatest orchestral concert they ever heard."[11]

Promoters also reached out to a wider range of concertgoers, tried to attract local supporters of the Boston Symphony Orchestra concerts, urged citizens to represent Springfield as a cultural community, and advertised Mahler as one of the best conductors in the world. Rather than market the concert as an evening primarily for the social elite, advertisements for this season guaranteed Mahler would create an exciting event and even interest those people "who do not usually care greatly for music."[12] Based on the enthusiasm shown during the concert in the previous year, the *Daily Republican* predicted the theater to be crowded and that "everybody" would be pleased with the entertainment.[13]

Articles encouraged patrons to mark Springfield as a community capable of not only enjoying musical comedy, but also appreciating refined music. Writers warned citizens that the possibility of future concerts depended on the success of the Philharmonic event, and unless a large audience appeared, Springfield would be in jeopardy of losing recognition as a cultural city. Compared to the previous year, the Philharmonic selected only two cities for the tour, and the *Daily News* believed, "Springfield should be considered especially favored to be included in the list."[14] Hope for establishing a tradition of the Philharmonic performing in Springfield appeared in advertisements marking the occasion as the "Second Annual Performance."[15]

With the Boston Symphony Orchestra as the dominant ensemble in New England, other orchestras struggled to gain local support. Although the Boston Symphony Orchestra planned a Springfield visit in late March, the writer of the *Daily Republican* believed this event offered no excuse to miss the upcoming New York Philharmonic concert. Continuing, he emphasized the quality of the orchestras as so entirely different that "one should by all means hear both."[16]

The writer noted the technical finish of the Boston Orchestra, but he also admired the power, impressiveness of style, and unique sound characteristic of the New York Philharmonic.[17] In the past the Boston Symphony Orchestra routinely brought forty-five men on tour, but the Philharmonic planned to arrive in Springfield with at least ninety musicians. Thus, newspaper writers requested readers to experience the difference in sound a larger orchestra offered, especially one with more heavily scored modern works. The writer of the *Daily Republican* created an analogy with a chorus singing softly versus a single singer. He continued to explain that a richer tone occurred with a large orchestra, such as the Philharmonic, and could not compare with the thinness of fewer instruments.[18] After his assessment, he recommended the only way to observe the vast difference was to attend the approaching concert.

The final method used to lure readers to the concert was to portray Mahler as an entertainer and capitalize on his image as a superior conductor of music. Even though Mahler stood approximately five feet tall, advertisements portrayed Mahler as "A Great Man with a Great Big Orchestra."[19] Some articles referred to Mahler as a genius who would give the best symphony concert of the season.[20] The *Homestead* proclaimed, "There was no better conductor or orchestra" in the United States.[21] To further entice the public the writer for the *Weekly Republican* recalled the image of Mahler's power from the previous performance in Springfield as he wrote, "No one who attended the concert last year is likely to forget either the splendid effect produced or the picturesque aspect of the fiery conductor, as he sat at the keyboard, sometimes playing, sometimes lifting a directing hand, much like a cavalry officer leading a charge."[22]

Dining in Springfield

Upon arriving in Springfield on the day of the concert, the musicians enjoyed ample time to relax and dine before the concert. In the *Musical Courier* Theodore Spiering, Philharmonic concertmaster, recounted the trip to Springfield and his experience when Mahler accepted his dinner invitation. At six o'clock in the evening when they met for dinner, Spiering insisted on selecting a meal for them that included specialties of New England cuisine as he ordered:

> By all means let us have some hors d'oeuvres and salted nuts to begin with. Also stuffed celery, but stuffed with Roquefort, if you please, and not with that villainous Canadian cheese that I usually encounter. Then we will have some Cape Cod oysters on the half shell, green turtle soup, broiled pompano, à la Marguery, with pommes frittes, sweetbreads with buerre noire, asparagus Hollandaise, roast young turkey—and mind we wish a whole turkey because there is not any too much meat on those juvenile birds—sweet potatoes Southern style and steeped in rum, artichokes vinaigrette, Roman punch, plum pudding,

black coffee, benedictine, and two Romeo y Julia perfectos. As for drinks, serve dry Martini cocktail as a starter, some Niersteiner with the fish, and Piper Heidseck, brut, with the rest of the meal.[23]

Mahler then returned to a discussion they had started on the train. Mahler remarked that the bass clarinet was not appropriate as a substitute for the cello, and he attempted to demonstrate this point with an example from Beethoven's Seventh Symphony. Realizing the score lay upstairs in his hotel room, Mahler excused himself to retrieve it. Mahler most likely brought the score to Springfield on this tour since the orchestra planned to perform it on the following Sunday, February 19, 1911. Rather than return to dinner with Spiering, Mahler ate his usual meal consisting of an apple, bread, and water in his room. Afterward, he took his usual pre-concert walk and arrived at the concert hall fifteen minutes prior to the concert. Meanwhile, when the enormous quantities of food arrived at Spiering's table, he decided to search for Mahler. After the desk clerk informed him he had already departed, Spiering returned to the table, ate some dinner, and paid the exorbitant bill. He quickly left for the hall, and upon his arrival Mahler whispered, "You were late. You know I require the presence of all my players fifteen minutes before we begin. Do not let it happen again."[24] Mahler tapped his baton and commenced the evening.

Reviews of the Springfield Concert

When the concert began, only a few hundred people appeared in the theater, "hardly enough present to make a respectably sized parlor audience."[25] Several critics could not explain why Mahler, as one of the greatest conductors in the world, and the New York Philharmonic drew only a small audience but several reasons should be considered. The writer for the *Homestead* noted, "Local people were slow to recognize a prophet who hailed from a land more distant than Boston."[26] The so-called New England spirit strongly supported ensembles from Boston but did not so eagerly endorse traveling orchestras from New York. Even when Walter Damrosch and the New York Symphony visited a month earlier in Springfield, the audience was not large.[27] Damrosch even included local talent in the program that featured Gabriel Pierne's *The Children at Bethlehem*. Unfortunately, the audience only "sprinkled about the lower floor" and made "a little better showing in the upper part of the house."[28]

The appearance of the famous Italian pianist Ferruccio Benvenuto Busoni in nearby Northampton on the same evening as the Philharmonic concert offered a second explanation for the dismal audience at the Philharmonic concert. Local advertisements noted Busoni as being "unsurpassed by any living pianist"[29] and forced music lovers to choose which event to attend. In addition, the following evening in Springfield offered a local amateur event featuring the fifth annual "Kapparappers" appearance in Captain Marshall's comedy *Second in Command* for the benefit of the local Day Nursery.[30] Even though the concert was publicized as the highlight of the season, the writer of the *Homestead* believed theatergoers were more drawn to the performance of the "Kapparappers" than to the Philharmonic.[31] The younger society of Springfield strongly supported this benefit concert and delighted in the annual occasion as they arrived as lace bedecked ingenues.[32] Those concertgoers who attended the Philharmonic concert, however, expressed no disappointment. If fact, many critics agreed the concert represented "one of the greatest ever offered to the Springfield public."[33]

Bach

The opening of Mahler's Bach Suite marked the second time listeners in Springfield heard the composition. Critics expressed opposing opinions on the inclusion of the reconfigured piano, but the critic for the *Daily News* approved of the instrument. He rated the effect as remarkable and believed the selection was "immeasurably enhanced by the peculiar accompaniment of the old instrument which masterful Mahler played vigorously, combined with impressive and dignified work on the part of the orchestra."[34] Unfortunately, the critic for the *Union* thought the selection demonstrated a look back into the musical past and appeared as only an "anachronistic novelty" which could have been left out of the program.[35] As the third movement the popular Air quickly captured the audience's attention. Rather than a soloist playing the melodic line on the violin, all the stringed instruments enriched the primary melody with more depth and fullness of tone. In a cynical comment regarding the cultural level of the community the critic for the *Union* remarked that the movement had such "a sensuous and poetic appearance even the tone deaf could appreciate."[36]

Beethoven

As the second selection Beethoven's Sixth Symphony soon became the audience's favorite work for the evening. According to the writer of the *Daily Republican*, this work had only been occasionally performed in Springfield and had not been heard in recent years.[37] As one of the final occasions when

Mahler conducted a work of Beethoven's, he created an interpretation some critics viewed as "nothing less than a revelation."[38] The critic for the *Weekly Republican* thought the symphony often disappointed listeners in the past, but with the "touch of a genius" such as Mahler, some listeners "were ready to say that they heard it for the first time."[39] The same writer summarized Mahler's approach to each movement of the symphony as he noted:

> It was the quintessence of Beethoven that he gave last week, and the spirit of the great composer might have been guiding the baton. How fresh and spontaneous was the pure flowing melody "Joyful impressions on arriving in the country!" How deliciously the water gurgled and the sweet birds sang in the "Scene by the brook!" How hearty and unbuttoned the dancing of the peasants in the "Merry making of the country fold." How tremendous and Beethovenish the bursting of the thunderstorm, how lovely and serene the clean landscape after the tempest![40]

Weber and Liszt

Critics in Springfield concentrated less on the concluding works in their reviews. Weingartner's arrangement of Weber's *Invitation to the Dance* featured the playing of lead cellist Leo Schulz, who frequently appeared as a soloist in Springfield. In a brief analysis of the rendition the *Union* noticed Mahler gave new meaning to the work, and the audience "quickly responded to the varying raptures of the youthful lovers."[41] The final selection, *Les Préludes* by Liszt, brought the evening to a brilliant close as the performance "was incomparably the greatest ever heard in Springfield."[42] Afterward, Mahler and the musicians quickly departed the stage in "a manner that portrayed a cheerful and agreeable sensation awakened by leaving the country."[43]

Despite the size of the audience, Mahler allowed "no evidence of disappointment or chagrin" to creep into "his rendition of the program."[44] Mahler's display of artistic conducting evoked the image of a "wizard as he mounted the conductor's rostrum."[45] The *Union* noticed that once Mahler began conducting the "audience as well as players falls immediately under the spell of his magical baton."[46] The *Weekly Republican* referred to Mahler as a "slender and wiry Napoleon" as he "rides the whirlwind and directs that storm."[47]

Once again the attendance did not generate enough revenue to meet the cost of producing a concert with such a large orchestra. Thus, reviewers feared the event would be the New York Philharmonic's second and, most likely, last concert in Springfield.[48] The writer for the *Homestead* opined that whatever excuse citizens had for not attending the concert, the result of poor attendance would damage the reputation of the musical taste and culture of Springfield.[49] Thus, high society feared outsiders would rank Springfield's cit-izens as uncultured and only capable of patronizing lowbrow entertainment.

The Hartford Concert on Thursday, February 16, 1911

On Thursday, February 16, 1911, Mahler and the Philharmonic traveled twenty-six miles south from Springfield, Massachusetts, to reach Hartford, Connecticut. As the capital of Connecticut, Hartford boasted several per-formance halls including the Parsons' Theater. From 1896 until 1936, Par-sons' Theater stood as "one of the most prominent playhouses in the East."[50] With a seating capacity of 1,700, the theater arose as "home of high class plays"[51] and easily accommodated orchestras on tour such as the Theodore Thomas Orchestra and the Boston Symphony Orchestra. With high hopes of establishing a musical tradition in Hartford, the Philharmonic promoted the concert as the "First Annual Appearance" and the "Symphonic Event of the Season."[52]

In addition to handling local arrangements for the concert in Springfield, William F. A. Engel also coordinated the Philharmonic's performance in Hartford. Compared to ticket prices in Springfield, which started at seventy-five cents,[53] Engel offered more affordable tickets in Hartford beginning at fifty cents.[54] In both cities, however, the most expensive tickets reached two dollars. Other attractions during February in Hartford included Minnie Mad-dern Fiske in the play *Becky Sharpe*, Edward Reynard the ventriloquist at Poli's Theater, and motion pictures at the Hartford Theatre.[55] Less than two weeks after the Philharmonic concert, the Boston Symphony Orchestra ar-rived in Hartford to offer their third and final concert of the season on Feb-ruary 27, 1911.[56]

Starting in 1885, the Boston Symphony Orchestra presented concerts in Hartford and formed a long-term relationship with local concertgoers. By the beginning of the twentieth century the orchestra annually offered three con-certs in Hartford. While a record of these visits appeared in historical re-sources, only Frances Hall Johnson's *Musical Memories of Hartford* provided any details surrounding Mahler's visit with the Philharmonic.[57]

Local articles and advertisements mimicked those produced for the news-papers in Springfield. At the beginning of February, news of the event ap-peared in the *Hartford Times*, *Hartford Globe*, *Hartford Evening Post*, and *Hart-ford Daily Courant*.[58] With the concert marking the Philharmonic's first Hartford appearance, many reports detailed the history of the orchestra and its conductor. Articles acknowledged the New York Philharmonic as the old-est and one of the most famous ensembles in the country and declared that "no orchestral organization in the country enjoys a greater reputation than the local music lovers are soon to have an opportunity to hear."[59] Readers soon learned how wealthy supporters of music in New York spared no ex-pense in financing the organization and engaging "eighty of the flower of metropolitan musicians" to reshape an orchestra now ranked "second to none."[60]

While Hartford citizens may not have been acquainted with Mahler, sev-eral feature stories displayed his photograph and recounted his accomplish-ments. The *Hartford Daily Courant* indicated that Mahler's conducting style differed from other well-known leaders, "but the striking effect and tremen-dous climaxes he obtains are of a character seldom equaled."[61] During this era concertgoers often expected a very animated conductor, yet the *Courant* de-scribed a different type of leader. The report painted Mahler as a reserved conductor whose power lay in his quietness; even so, he "never fails to arouse a high pitch of enthusiasm."[62]

Several days later the *Courant* further elaborated on Mahler's achieve-ments. After noting Mahler as an accomplished composer of symphonic works, the article recognized him as a modern composer whose works aroused a "marked difference of opinions" among critics.[63] Furthermore, the writer believed Mahler's leadership as a conductor rather than a composer would forever assure him a place in music.[64]

The *Hartford Evening Post* noted Mahler's rule over the Philharmonic dur-ing the past two seasons achieved "a precision of attack and an ensemble, a perfection of finish and style suggestive of the famous Old World symphony orchestras, as, for example, the Berlin Philharmonic."[65] Mahler's success as a conductor in America and the Philharmonic's growth became apparent as concert attendance in New York increased considerably starting in 1909.

The newspaper articles inspired readers to attend the concert, and when ticket sales opened, preliminary reports indicated sales progressing on or above target. The *Evening Post* recorded that the enthusiasm for the Philhar-monic increased by "leaps and bounds since the first announcement"[66] and the coming engagement promised to deliver a tremendous success.[67]

Reviews of the Hartford Concert

Hartford encountered a night of severe cold on February 16, 1911.[68] Perhaps as a result of the weather, an audience "not as large as it should have been" arrived at Parsons' Theater before the concert commenced at eight fifteen in the evening.[69] Regardless, patrons expressed appreciation for Mahler and warmly greeted him with a round of applause.[70] In contrast to the orchestra's reception in Springfield, concertgoers in Hartford displayed sheer approval for Mahler and the New York Philharmonic. The *Courant* observed after one selection that the applause became so insistent that "the members of the orchestra were called on to rise to share it with their leader, and they, as well as he, fully merited the audience's appreciation."[71]

Bach

Mahler's Bach Suite opened the evening, but unfortunately no records indicate if Mahler incorporated a temporary or permanent organ at this concert. Similar to other performances, Mahler played and conducted from the reconfigured piano. Since the instrument visually represented a typical twentieth-century baby grand piano, listeners anticipated a big and brilliant tone with fine sustained effects and were surprised when the instrument produced a muffled and tinkling sound.[72]

An extensive description in the *Hartford Daily News* noted the rendition as more of a study of former music rather than a piece of concert music. The critic recorded that Mahler even played the piano "in the manner of the modified instrument."[73] Although the sound appeared at times insufficient, thin, and rather foreign to listeners, the reviewer concluded the interpretation "interesting and carried through in a rounded manner, and with much finish and style."[74]

Beethoven

Beethoven's Sixth Symphony followed and quickly won the audience's praise, as they displayed "prolonged applause" after its completion.[75] In recent years, music lovers heard several performances of the work; yet, as the critic for the *Daily News* concluded, "One has often heard—all have often heard—the sixth symphony. But hear Mahler play it. It is a different thing. It discloses wonders not dreamt of before."[76] The writer from the *Evening Post* commended Mahler's interpretation and remarked that such a rendition had never before been heard in Hartford when, during the allegro movement, "the orchestra rose to the heights of its marvelous power as perhaps in no other number during the evening."[77]

Unlike the Bach selection, the Beethoven work required a larger group of instruments and demanded a greater dramatic contrast in dynamics and timbre. Concertgoers could not help but evaluate Mahler's conducting technique. As the *Daily News* recorded, Mahler created "a piety of reproduction, a careful study of intentions, a reserve of effects, then. Beyond that, a throwing of himself and his musicians into the sentiment, the feeling of the piece."[78] While other directors managed to merely conduct the bare score, Mahler appeared "engrossed in the poetic intent," which included the sentiment and intellectuality of the work.[79]

An article in the *Courant* captured the variety of contrasting sound the Philharmonic produced, as the reviewer wrote:

> All the graces and beauties of the delicate pictorial passages were clearly, gracefully and beautifully played and the splendid storm picture was painted in all the glories of crashing black thunder tones relieved by the screaming yellows of the lightning flashes and the lovely gray tints of the slanting rain.[80]

After recounting previous performances of the Sixth Symphony by other orchestras, the writer of the *Daily News* concluded, "They are all too plain, and we have heard them again and again since Thomas played them here. But never so vividly, so picturesquely, as last night."[81]

Weber

Moving ahead into the Romantic period, Mahler selected Weingartner's arrangement of *Invitation to the Dance* by Weber as the third selection. Noted by critics as less familiar to listeners in Hartford than the Beethoven selection, Mahler once again gained the admiration of concertgoers. Reporting for the *Daily News*, the critic noticed the work almost carried the audience off its feet, as the music was "so electric, so full of life and movement, so brilliant in its sweeps."[82] The article continued to elaborate on how the Philharmonic performed the work with charm and modesty, which allowed some parts to become "exquisite, rich, gliding, languorous, and again extravagantly high spirited, full of impetus and of palpitating joy."[83]

While musicians from the Philharmonic recalled how Mahler often demanded a loud sound in various works, they emphasized how he never lost sight of the music. The *Courant* confirmed the tremendous volume of sound created in the dance measures and noted that Mahler had not lost awareness for the rhythmic grace as the "charm of the dialogue and of the quiet ending of the episode was most potent."[84] The critic for the *Evening Post* voiced a similar opinion regarding Mahler's interpretation. While some passages in the composition were familiar to the audience, under Mahler's direction the "real beauties of this familiar number have never been heard before."[85]

Liszt

The evening concluded with the symphonic poem *Les Préludes* by Liszt. Even though some critics did not evaluate this selection as meticulously as other works, it received overwhelming praise as the musicians demonstrated their expertise. A critic from the *Daily News* observed, "It was an ocean of sound, and yet it was held by artistic harmonies, tender expressive plaints, and molded by sentiment. If there were pure artists and wonderful scene painters in playing Beethoven, they became magicians in playing Liszt."[86] Afterward, listeners rejoiced in Mahler's rendition and produced a thunderous applause, which brought Mahler back to the stage. The *Courant* concluded that the audience fully recognized his "powers as a conductor, as well as a realization of the general excellence of the huge orchestra of the Philharmonic Society of New York."[87]

From the glowing reviews in Hartford newspapers the first annual New York Philharmonic concert proved victorious. The only negative aspect seemed to be the low attendance, since New England audiences overwhelmingly supported the Boston Symphony Orchestra. When compared with the attendance at a New York Symphony concert from earlier in the year, the Philharmonic received adequate patronage from local citizens. When Damrosch and the New York Symphony offered a concert at Parsons' Theater on February 1, 1911, the *Evening Post* reported a remarkable artistic performance with not more than a third of the hall occupied.[88] Here again, the critic believed citizens neglected taking advantage of a delightful evening.[89]

Programming a famous soloist frequently attracted a wider range of concertgoers and kept loyal patrons returning to the concert hall. When the Boston Symphony Orchestra arrived in Hartford on February 27, 1911, to give its final concert for the season, the orchestra used the renowned pianist Ferruccio Benvenuto Busoni. The orchestra attracted an audience "huge in size and vehement in its expression of approval."[90] Concertgoers demonstrated their praise for the leading musicians as "Mr. Fiedler was applauded to the echo, and Mr. Busoni, the soloist, had the unusual Hartford experience of being recalled seven times to the platform."[91]

If the Philharmonic had added Busoni, or another renowned soloist to the Hartford concert, a larger audience may have attended. Nevertheless, Mahler and the New York Philharmonic successfully introduced the orchestra to audiences far beyond the greater New York area and gained the respect of critics and concertgoers in Springfield and Hartford.

Notes

1. *Carnegie Hall: Collection of Ledgers and Cash Book Covering the Period 1891–1925*, vol. 6, 211. Fine Arts Division of the New York Public Library.

2. The concert included Mendelssohn's Violin Concerto in E Minor, op. 64, with Fredric Fradkin as soloist, Weber's Overture to *Oberon*, Beethoven's Symphony No. 7 in A Major, op. 92, and Liszt's *Les Préludes*.

3. Alma Mahler, *Gustav Mahler—Memories and Letters*, 3rd ed., ed. Donald Mitchell, trans. Basil Creighton (Seattle: University of Washington Press, 1975), 189.

4. "William Malloch's 'I Remember Mahler'" in *New York Philharmonic: The Mahler Broadcasts 1948–1987*, The Philharmonic-Symphony Society of New York, NYP 9813, 1998, compact disc.

5. "The Philharmonic Concert," *Springfield Weekly Republican*, 23 February 1911, 6.

6. Frances Hall Johnson, *Musical Memories of Hartford* (Hartford, CT: Finlay Brothers Press, 1931), 236.

7. "The Local Entertainment Field," *Hartford Evening Post*, 13 February 1911, 5.

8. Letter from Gustav Mahler, Savoy, NY, to Director Emil Hertzka, Vienna, received in Vienna on February 21, 1911, in Hans Moldenhauer, "Unbekannte Briefe Gustav Mahler an Emil Hertzka," *Neue Zeitschrift für Musik* 135, no. 9 (Summer 1974), 548; quoted in Zoltan Roman, *Gustav Mahler's American Years, 1907–1911* (Stuyvesant, NY: Pendragon Press, 1989), 452.

9. Felix von Weingartner (1863–1942) appeared as a guest conductor with the New York Philharmonic between 1905 and 1907. In 1908, he succeeded Mahler at the Vienna Court Opera and conducted the Vienna Philharmonic until 1927. Throughout his career he composed, conducted, and wrote numerous articles.

10. The *N. W. Ayer and Son's Newspaper Annual Directory of 1910* (Philadelphia: N. W. Ayer and Son, 1910) printed the daily/weekly circulation of each paper as follows on page 392: *Springfield Daily Republican*, 16,102; *Springfield Union*, 25,000; *Springfield Daily News*, 10,243; *Springfield Weekly Republican*, 17,415; and *Springfield Homestead* (Monday, Wednesday, and Saturday), 5,000.

11. "Mahler and the New York Philharmonic to Appear in Springfield," *Springfield Daily Republican*, 3 February 1911, 4.

12. "Mahler and the New York Philharmonic to Appear in Springfield," 4.

13. "The Philharmonic Society," *Springfield Daily Republican*, 15 February 1911, 6.

14. "Plays, Players, and Coming Attractions: Mahler and Philharmonic," *Springfield Daily News*, 9 February 1911.

15. "Amusements, Meetings, Etc.," *Springfield Daily Republican*, 13 February 1911, 3.

16. "The Notable Concert which the New York Philharmonic Society will give under Gustav Mahler," *Springfield Daily Republican*, 10 February 1911, 4.

17. "The Philharmonic Society," 6.

18. "The Philharmonic Society," 6.

19. "Amusements, Meetings, Etc.,", 3. This slogan also ran in the *Springfield Daily Republican* on February 14, 1911, and February 15, 1911.

20. "New York Philharmonic Tonight," *Springfield Homestead*, 15 February 1911, 7.

21. "New York Philharmonic Tonight," 7.

22. "Of Music and Musicians: Gustav Mahler's Program," *Springfield Weekly Republican*, 9 February 1911, 6.

23. "Variations," *Musical Courier* 65, no. 17 (23 October 1912): 27.

24. "Variations," 27.

25. "The Theaters: Orchestral Concert," *Springfield Union*, 16 February 1911, 4.

26. "The Theaters," *Springfield Homestead*, 18 February 1911, 10.

27. "Damrosch and Orchestra," *Springfield Homestead*, 1 February 1911, 2. Damrosch appeared at the Court Square Theater on January 31, 1911.

28. "Damrosch and Orchestra," 2.

29. "Local Musical Matters: Busoni's Program at Northampton," *Springfield Daily Republican*, 12 February 1911, 5.

30. "Amusements," *Springfield Daily Republican*," 22 February 1911, 22.

31. "The Theaters," *Springfield Homestead*, 18 February 1911, 10.

32. "The Theaters," 10.

33. "The Philharmonic Concert," *Springfield Weekly Republican*, 23 February 1911, 6.

34. "Memorable Concert," *Springfield Daily News*, 16 February 1911, 4.

35. "The Theaters: Orchestral Concert," 3.

36. "The Theaters: Orchestral Concert," 3.

37. "Local Musical Matters: The Concert to Be Given at Court Square Theater Wednesday Evening by the New York Philharmonic Society, Conducted by Gustav Mahler," *Springfield Daily Republican*, 12 February 1911, 5.

38. "The Philharmonic Concert," 6.

39. "The Philharmonic Concert," 6.

40. "The Philharmonic Concert," 6.

41. "The Theaters: Orchestral Concert," 3.

42. "The Philharmonic Concert," 6.

43. "The Philharmonic Concert," 6.

44. "Memorable Concert," 4.

45. "The Theaters: Orchestral Concert," 3.

46. "The Theaters: Orchestral Concert," 3.

47. "The Philharmonic Concert," 6.

48. "The Philharmonic Concert," 6.

49. "The Theaters," 10.

50. *Hartford in 1912: Story of the Capital City, Present and Prospective* (Hartford: Hartford Post, 1912), 22.

51. "Entertainments," *Hartford Daily Courant*, 15 February 1911, 7.

52. "Entertainments," 7.

53. "Amusements," *Springfield Daily News*, 15 February 1911, 9.

54. "Amusements," *Hartford Daily Times*, 13 February 1911, 7.

55. "Amusements," *Hartford Daily Times*, 13 February 1911, 7.

56. The orchestra gave this concert at the Parsons' Theater. The Boston Symphony Orchestra offered two other concerts during the season on November 14, 1910, and January 16, 1911.

57. Johnson, 236.

58. *N. W. Ayer and Son's Newspaper Annual Directory of 1910*, 102. Circulations for the papers included the *Hartford Times*, 19,846; *Hartford Globe*, 14,743; *Hartford Evening Post*, 12,000; and the *Hartford Daily Courant* (morning), 13,500.

59. "The Parsons Theater: 'Our World' This Evening—Coming Attractions," *Hartford Daily Courant*, 10 February 1911, 6.

60. "The Local Entertainment Field: New York Philharmonic Orchestra," *Hartford Evening Post*, 13 February 1911, 5.

61. "The Parsons Theater: 'Our World' This Evening—Coming Attractions," 6.

62. "The Parsons Theater: 'Our World' This Evening—Coming Attractions," 6.

63. "The Parsons Theater: New York Philharmonic Concert," *Hartford Daily Courant*, 15 February 1911, 6.

64. "The Parsons Theater: New York Philharmonic Concert," 6.

65. "The Local Entertainment Field: New York Philharmonic Orchestra," *Hartford Evening Post*, 13 February 1911, 5.

66. "The Local Entertainment Field: New York Philharmonic," 5.

67. "The Local Entertainment Field: New York Philharmonic," 5.

68. Johnson, 236.

69. "Unusual Musical Event: New York Philharmonic," *Hartford Daily News*, 17 February 1911, 7.

70. "Unusual Musical Event: New York Philharmonic," 7.

71. "N.Y. Philharmonic Orchestra's Success," *Hartford Daily Courant*, 17 February 1911, 10.

72. "N.Y. Philharmonic Orchestra's Success," 10.

73. "Unusual Musical Event: New York Philharmonic," 7.

74. "Unusual Musical Event: New York Philharmonic," 7.

75. "N.Y. Philharmonic Orchestra's Success," 10.

76. "Unusual Musical Event: New York Philharmonic," 7.

77. "The Local Entertainment Field: New York Philharmonic," *Hartford Evening Post*, 17 February 1911, 5.

78. "Unusual Musical Event: New York Philharmonic," 7.

79. "Unusual Musical Event: New York Philharmonic," 7.

80. "N.Y. Philharmonic Orchestra's Success," 10.

81. "Unusual Musical Event: New York Philharmonic," 7.

82. "Unusual Musical Event: New York Philharmonic," 7.

83. "Unusual Musical Event: New York Philharmonic," 7.

84. "N.Y. Philharmonic Orchestra's Success," 10.

85. "The Local Entertainment Field: New York Philharmonic," 5.

86. "Unusual Musical Event: New York Philharmonic," 7.

87. "N.Y. Philharmonic Orchestra's Success," 10.

88. Mac Henry, "Walter Damrosch," *Hartford Evening Post*, 2 February 1911, 4.

89. Henry, 4.

90. "Last Concert by Boston Symphony," *Hartford Daily Courant*, 28 February 1911, 6.

91. "Last Concert by Boston Symphony," 6.

~

Epilogue

Several issues distracted researchers from thoroughly documenting Mahler's last tour during the winter of 1911. As early as December 1910 conflicting reports surfaced in the media regarding Mahler's replacement.[1] In a letter written to Emil Gutmann, Mahler seemed certain and determined to spend another season in New York.[2] At the end of January 1911, however, the *Musical Courier* reported that the guarantors were still searching for a conductor. The writer considered Mahler a strong possibility and the "favorite selection of the greatest number of music lovers in the metropolis," but as of that time, the committee announced no definite intentions.[3] Even as late as March, weeks after Mahler fell ill, major music periodicals such as the *New Music Review and Church Music Review* and *Musical America* reported, "It is stated positively that Gustav Mahler has been engaged for another year as conductor of the Philharmonic Society."[4] Furthermore, the reporter commended Mahler on the larger audiences seen lately at concerts. The article also indicated violinist Franz Kneisel as the only other individual rumored as a possible contender.[5] Other sources such as the *New York Times* confirmed that the Philharmonic engaged Mahler for a third season, even though some matters still needed to be resolved with the directors of the society.[6]

As several sources documented, and as Alma Mahler noted, in the middle of February Mary Sheldon summoned Mahler and declined to renew his contract for the following season. After becoming critically ill on February 21, 1911, Mahler remained in New York for six additional weeks and finally departed for Europe on April 8, 1911. He died in Vienna on May 18, 1911, and was buried in the Grinzing Cemetery.

Selecting a New Director

Ironically, in the same issue of *Musical America* on May 13, 1911, that reported "Gustav Mahler's Illness Critical," another article on the same page verified that two cables were received in New York confirming the appointment of Joseph Stransky as the Philharmonic's new director. The orchestra's management, however, refrained from making any official announcement of the appointment until several weeks later. In a subsequent issue of *Musical America* dated May 27, 1911, a headline on the front page announced "Gustav Mahler's Untimely Death" and further down on the page Loudon Charlton confirmed Stransky as the Philharmonic's new leader. Stransky agreed to take the position for $22,000 a year and reigned as conductor until 1922.

Charlton Leaves

Although some writers criticized the grueling schedule Charlton designed for Mahler, life as a manager of musical artists also proved strenuous. For more than thirty years, Charlton managed the career of international artists. With the toll of the Great Depression and substantial market losses, however, Charlton encountered difficult times. On April 27, 1931, after waking up and greeting his wife, singer Helen Stanley, Charlton placed three pillows on the bedroom floor and shot himself in the head with a .32 caliber bullet.[7] Unfortunately, none of the documents from Charlton's business transactions survive in the archives of the New York Philharmonic, Carnegie Hall, or the New York Public Library.

Mary Sheldon—Records and Financial Support

As indicated earlier many records and articles from the 1910–1911 season remained incomplete. Although it was believed that one of the women on the committee collected newspaper articles related to the orchestra's activity, it appears certain that Sheldon took on the responsibility of keeping the orchestra's records and financial papers. Sheldon proved to be irreplaceable in raising money to cover the guarantee fund for three seasons. At the end of December 1910 she became extremely ill and was rushed to the hospital for emergency surgery. At the same time Sheldon discontinued maintaining records and documents of the Philharmonic, and hence, even today, this period remains incomplete in the Philharmonic's collection.

Many writers criticized Sheldon for her actions toward Mahler during his final months. Nevertheless, Sheldon persuaded Mahler to join the Philharmonic in the first place and raised enough money to ensure the orchestra's future for three years. Despite Sheldon's efforts, her health continued to deteriorate, and more than two years after Mahler's death, Sheldon passed away on June 16, 1913.[8]

Before Sheldon's death, however, the Philharmonic received news of a bequest from Joseph Pulitzer of $500,000 from his estate valued at more than thirty million dollars. The Metropolitan Museum of Art represented the only other cultural institution that received a gift of equal value from Pulitzer.[9] Just as the guarantor fund dwindled, this generous contribution placed the Philharmonic on solid financial ground, and the *New York Times* announced that the money "Will Save Philharmonic" and "Makes City's Oldest Musical Society Very Much Alive."[10]

Mahler's Legacy

This period in Mahler's career presents an exciting time in America's cultural development, as musicians immigrated and orchestras formed throughout the country. With a constellation of special circumstances, concertgoers from New York and more than a dozen other cities witnessed Mahler as a leading conductor of symphonic music. These fortunate opportunities occurred only a brief time before Mahler's death and the onset of World War I. With the reorganization of the Philharmonic, a renewed level of enthusiasm among the public, and a boost in financial contributions, the Philharmonic entered a new era. With the efforts of managers Leifels and Charlton, Mary Sheldon and a group of guarantors, and a renowned conductor, Gustav Mahler, the Philharmonic faced a prosperous future.

These years brought about a series of firsts for Mahler and the New York Philharmonic. During Mahler's period the orchestra embarked on their first tours. Compared with other traveling ensembles, the Philharmonic was one of the first orchestras to travel with one hundred musicians. For the first time in years the Philharmonic experienced no deficits on its balance sheet, and as a result of the restructuring, the musicians became full-time employees for the first time. Throughout the tours audiences heard some selections for the first time and especially enjoyed Mahler's performances of his Bach Suite.

Mahler's impact in America continued and flourished beyond his lifetime. Beginning with a renewed interest in Mahler's music after World War II, major and even minor orchestras now regularly program his music. As a conductor, Mahler improved the performance standards of the New York Philharmonic, preserved the intentions of composers, broadened the audience base beyond New York City, and transformed the orchestra into a leading orchestra in America. These accomplishments led the Philharmonic, the oldest orchestra in the United States, to a bright future.

Notes

1. Zoltan Roman, *Gustav Mahler's American Years: 1907–1911* (Stuyvesant, NY: Pendragon Press, 1989), 380.

2. Knud Martner, ed., *Selected Letters of Gustav Mahler*, 2d ed., trans. Eithne Wilkins, Ernst Kaiser, and Bill Hopkins (London: Ebenezer Baylis and Son, 1979), 370. Emil Gutmann (1877–1922) was a German impresario and organized the premiere of Mahler's Eighth Symphony in Munich. During his career he worked primarily in Berlin and Munich.

3. *The Musical Courier* 62, no. 4 (January 25, 1911): 20.

4. "Facts, Rumors, and Remarks," *The New Music Review and Church Music Review* 10, no. 112 (March, 1911): 204.

5. "Facts, Rumors, and Remarks," 204.

6. "Mr. Mahler Still Absent," *New York Times*, May 11, 1911, 13.

7. "Loudon Charlton is [sic] Suicide in Home," *New York Times*, April 28, 1931, 56. Additional obituary articles are available in the Music Division of the New York Public Library for the Performing Arts, Astor, Lenox and Tilden Foundations.

8. "Mrs. G. R. Sheldon Dead," *New York Times*, June 17, 1913, 7.

9. "Pulitzer Paper Left in Trust," *New York Times*, November 14, 1911, 1.

10. "Will Save Philharmonic," *New York Times*, November 14, 1911, 2.

∼

Reconstructed Programs

Monday, January 17, 1910   **Academy of Music—Philadelphia**

Symphony No. 5 in C Minor, Op. 67   Ludwig van Beethoven
  Allegro con brio   (1770–1827)
  Andante con molto
  Allegro
  Allegro
Overture to *The Bartered Bride*   Bedřich Smetana
    (1824–1884)

Till Eulenspiegels lustige Streiche   Richard Strauss
    (1864–1949)

Prelude to *Die Meistersinger von Nürnberg*   Richard Wagner
    (1813–1883)

Wednesday, February 23, 1910   **Woolsey Hall—New Haven**

Symphonie Fantastique, Op. 14   Hector Berlioz
  Rêveries, passions   (1803–1869)
  Un bal
  Scène aux champs
  Marche au supplice
  Songe d'une nuit de sabbat

Suite for Orchestra   Johann Sebastian Bach
   Overture from Orchestral Suite No. 2 in B Minor   (1685–1750)
   [BWV 1067]
   Rondeau from Orchestral Suite No. 2   Arr. Gustav Mahler
   Air from Orchestral Suite No. 3 in D Major [BWV 1068]   (1860–1911)
   Gavotte from Orchestral Suite No. 3
              Gustav Mahler, Harpsichord
               Harry Jepson, Organ
Piano Concerto in A Minor, Op. 16   Edvard Grieg
   Allegro molto moderato   (1843–1907)
   Adagio
   Allegro moderato molto e marcato
             Olga Samaroff, Piano
Till Eulenspiegels lustige Streiche   Richard Strauss
                         (1864–1949)

Thursday, February 24, 1910 Court Square Theater—Springfield

Symphonie Fantastique, Op. 14   Hector Berlioz
   Rêveries, passions   (1803–1869)
   Un bal
   Scène aux champs
   Marche au supplice
   Songe d'une nuit de sabbat
Suite for Orchestra   Johann Sebastian Bach
   Overture from Orchestral Suite No. 2 in B Minor   (1685–1750)
   [BWV 1067]
   Rondeau from Orchestral Suite No. 2   Arr. Gustav Mahler
   Air from Orchestral Suite No. 3 in D Major,   (1860–1911)
   [BWV 1068]
   Gavotte from Orchestral Suite No. 3
            Gustav Mahler, Harpsichord
"Quanto dolci" from *Flavio*   George Frideric Handel
                         (1685–1759)
"Voi che sapete" from *Le Nozze di Figaro*   Wolfgang Amadeus Mozart
                         (1756–1791)

            Corrine Rider-Kelsey, Soloist
Till Eulenspiegels lustige Streiche   Richard Strauss
                         (1864–1949)

Prelude to *Die Meistersinger von Nürnberg*   Richard Wagner
                         (1813–1883)

Friday, February 25, 1910   Infantry Hall—Providence

Symphonie Fantastique, Op. 14   Hector Berlioz
    Rêveries, passions   (1803–1869)
    Un bal
    Scène aux champs
    Marche au supplice
    Songe d'une nuit de sabbat
Violin Concerto No. 5 in A Minor, Op. 37 (*Grétry*)   Henri Vieuxtemps
    Allegro non troppo   (1820–1881)
    Adagio
    Allegro con fuoco
       Theodore Spiering, Violin
Till Eulenspiegels lustige Streiche   Richard Strauss
    (1864–1949)

Prelude to *Die Meistersinger von Nürnberg*   Richard Wagner
    (1813–1883)

Saturday, February 26, 1910   Symphony Hall—Boston

Symphonie Fantastique, Op. 14   Hector Berlioz
    Rêveries, passions   (1803–1869)
    Un bal
    Scène aux champs
    Marche au supplice
    Songe d'une nuit de sabbat
Suite for Orchestra   Johann Sebastian Bach
    Overture from Orchestral Suite No. 2 in B Minor   (1685–1750)
    [BWV 1067]
    Rondeau from Orchestral Suite No. 2   Arr. Gustav Mahler
    Air from Orchestral Suite No. 3 in D Major [BWV 1068]   (1860–1911)
    Gavotte from Orchestral Suite No. 3
       Gustav Mahler, Harpsichord
Overture No. 3 to *Leonore*, Op. 72   Ludwig van Beethoven
    (1770–1827)

Till Eulenspiegels lustige Streiche   Richard Strauss
    (1864–1949)

Monday, March 14, 1910   **Academy of Music—Philadelphia**

Symphonie Fantastique, Op. 14	Hector Berlioz
Rêveries, passions	(1803–1869)
Un bal	
Scène aux champs	
Marche au supplice	
Songe d'une nuit de sabbat	
Violin Concerto in D Major, Op. 61	Ludwig van Beethoven
Allegro ma non troppo	(1770–1827)
Larghetto	
Rondo	

Fritz Kreisler, Violin

Overture to *Tannhäuser*	Richard Wagner
	(1813–1883)

Monday, December 5, 1910   **Soldiers and Sailors**
Memorial Hall—Pittsburgh
Tuesday, December 6, 1910   Grays Armory—Cleveland
Wednesday, December 7, 1910   Convention Hall—Buffalo
Thursday, December 8, 1910   Convention Hall—Rochester
Friday, December 9, 1910 New Wieting Opera House—Syracuse
Saturday, December 10, 1910   Majestic Theater—Utica

Suite for Orchestra	Johann Sebastian Bach
Overture from Orchestral Suite No. 2 in B Minor	(1685–1750)
[BWV 1067]	
Rondeau from Orchestral Suite No. 2	Arr. Gustav Mahler
Air from Orchestral Suite No. 3 in D Major [BWV 1068]	(1860–1911)
Gavotte from Orchestral Suite No. 3	

Gustav Mahler, Harpsichord

Symphony No. 6 in F Major, Op. 68 (*Pastoral*)	Ludwig van Beethoven
Allegro ma non troppo	(1770–1827)
Andante molto moto	
Allegro	
Allegretto	
Prelude and Liebestod from *Tristan und Isolde*	Richard Wagner
	(1813–1883)
Siegfried Idyll	Richard Wagner
Prelude to *Die Meistersinger von Nürnberg*	Richard Wagner

Monday, January 23, 1911   Academy of Music—Philadelphia
Tuesday, January 24, 1911   New National Theatre—Washington, DC

Featuring Music by Richard Wagner (1813–1883)

Overture to *Rienzi*
Overture to *Der Fliegende Holländer*
Prelude to *Lohengrin*
Overture to *Tannhäuser*
Elisabeth's aria from *Tannhäuser*
Elsa's Dream from *Lohengrin*

Johanna Gadski, Soloist

Siegfried Idyll
Prelude and Liebestod from *Tristan und Isolde*

Johanna Gadski, Soloist

Prelude to *Die Meistersinger von Nürnberg*

Wednesday, February 15, 1911   Court Square Theater—Springfield
Thursday, February 16, 1911   Parsons' Theater—Hartford

Suite for Orchestra	Johann Sebastian Bach
Overture from Orchestral Suite No. 2 in B Minor	(1685–1750)
[BWV 1067]	
Rondeau from Orchestral Suite No. 2	Arr. Gustav Mahler
Air from Orchestral Suite No. 3 in D Major [BWV 1068]	(1860–1911)
Gavotte from Orchestral Suite No. 3	

Gustav Mahler, Harpsichord

Symphony No. 6 in F Major, Op. 68 (*Pastoral*)	Ludwig van Beethoven
Allegro ma non troppo	(1770–1827)
Andante molto moto	
Allegro	
Allegro	
Allegretto	

II

Invitation to the Dance	Carl Maria von Weber
	(1786–1826)
	Arr. Felix Weingartner
	(1863–1942)

Leo Schulz, Cello

Les Préludes, R.414	Franz Liszt
	(1811–1886)

APPENDIX B

∼

Concert Halls

Academy of Music, Philadelphia

Still a center of cultural life in Philadelphia, the Academy of Music is the oldest grand opera house in America. Through an appeal made to the general public in 1852, funds were raised for its construction, which began on June 18, 1855. The Academy officially opened on January 26, 1857, with a Grand Ball and Promenade Concert. Napoleon Le Brun and Gustavus Runge designed the hall based on the horseshoe shape of La Scala. Located in the heart of Philadelphia at Broad and Locust Avenue, the hall offers 2,897 seats to concertgoers. The balconies are recessed and supported with fourteen Corinthian columns. A three-foot thick brick wall surrounds the auditorium, and a 5,000-pound crystal chandelier adorns the hall's interior. Originally constructed with 240 gas burners, the chandelier was electrified in 1900 and rewired in 1957. Since 1900, the Philadelphia Orchestra Association has owned the building.[1]

Nicknamed the "Old Lady of Locust Street," the Academy was designated as a National Historical Landmark in 1963. Money for funding the restoration projects and maintenance is raised through the annual Anniversary Concert and Ball. Beginning in 1994, a $31 million renovation, known as the Twenty-first Century Project, restored the Academy's ceiling, enhanced the acoustics, paid for the installation of a new wooden stage floor, and provided seating for the physically disabled.

Gustav Mahler conducted three Philharmonic concerts at the Academy on Monday, January 17, 1910; Monday, March 14, 1910; and Monday, January

23, 1911. He made his first appearance at the Academy on February 18, 1908, when he conducted the Metropolitan Opera in a production of Mozart's *Don Giovanni*.

Woolsey Hall, New Haven, Connecticut

Since 1902, Woolsey Hall has been used as a concert hall and remains the home of the New Haven Symphony Orchestra. As part of Yale University, the hall was named in honor of Theodore Dwight Woolsey, president of Yale from 1846 to 1871. The Hutschings-Votey Organ Company of Boston[2] constructed the Newberry Memorial Organ in Woolsey Hall during the 1902–1903 academic year. Helen Handy Newberry of Detroit, Michigan, provided the funds for the organ and dedicated the instrument in memory of her late husband John Stoughton Newberry.[3] Professor Jepson and Professor Sanford authorized the specifications and installation of the organ.

Even today the original wooden seats and hardwood floor, present when Mahler conducted the Philharmonic on February 23, 1910, still exist in Woolsey. The hall is 126 feet long from the front of the organ to the back wall, ninety-three feet wide, and fifty-six feet high. The arched ceiling provides the hall with a resonance of four seconds when the hall is empty and two seconds when the hall is full. Woolsey Hall offers 2,683 seats with 1,109 in the orchestra section, 372 in the parquet, 867 in the first balcony, and 335 in the second balcony.

Court Square Theater, Springfield, Massachusetts

On Thursday, February 24, 1910, and Wednesday, February 15, 1911, Gustav Mahler conducted the New York Philharmonic at the Court Square Theater. Originally located at 378 Main Street near Elm Street, the Court opened on September 5, 1892. After Dwight Gilmore purchased the property, he hired J. B. McElfatrick and Sons of New York to design the theater. When Gilmore died in 1918, his nephew Dwight O. Gilmore ran the theater under Gilmore and Associates. In 1937, E. M. Loew's Theaters of Boston leased the building as a movie house, and starting in 1941, the Playgoers of Springfield offered occasional Broadway shows and road attractions. After restoration, Samuel Wasserman leased the Court in 1953, and in 1955, Owen Holmes made one last attempt to revitalize the facility. After the 30,000 square feet of space was demolished in 1956, the Meyers' Brothers Parking System turned the property into a parking lot in 1958.[4]

Built with Blanford buff brick, the Court stood five stories high. The stage ran eighty feet wide and seventy feet long. Complete with twenty-eight dressing rooms and gorgeous painted stage scenes, the theater also included a main curtain that depicted Springfield's Old Elm Street in the late nineteenth century. The hall accommodated 1,860 people and offered 725 seats on the main floor, 535 seats on the first balcony, 500 in the upper balcony, and 100 in the gallery. Beautiful frescoes decorated the ceiling, and concertgoers enjoyed elegantly furnished restrooms. A promenade of seventy-five feet extended the rear of the house, and a separate entrance led audiences to the balconies.[5]

Infantry Hall, Providence, Rhode Island

On May 12, 1879, the First Light Infantry laid the cornerstone for the Infantry Hall on South Main Street. George W. Cady designed the building to accommodate 2,000 people, and it officially opened in January 1880. The infantry used the building as their armory and remained the owners until its destruction by fire on October 4, 1942. Infantry Hall served as the scene of Providence's musical, political, and sporting events. Although Mahler conducted only one concert at the hall on February 25, 1910, from 1882 to 1926 the Boston Symphony Orchestra offered more than 200 concerts at the hall.

The building was constructed of brick with a four-story façade and a tower at the center. At one end of the hall the stage and dressing rooms stood, and galleries surrounded the remaining three sides. The assembly room occupied the second floor of Infantry Hall, stretching seventy-five feet wide and one hundred and forty feet long.[6]

Between 1910 and 1920 the facility became known as a leading sports center in New England. After a decline in the 1920s and several changes in management, it closed in 1926.[7] The hall escaped several threats of demolition and reopened after a renovation in 1929. During this period the hall featured wrestling, basketball, and boxing, while its top floor served as the headquarters for the Catholic Youth Organization. Prior to its destruction in 1942 the hall was used as a roller-skating rink.

Symphony Hall, Boston, Massachusetts

Symphony Hall became home to the Boston Symphony Orchestra when it opened on October 15, 1900. When Major Henry Lee Higginson decided to give his orchestra a permanent home, he formed a corporation to raise $750,000 for the hall. McKim, Mead and White of New York designed the hall and created an auditorium that used "scientifically-derived acoustical principles."[8] Located at 301 Massachusetts Avenue, the hall was encased in two layers of concrete to reduce traffic noise. The rectangular auditorium features two balconies and, except for the wooden floor, is supported with brick, tile, and plaster. Although minimal decoration appears in the hall, the red railings, carpeting, and deep maroon walls from the floor to the first balcony enliven it. Originally, the upper walls appeared in shades of gray and cream while five large chandeliers adorned the ceiling. Within two years after the building opened, sixteen replicas of Greek and Roman statues occupied the niches around the hall and provided an important factor in the hall's acoustics. In 1949, an Aeolian-Skinner Organ designed by G. Donald Harrison was installed in the hall. The 2,625 original leather seats were replaced with tables and chairs for the Boston Pops concerts, which can accommodate 2,371 concertgoers.[9]

Although Mahler directed the Metropolitan Opera in Boston during April 1908, he conducted only one Philharmonic concert at Symphony Hall, on February 26, 1910.

Soldiers and Sailors Memorial Hall, Pittsburgh

Located in the heart of downtown Pittsburgh at 4141 Fifth Avenue, the hall was created as a memorial to the soldiers and sailors who fought during the Civil War. Although it took forty-five years to complete, the dream for the hall took shape in 1891 when the twenty-eight military posts formed the Allegheny County Grand Army Association. Upon the hall's completion, a religious service was held on October 9, 1910, followed by the actual dedication exercises on October 11, 1910. Styled after the mausoleum of Halicarnassus, the building that Plamer and Hornbostel designed cost $1,562,500.

Memorial Hall occupies a four-acre city block with 280 feet facing Fifth Avenue. The exterior of the building has a width of 240 feet and a depth of 210 feet with a pyramided roof that tops approximately 106 feet above Fifth Avenue.[10] In front of the building are two stone tablets, one on each side of the pillars, fifty-one feet high by five feet wide. The hall is 110 by 120 feet with a ceiling sixty-five feet high. The square hall offers 2,378 seats with 1,562 seats on the first floor and another 816 in the balcony. In addition, the stage of twenty-eight by seventy-eight feet can accommodate another three hundred people. Stretching seventy by eight feet across the back wall of the stage is the largest reproduction of Lincoln's Gettysburg Address. The building remains open to the public and is frequently used for local graduations. Along the left corridor in the ninth showcase, which contains Abraham Lincoln's death mask, are two original concert chairs from when Mahler conducted the Philharmonic on Tuesday, December 5, 1910.

Grays Armory, Cleveland

Located only a few blocks from Jacobs Field at the corner of Bolivar Street near Prospect Avenue, Grays Armory has been a part of Cleveland's history since it opened in 1893. Local architect Fenimore C. Bates designed the building for the private military company, the Cleveland Grays. The Grays planned to use the building primarily as a meeting lodge and as a place for training men for the military. With fairly decent acoustics in the Armory, many groups performed there including Gustav Mahler and the New York Philharmonic on December 6, 1910. Throughout the past century the Armory held events ranging from chicken shows, which included contests for the best breeds, to symphonic concerts. Today the Armory can still be rented for various functions and offers several educational programs.

The Armory is a stone building shaped like a typical drill hall with a five-story tower. The hall contains no permanent seating, but at the turn of the twentieth century approximately 5,000 stiff wooden chairs were arranged for concerts. Even though the Armory was never intended to be a concert hall, it served as home of The Cleveland Orchestra until Severance Hall opened in 1923.[11] As various theaters and concert halls opened in Cleveland, the Armory became less popular as a performance space. In 1963, the Warner Brothers donated a Wurlitzer theater pipe organ from Erie, Pennsylvania, to the armory and began offering organ concerts. Grays Armory still offers organ concerts several times throughout the year.

Convention Hall, Buffalo

Today on the northeast corner of Virginia and Elmwood Avenue in Buffalo stands a Rite Aid Pharmacy, but when Mahler visited Buffalo on December 7, 1910, Convention Hall occupied this site. With assistance from architect Robert A. Bethune, the Seventy-Fourth Regiment of New York founded the building in 1887. When the regiment outgrew the building in 1901, the city took over the management under the name Convention Hall. In the same year J. N. Adams gave the hall the organ from the Pan-American Exposition in Buffalo. The stage was remodeled to accommodate the organ, and after its installation, a series of Sunday afternoon organ concerts marked the hall's first musical programs. Located on Elmwood Avenue, Convention Hall officially became known as the Elmwood Music Hall in 1912.

Until 1938, Convention Hall offered programs featuring fine soloists, orchestras, and operas. Even though the hall could accommodate approximately 5,000 concertgoers, it did not remain a success. Located on an extremely busy avenue in Buffalo, streetcars could be heard throughout the building and provided a constant distraction during the performances. The hall's popularity continued to decline, and on February 25, 1938, Nelson Eddy performed the last concert. Shortly thereafter, the building was condemned.[12]

Convention Hall, Rochester, New York

Once known as Convention Hall, the building at 168 South Clinton Avenue, on the south side of Rochester's Washington Square, was built in 1871 to house the Fifty-fourth Regiment of the New York National Guard. The facility, however, changed owners a number of times over the past century. When the guard moved to a new location in 1907, the city took over the building and on March 18, 1908, opened it as Convention Hall. In addition, they constructed an annex on the back in 1909. Although the facility was too small to accommodate large conventions between 1909 and 1938, Convention Hall welcomed entertainment, political debates, rallies, and musical events, including a concert that featured Mahler and the New York Philharmonic on December 8, 1910. Even political leaders such as Franklin D. Roosevelt, William Jennings Bryan, Theodore Roosevelt, and William Howard Taft appeared at the hall for various conventions.

The hall consists of 38,000 square feet and in 1910 could accommodate 3,000 concertgoers. A marble staircase leads from the first floor to a mezzanine balcony.[13] Prior to the construction of the Eastman Theater, the Rochester Orchestra performed in the hall. In the 1920s, George Eastman converted the facility into a free tonsil clinic, and during the Great Depression the Welfare Department used the annex to dispense clothing and food. From 1949 to 1969 the Naval Militia leased the hall, razing the two towers and creating skeletal steel towers for radars. The GeVa Players purchased the hall from the city for one dollar in 1982 and operate it today as the Richard Pine Theater.[14]

New Wieting Opera House, Syracuse

Constructed in 1897, the New Wieting Opera House, where Mahler performed on December 9, 1910, was the fourth and last Wieting Opera House built on the site. After an enormous fire on the Wieting block in 1851, Dr. John M. Wieting purchased the property and opened the first Wieting Hall on December 16, 1852. Less than four years later, in 1856, the hall burned to the ground, and with only the left wall remaining, Wieting reconstructed the building and opened the second Wieting on December 9, 1856. In 1870, the Wieting was renovated and renamed the Wieting Opera House on September 19, 1870. After Wieting's death, another fire engulfed the hall in 1895. Then Mrs. Wieting hired architect Oscar Cobb and builder Amos L. Mason to rebuild the hall for the fourth time.[15]

The hall featured 2,150 seats with 750 available on the orchestral level, 250 on the entresol, 400 in the balcony, and 750 in the gallery. The balcony floor provided standing room for 300 additional people. The auditorium was decorated in a pale green and gold color scheme and offered a small stage.[16] When the building opened, it had a "larger seating capacity than any of best theaters in New York."[17] The site of the theater is now in the Atrium Building on Water Street directly across from Clinton Square.

Majestic Theater, Utica, New York

The Majestic Theater originally opened as the Utica Opera House in 1870 on the corner of Lafayette and Washington Streets. After it was partially torn down in 1900, the remaining walls formed the beginning of the Majestic Theater. Schubert Management operated the theater and arranged for numerous attractions that made the Majestic the most popular theater in Utica. Wilmer and Vincent took over the lease in 1905, and in later years B. L. Burt managed the building and offered motion pictures and vaudeville shows.[18] In the 1950s the Hotel Pershing stood on the site, but eventually the building was turned into a parking lot.[19]

The auditorium was sixty-seven feet wide and seventy-eight feet deep. The main floor featured 420 seats on a sloping floor and a group of twelve boxes. A marble staircase led to the balcony level that looked down into the lobby and contained 425 seats. The gallery could be accessed from Washington Street and offered 500 seats with two rows of reserved seats and nine rows of benches. The unique "gallerette" on the fourth floor offered standing room and seventy-five seats immediately in front of the gallery.[20] The stage was forty feet in depth and sixty-seven feet wide with a height of sixty-seven feet. Contained in the theater were fifteen complete sets of scenery. Mahler led the New York Philharmonic in a concert at the Majestic on December 10, 1910.

New National Theatre, Washington, D.C.

Recognized as the oldest cultural center in Washington, D.C., the National Theatre was founded by William Corcoran in 1835. Located only three blocks east of the White House at 1321 Pennsylvania Avenue, the National Theatre is known as "The Theatre of Presidents." From its beginning, every U.S. president has attended an event at the theater. On January 24, 1911, First Lady Mrs. Helen Taft appeared in the audience as Mahler led the New York Philharmonic in a concert.

During the nineteenth century fire damaged, and even destroyed, the building several times. Hence, when the theater reopened for the fifth time in 1885 with a 1,900 seat interior, some writers referred to the hall as the New National Theatre, New National Hall, or Grover's National Theater.[21] Today's theater is the sixth renovation of the building and dates back to the 1920s. The renovation in 1984 replaced the original dressing room wing and the stage alley and added a rehearsal room and a stage security office. In addition, the lobby was expanded to four times its original size. In 1983 designer Oliver Smith created the present interior décor.

The Schubert Organization currently manages the theater for the nonprofit National Theatre Corporation. Inside the hall 820 seats are available on the orchestral level, 446 in the mezzanine, 346 in the balcony, and 44 in the boxes giving a total of 1,656 seats.

Parsons' Theater, Hartford, Connecticut

On February 16, 1911, Mahler conducted his last concert outside New York at Parsons' Theater. Herbert C. Parsons started building the theater in the fall of 1895, and it opened on April 1, 1896. Noted as the location where the best shows performed and one of the first stops for performances outside New York City, the theater soon gained the reputation as "one of the best of the high-class theatres in the eastern states."[22] Located on the corner of Central Row and Prospect Street, Parsons' could accommodate 1,700 concertgoers. After a small fire in 1915, Parsons spent approximately twenty thousand dollars to update and refurbish the interior. The theater reopened in October 1915.[23]

Although Parsons originally owned the building, the Schubert Organization took over the theater in the 1920s. After the theater encountered difficult financial times from the Depression, it was demolished to make way for the Constitution Plaza complex. A New Parsons' Theater opened in 1951 on Main Street but went out of business by 1953.

Notes

1. Herbert Kupferberg, *Those Fabulous Philadelphians* (New York: Charles Scribner's Sons, 1969), 152.

2. George Sherburn Hutchings started an organ company in 1860 called the J. H. Wilcox Company. Following several reorganizations, the company built a new factory and formed the Hutchings-Votey Organ Company in 1901. After financial difficulties, the company folded in 1919. For more information see Barbara Owen, "Hutchings, George Sherburn," *The New Grove Dictionary of Music and Musicians*, ed. Stanley Sadie, 2d ed. (London: Macmillan, 2001), 11:896.

3. Edward W. Flint, *The Newberry Memorial Organ at Yale University* (New Haven: Yale University Press, 1930), 13.

4. David J. Williams, "Arrival of Metropolitan Opera Seats Recalls Theatrical Era of Grandeur," *Springfield Sunday Republican*, 26 February 1969, sec.1, 11.

5. "Dwight O. Gilmore," *The Leading Citizens of Hampden County Massachusetts* (Boston: Biographical Review Publishing Company, 1895), 484.

6. John Hutchins Cady, *The Civic and Architectural Development of Providence: 1635–1950* (Providence: The Book Shop, 1957), 154.

7. "Famed Personages of World Once Seen in Infantry Hall," *Providence Journal*, 5 October 1942, 5.

8. Leaflet, "Symphony Hall—A Brief History," Boston Symphony Orchestra Archives, n.d.

9. H. Earle Johnson, *Symphony Hall, Boston* (Boston: Little, Brown and Company, 1950), 12.

10. *Soldiers and Sailors Memorial Hall: Yesterday and Today* (Pittsburgh: Board of Managers and Board of Commissioners of the Soldiers and Sailors Memorial Hall, 1983), 6.

11. David D. VanTassel and John J. Grabowski, eds., *The Encyclopedia of Cleveland History* (Bloomington: Indiana University Press, 1987), s.v. "Grays Armory."

12. Mildred E. Wolf, *History of Music in Buffalo: 1820–1945* (Buffalo: Kleinhans Musical Hall Management, 1945), 18.

13. "Plan for 'Convention Hall' in Duffy-Powers Site Told," *Rochester Democrat and Chronicle*, 12 September 1940, 19.

14. "Reminiscing Rochester: Arsenal, Convention Hall, Theatre," *Rochester Democrat and Chronicle*, 20 November 1999, sec. 2, 5.

15. Franklin H. Chase, *Syracuse and Its Environs: A History*, vol. 1 (New York: Lewis Historical Publishing Company, 1924), 237.

16. George Hawley, Syracuse, to Mary H. Wagner, Syracuse, 31 January 2000.

17. "Finest of Playhouses," *Syracuse Standard*, 8 September 1897.

18. "Large audience at Majestic Reopening," *Utica Herald-Dispatch*, 7 January 1916.

19. "Utica Area Offers Rich History of Old Music Theaters," *Utica Observer-Dispatch*, 25 April 1999, sec. G, 2.

20. John J. Walsh, *Vignettes of Old Utica* (Utica, NY: Utica Public Library, 1982), 363.

21. Douglas Bennett Lee, Roger L. Meersman, and Donn B. Murphy, *Stage for a Nation: The National Theatre, 150 Years* (New York: University Press of America, 1985), 135.

22. Marion Hepburn Grant, *In and About Hartford: Tours and Tales* (Hartford, CT: Connecticut Historical Society, 1978), 148.

23. "Parsons' Theatre: Twentieth Anniversary Historical Souvenir, 1 April 1916," Box Programs, "Parsons' Theatre," Connecticut Historical Society, Hartford, Connecticut.

~

Bibliography

Books and Dissertations

Aldrich, Richard. *Concert Life in New York: 1902–1923*. New York: G.P. Putnam's Sons, 1941.

Alexander, J. Heywood. *It Must Be Heard: A Survey of Musical Life of Cleveland, 1836–1918*. Cleveland: The Western Reserve Historical Society, 1981.

Amory, Cleveland. *The Proper Bostonians*. Orleans, MA: Parnassus Imprints, 1947.

Arian, Edward. *Bach, Beethoven, and Bureaucracy: The Case of the Philadelphia Orchestra*. Tuscaloosa: University of Alabama Press, 1971.

[Ayer.] *N. W. Ayer and Son's Newspaper Annual and Directory of 1910*. Philadelphia: N. W. Ayer and Son, 1910.

Bauer, Jr., Frank. *At the Crossroads: Springfield, Massachusetts, 1636–1975*. Springfield, MA: Bicentennial Committee of Springfield, 1975.

Baynham, Edward G. "A History of Pittsburgh Music 1758–1958." 2 vols. (photocopy). Music and Art Department, Carnegie Library, Pittsburgh.

Blaukopf, Kurt, and Herta Blaukopf, eds. *Mahler: His Life Work, and World*. New York: Thames and Hudson, 2000.

Broyles, Michael. *"Music of the Highest Class": Elitism and Populism in Antebellum Boston*. New Haven: Yale University Press, 1992.

Burns, Sarah. *Inventing the Modern Artist: Art and Culture in Gilded Age America*. New Haven: Yale University Press, 1996.

Cady, John Hutchins. *The Civic and Architectural Development of Providence: 1635–1950*. Providence, RI: The Book Shop, 1957.

Carr, Jonathan. *Mahler: A Biography*. Woodstock, NY: Overlook Press, 1999.

Chase, Franklin H. *Syracuse and Its Environs: A History*. 4 vols. New York: Lewis Historical Publishing Company, 1924.

Conley, Patrick T., and Paul R. Campbell. *Providence: A Pictorial History*. Norfolk, VA: Donning, 1982.

Cooke, Deryck. *Gustav Mahler: An Introduction to His Music*. London: Faber Music, 1980.

Damrosch, Walter. *My Musical Life*. New York: Charles Scribner's Sons, 1923.

Dizikes, John. *Opera in America*. New Haven: Yale University Press, 1993.

Dunn, Samuel O. *Current Railway Problems*. New York: Railway Age Gazette, 1911.

Eaton, Quaintance. *The Boston Opera Company*. New York: Appleton-Century, 1965.

_____. *Opera Caravan: Adventures of the Metropolitan Company on Tour*. New York: The Metropolitan Opera Guild, 1957.

Ellis, David M., James A. Frost, Harold C. Syrett, and Harry J. Carman. *A History of New York State*. Ithaca, NY: Cornell University Press, 1967.

Erskine, John. *The Philharmonic-Symphony Society of New York: Its First Hundred Years*. New York: The Macmillan Company, 1943.

Filler, Susan Melanie. *Gustav and Alma Mahler: A Guide to Research*. New York: Garland Publishing, 1989.

Flint, Edward W. *The Newberry Memorial Organ at Yale University*. New Haven: Yale University Press, 1930.

Floros, Constantin. *Gustav Mahler: The Symphonies*. Translated by Vernon and Jutta Wicker. Edited by Reinhard G. Pauly. Portland, OR: Amadeus Press, 1993.

Foreman, Howard R., ed. *Centennial History of Rochester, New York*. 3 vols. Rochester, NY: Rochester Historical Society, 1932.

Franklin, Peter. *The Life of Mahler*. Cambridge: Cambridge University Press, 1997.

Gartenberg, Egon. *Mahler: The Man and His Music*. New York: Schirmer, 1978.

Giroud, Françoise. *Alma Mahler or the Art of Being Loved*. Translated by R. M. Stock. Oxford: Oxford University Press, 1991.

Grant, Marion Hepburn. *In and About Hartford: Tours and Tales*. Hartford, CT: Connecticut Historical Society, 1978.

Grant, Mark N. *Maestros of the Pen*. Edited by Eric Friedheim. Boston: Northeastern University Press, 1998.

Gregory, Winifred. *American Newspapers 1821–1936: A Union List of Files Available in the United States and Canada*. New York: The H.W. Wilson Company, 1937.

Grossman, F. Karl. *A History of Music in Cleveland*. Cleveland: Case Western Reserve University, 1972.

Harris, Neil. *Cultural Excursions: Marketing Appetites and Cultural Tastes in Modern America*. Chicago: University of Chicago Press, 1990.

Hart, Philip. *Orpheus in the New World: The Symphony Orchestra as an American Cultural Institution*. New York: W. W. Norton, 1973.

Heilbrun, James. *The Economics of Art and Culture: An American Perspective*. Cambridge: Cambridge University Press, 1993.

Horowitz, Joseph. *Wagner Nights: An American History*. Berkeley: University of California, 1994.

Howe, M. A. DeWolfe. *The Boston Symphony Orchestra 1881–1931*. 2d ed. Revised and extended with John N. Burk. Cambridge: The Riverside Press, 1931.

Hughes, Adella Prentiss. *Music Is My Life*. Cleveland: World Publishing Company, 1947.

Huneker, James Gibbons. *The Philharmonic Society of New York and Its Seventy-fifth Anniversary: A Retrospect*. New York, 1917.

Ingersoll, Ernest. *Rand McNally and Company's Handy Guide to New York City*. New York: Rand McNally, 1912.

Johnson, Frances Hall. *Musical Memories of Hartford*. Hartford, CT: Finlay Brothers Press, 1931.

Johnson, Gerald W. "The Muckraking Era." In *Pittsburgh: The Story of an American City*, ed. Stefan Lorant. Garden City NY: Doubleday, 1964.

Johnson, H. Earle. *Symphony Hall, Boston*. Boston: Little, Brown and Company, 1950.

Kennedy, Michael. *Mahler*. London: Dent, 1974.

King, William G. *The Philharmonic Symphony Orchestra of New York*. Drawings by Lintott. New York: Press of R. Joffe, 1939.

Kraut, Alan M. *The Huddled Masses: The Immigrant in American Society, 1880–1921*. The American History Series. Wheeling, IL: Harlan Davidson, 1982.

Kupferberg, Herbert. *Those Fabulous Philadelphians: The Life and Times of a Great Orchestra*. New York: C. Scribner's Sons, 1969.

La Grange, Henry-Louis de. *Gustav Mahler: chronique d'une vie*. 3 vols. Paris: Fayard, 1973–84.

_____. *Mahler*. Vol. I. London: Gollancz, 1974; *Gustav Mahler,* Vol. II, *Vienna: The Years of Challenge (1897–1904)*. Oxford: Oxford University Press, 1995; *Gustav Mahler,* Vol. III, *Triumph and Disillusion (1904–1907)*. Oxford: Oxford University Press, 1999.

The Leading Citizens of Hampden County Massachusetts. Boston: Biographical Review Publishing Company, 1895.

Lebrecht, Norman. *The Maestro Myth: Great Conductors in Pursuit of Power*. Secaucus, NJ: Carol Publishing Group, 1991.

_____. *Mahler Remembered*. New York: W.W. Norton and Company, 1988.

_____. *Who Killed Classical Music? Maestros, Managers, and Corporate Politics*. Secaucus, NJ: Carol Publishing Group, 1997.

Lee, Douglas Bennett, Roger L. Meersman, and Donn B. Murphy. *Stage for a Nation: The National Theatre, 150 Years*. New York: University Press of America, 1985.

Levine, Lawrence W. *Highbrow/Lowbrow: The Emergence of Cultural Hierarchy in America*. Cambridge, MA: Harvard University Press, 1988.

Lynes, Russell. *The Lively Audience: A Social History of the Visual and Performing Arts 1890–1950*. The New American Nation Series, Henry Steele Commager and Richard B. Morris, eds. New York: Harper and Row, 1985.

Mahler, Alma, ed. *Gustav Mahler: Briefe 1879–1911*. Translated by K. Martner. Berlin: Zsolnay, 1924.

_____. *Gustav Mahler Memories and Letters*. Introduction by Donald Mitchell. Translated by Basil Creighton. London: Cox and Wyman, 1946.

Mahler, Gustav. *Die drei Pintos: Based on Sketches and Original Music of Carl Maria von Weber.* Edited by James L. Zychowicz. Madison WI: A-R Editions, 2000.

_____. *Letters to his Wife.* 2d ed. Edited by Henry-Louis de La Grange and Günther Weiss, in collaboration with Knud Martner. Translated by Antony Beaumont. Ithaca, NY: Cornell University Press, 2004.

Marsh, Robert C. *The Cleveland Orchestra.* Foreword by George Szell. Cleveland: World Publishing Company, 1967.

Martin, George. *The Damrosch Dynasty.* Boston: Houghton Mifflin, 1983.

Martner, Knud, ed. *Selected Letters of Gustav Mahler.* 2d ed. Translated by Eithne Wilkins, Ernst Kaiser, and Bill Hopkins. London: Ebenezer Baylis and Son, 1979.

_____. *Gustav Mahler im Konzertsaal.* Kopenhagen: Martner, 1985.

McKelvey, Blake. *Rochester: The Quest for Quality 1890–1925.* Cambridge, MA: Harvard University Press, 1956.

Millington, Barry, ed. *The Wagner Compendium: A Guide to Wagner's Life and Music.* London: Thames and Hudson, 1992.

Mitchell, Donald. *Gustav Mahler.* Vol. 1, *The Early Years.* 2d ed. Edited and revised by Paul Banks and David Matthews. Berkeley: University of California Press, 1980; reprint, Berkeley: University of California Press, 1995.

_____. *Gustav Mahler.* Vol. 2, *The Wunderhorn Years.* Berkeley: University of California Press, 1975; reprint, Berkeley: University of California Press, 1995.

Mitchell, Donald, and Andrew Nicholson, eds. *The Mahler Companion.* Oxford: Oxford University Press, 1999.

Moses, Montrose. *The Life of Heinrich Conried.* New York: Arno Press, 1977.

Mueller, John H. *The American Symphony Orchestra: A Social History of Music Taste.* Bloomington: Indiana University Press, 1951.

Mussulman, Joseph A. *Music in the Cultured Generation: A Social History of Music in America 1870–1900.* Studies in American Music. Evanston, IL: Northwestern University Press, 1971.

Newlin, Dika. *Bruckner, Mahler, Schoenberg.* 2d ed. New York: W.W. Norton and Company, 1978.

Palmer, Larry. *Harpsichord in America: A Twentieth-Century Revival.* Bloomington: Indiana University Press, 1989.

Reeb, Mary. "Adella Prentiss Hughes and the Founding, Fostering and Financing of the Cleveland Orchestra." *Gamut* 5, no. 2 (Spring/Summer 1985): 62–67.

Robinson, Francis. *Celebration: The Metropolitan Opera.* Garden City, NY: Doubleday and Company, 1979.

Roman, Zoltan. *Gustav Mahler's American Years 1907–1911.* Stuyvesant, NY: Pendragon Press, 1989.

Rose, William Ganson. *Cleveland: The Making of a City.* Cleveland: New World Publishing Company, 1950.

Rosenberg, Donald. *The Cleveland Orchestra Story: Second to None.* Cleveland: Gray and Company, 2000.

Roussel, Hubert. *The Houston Symphony Orchestra: 1913–1971.* Austin: University of Texas Press, 1972.

Russell, Charles Edward. *The American Orchestra and Theodore Thomas*. Garden City, NY: Doubleday, Page, 1927.

Sabin, Robert, ed. *The International Cyclopedia of Music and Musicians*. New York: Dodd, Mead, and Company, 1964.

Sabin, Stewart B. *Music in Rochester: From 1909 to 1924*, The Rochester Historical Society Fund Series. Edited by Edward R. Foreman, vol. 3. Rochester: Rochester Historical Society, 1924.

Sadie, Stanley, ed. *The New Grove Dictionary of Music and Musicians*. 20 vols. London: Macmillan, 1980.

_____. *The New Grove Dictionary of Music and Musicians*. 2d ed. 29 vols. London: Macmillan, 2001.

Schabas, Ezra. *Theodore Thomas: America's Conductor and Builder of Orchestras 1835–1905*. Urbana: University of Illinois Press, 1989.

Schickel, Richard. *The World of Carnegie Hall*. New York: Julian Messner, 1960.

Seckerson, Edward. *Mahler: His Life and Times*. New York: Hippocrene, 1982.

Shanet, Howard. *Philharmonic: A History of New York's Orchestra*. Garden City, NY: Doubleday, 1975.

Slonimsky, Nicolas, ed. *Baker's Biographical Dictionary of Music and Musicians*. 5th ed. New York: G. Schirmer, 1958.

Soldiers and Sailors Memorial Hall: Yesterday and Today. Pittsburgh: Board of Managers and Board of Commissioners of the Soldiers and Sailors Memorial Hall, 1983.

Stokowski, Olga Samaroff. *An American Musician's Story*. New York: W.W. Norton and Company, 1939.

Stover, John F. *American Railroads*. 2d ed. Chicago: University of Chicago Press, 1997.

Tebbel, John. *The Media in America*. New York: Thomas Y. Crowell Company, 1974.

Thomas, Rose Fay. *Memoirs of Theodore Thomas*. New York: Moffett, Yard, 1911.

Thomas, Theodore. *Theodore Thomas: A Musical Autobiography*. Edited by George P. Upton. New York: Da Capo Press, 1964.

Tibbetts, John C., ed. *Dvořák in America: 1892–1895*. Portland, OR: Amadeus Press, 1993.

Van Tassel, David D., and John J. Grabowski, eds. *The Encyclopedia of Cleveland History*. Bloomington: Indiana University Press, 1987.

von Deck, Marvin L. "Gustav Mahler in New York: His Conducting Activities in New York City, 1908–1911." Ph.D. diss., New York University, 1973.

Wagner, Mary. "Early Orchestras in Cleveland." Master's thesis, Kent State University, 1998.

Walsh, John J. *Vignettes of Old Utica*. Utica: Utica Public Library, 1982.

Walter, Bruno. *Gustav Mahler*. New York: Alfred A. Knopf, 1958.

Whitesitt, Linda. "The Role of Women Impresarios in American Concert Life, 1871–1933." *American Music* 7, no. 2 (Summer 1989): 159–180.

Witchey, Holly Rarick, and John Vacha. *Fine Arts in Cleveland*. Bloomington: Indiana University Press, 1994.

Wolf, Mildred E. *History of Music in Buffalo: 1820–1945*. Buffalo: Kleinhans Musical Hall Management, 1945.

Newspapers and Journals

Boston Advertiser, 31 January–28 February 1910.
Boston American, 31 January–28 February 1910.
Boston Corbett's Herald, 31 January–28 February 1910.
Boston Germania, 31 January–28 February 1910.
Boston Globe, 31 January–28 February 1910.
Boston Herald, 31 January–28 February 1910.
Boston Post, 31 January–28 February 1910.
Boston Transcript [includes *Daily Evening Transcript, Boston Daily Evening Transcript,* and *Boston Evening Transcript*], 31 January–28 February 1910.
Brighton-Pittsford Post.
Buffalo Courier, 3 December–8 December 1910.
Buffalo Enquirer, 23 November–8 December 1910.
Buffalo Evening News, 3 December–8 December 1910.
Buffalo Evening Times, 20 November–8 December 1910.
Buffalo Freie Presse, 3 December–8 December 1910.
Buffalo Morning Express, 4 September–8 December 1910.
Buffalo Morning Journal, 3 December–8 December 1910.
Buffalo Tribune, 3 December–8 December 1910.
Buffalo Volksfreund, 3 December–8 December 1910.
Buffalo Weekly Courier, 3 December–8 December 1910.
Christian Science Monitor, 31 January–28 February 1910.
Cleveland Leader, 18 September–10 December 1910.
Cleveland News, 1 October–10 December 1910.
Cleveland Plain Dealer, 3 December–10 December 1910.
Cleveland Town Topics, 26 November–10 December 1910.
Cleveland Wächter und Anzeiger, 3 December–10 December 1910.
Hartford Daily Courant, 10 February–28 February 1911.
Hartford Daily Times, 10 February–28 February 1911.
Hartford Evening Post, 10 February–28 February 1911.
Hartford Globe, 10 February–28 February 1911.
Lockport Union-Sun, 1 December–8 December 1910.
Musical America.
Musical Courier.
New Haven Columbian Weekly Register, 19 February–24 February 1910.
New Haven Evening Leader, 9 February–24 February 1910.
New Haven Morning Journal Courier, 9 February–24 February 1910.
New Haven Register [includes *New Haven Evening Register* and *New Haven Sunday Register*], 9 February–24 February 1910.

New Haven Times Leader, 9 February–24 February 1910.

New Haven Union, 9 February–24 February 1910.

New York Herald.

New York Times, 28 November 1888–28 April 1931.

New York Tribune.

Philadelphia Evening Bulletin, 1 January 1910–24 January 1911.

Philadelphia Evening Star, 1 January 1910–24 January 1911.

Philadelphia Evening Telegram, 1 January 1910–24 January 1911.

Philadelphia Evening Times, 1 January 1910–24 January 1911.

Philadelphia Inquirer, 19 February 1908–24 January 1911.

Philadelphia Press, 1 January 1910–24 January 1911.

Philadelphia Public Ledger, 1 January 1910–3 March 1916.

Philadelphia Record, 1 January 1910–24 January 1911.

Philadelphia Sunday Dispatch, 1 January 1910–24 January 1911.

Philadelphia Sunday Item, 1 January 1910–24 January 1911.

Pittsburgh Bulletin, 18 November–12 December 1910

Pittsburgh Chronicle Telegraph, 1 December–12 December 1910.

Pittsburgh Daily Dispatch, 1 December–12 December 1910.

Pittsburgh Gazette Times, 25 September–12 December 1910.

Pittsburgh Index, 1 December 1910–11 October 1934.

Pittsburgh Leader, 1 December–12 December 1910.

Pittsburgh Post, 1 December–12 December 1910.

Pittsburgh Press, 2 October–12 December 1910.

Pittsburgh Volksblatt und Freiheits-Freund, 1 December–12 December 1910.

Providence Evening Bulletin, 13 February–26 February 1910.

Providence Evening News, 13 February–26 February 1910.

Providence Evening Tribune, 13 February–26 February 1910.

Providence Journal, 13 February 1910–5 October 1942.

Providence News and News Tribune, 13 February–26 February 1910.

Providence Telegram, 13 February–26 February 1910.

Rochester Daily Record, 1 December–9 December 1910.

Rochester Democrat and Chronicle, 1 December–20 November 1999.

Rochester Herald, 21 August–9 December 1910.

Rochester Post Express, 1 December–9 December 1910.

Rochester Union and Advertiser, 5 November–9 December 1910.

Springfield Daily News, 10 February 1910–23 February 1911.

Springfield Daily Republican, 10 February 1910–23 February 1911.

Springfield Evening Union, 10 February 1910–23 February 1911.

Springfield Homestead, 10 February 1910–23 February 1911.

Springfield Sunday Republican, 10 February 1910–26 February 1969.

Syracuse Herald, 2 December–10 December 1910.

Syracuse Journal, 2 December 1910–14 January 1935.

Syracuse Post-Standard, 8 September 1897–10 December 1910.

Utica Daily Press, 3 December–12 December 1910.
Utica Herald Dispatch, 3 December 1910–7 January 1916.
Utica Observer, 3 December 1910–25 April 1999.
Utica Saturday Globe, 1 December–12 December 1910.
Utica Sunday Tribune, 1 December–12 December 1910.
Washington Herald, 1 January 1910–29 March 1911.
Washington Post, 4 December 1910–29 March 1911.
Washington Star, 1 January 1910–29 March 1911.
Washington Times, 1 January 1910–29 March 1911.
Yale Daily News, 16 February–24 February 1910.

Index

~

About the Author

Mary H. Wagner is an assistant professor of music at the University of Michigan at Flint. She received her Ph.D. in musicology/ethnomusicology from Kent State University. Her credentials also include a master of music in voice, a master of arts in musicology, and a master of business administration. At the University of Michigan–Flint, Dr. Wagner teaches courses in music history, world music, and women in music. Articles by Dr. Wagner have recently appeared in *Michigan History*, *Naturlaut*, and *Jazz Education*. Dr. Wagner is involved in music throughout Michigan, where she provides preconcert lectures, program notes, and singing and participates as a board member of the Saginaw Bay Symphony Orchestra.